DELHI
AGRA & JAIPUR

Louise Nicholson is the author of the bestselling *India in Luxury: a practical guide for the discerning traveller*, published in 1985. More recently, her *London: Louise Nicholson's Definitive Guide* won the London Tourist Board prize for the best book on the city in 1988, and was short-listed for the Thomas Cook Award. Her other books on India include *The Red Fort, Delhi* (1989).

For William

The author would particularly like to thank the Taj Group of Hotels for their hospitality while researching this book.

DELHI, AGRA & JAIPUR

Louise Nicholson

Photographs by Steve Vidler
Original illustrations by Mohan Lal Soni

ODYSSEY GUIDES
Hong Kong

Distribution in the UK, Ireland, Europe and certain Commonwealth countries by
Hodder & Stoughton, Mill Road, Dunton Green, Sevenoaks, Kent, TN13 2YA

The author would like to thank the Taj Group of Hotels for their hospitality while
researching this book.

Grateful acknowledgement is made to the following authors and publishers
for permissions granted:

HarperCollins Publishers for
A Princess Remembers © Gayatri Devi and Santha Rama Rau 1976

Penguin Books Ltd. for
A Situation in New Delhi © Nayantara Sahgal 1977, 1988
and
Broken Song by Rabindranath Tagore, from his Selected Poems,
translated by William Radyce

Victor Gollancz Ltd. and Murray Pollinger for
The Wedding of Jayanthi Mandel © Sara Banerji 1987, published
by Victor Gollancz Ltd. and Arrow Books

The Wallace Literary Agency Inc. and Penguin USA for
The Guide © 1958 R K Narayan. Published in the USA by Viking Press
and in the UK by Heinemann

Aitken & Stone Ltd. for
An Area of Darkness © V S Naipaul 1964

Series Editor: May Holdsworth, Ralph Kiggell and Toby Sinclair
Picture Editor: Carolyn Watts
Map Design: Bai Yiliang
Design: Unity Design Studio
Cover Concept: Raquel Jaramillo and Aubrey Tse
Artwork: Au Yeung Chui Kwai
Photography: Steve Vidler. Original illustrations by Mohan Lal Soni;
Back cover by Sarah Lock

ISBN: 962-217-179-6

British Library Cataloguing in Publication Data has been applied for.

Produced by Twin Age Ltd
Printed in Hong Kong

Cover: The Taj Mahal at sunset

Contents

Excerpts

Delhi, Agra and Jaipur
Three Cities Intertwined through the Centuries

The stories of Delhi, Agra and Jaipur are quite different, yet interwoven. Delhi's starts with misty myth and, through a succession of now-deserted strongholds, concludes triumphantly when it was adopted as independent India's capital with twin living cities: a purpose-built Mughal fort-city and a British-designed imperial capital. Agra was barely founded when the great Mughal emperors made it their magnificent capital during a century of empire-building; when they forsook it for Delhi, it never recovered. Jaipur and its predecessor Amber were built with wealth gained from astute alliances between Jaipur rulers and Mughal emperors, deals so successful that flourishing Jaipur city was later the obvious choice as the capital of Rajasthan state. To help clarify the confusion, see the dynastic chart on page 182.

Delhi, the Irresistible Capital
For the origins of the capital of the world's largest democracy, myth and reality fuse. The great Hindu epic, the *Mahabharata*, tells of the five Pandava brother heroes founding Indraprastha beside the River Yamuna in around 1450 BC. And modern archaeologists have found pottery suggesting that a town flourished around the first millennium BC. The site is on the west bank of the shifting channel of the Yamuna, a major tributary of the River Ganga which nourishes the vast and fertile plain of north India. The Aravalli Hills border it to the west and south, with a finger poking round to the north known as North Ridge.

This strategic position became the gateway to the sub-continent for conquerors from the north. Fought over repeatedly, Delhi became the capital for a succession of empires and kingdoms, a triumphant conqueror often abandoning his defeated city to build a fresh symbol of power on neighbouring virgin land.

The string of cities — seven major ones but up to 15 counting the smaller strongholds — began with Dilli, the Tomar Rajputs' capital in the eighth to tenth centuries. The Chauhan Rajputs ruled next. But in 1192 their hero-king Prithviraj III was defeated by the Turkish invader Qutb-ud-din Aibak. This had a massive social impact on Delhi and the territories ruled by its subsequent conquerors. Hindu rule ended; Islam was dominant. As the successive Muslim conquerors poured down over the Hindu Kush, the Slave, Khalji, Tughluq, Sayyid and Lodi sultanates (together known as the Delhi Sultanate, 1206–1526) succeeded one another and the two cultures fused to create a rich Indo-Islamic society focused on Delhi.

Early in the 16th century, the Lodis quit Delhi for Agra, which became the Mughal glory. But Delhi proved irresistible even for the Mughals. The second emperor, Humayun (ruled 1530–40, 1555–6), returned to build the city of

Dinpanah, lost it to Sher Shah Sur in 1540, regained it in 1555 and died there. Akbar and Jahangir were not tempted by Delhi. But the fifth Mughal emperor was: in 1648 Shah Jahan (ruled 1627–58) entered his sparkling, newly-built Shahjahanabad, now called Old Delhi, the last of Delhi's Muslim cities and the only one still thriving today.

This century an eighth Delhi was built. Following the demise of the later Mughal rulers and the rise of British power in India, Old Delhi, with its British cantonment to the north, was a backwater while Calcutta shone. Then, in 1911, the king-emperor George V announced the move back to Delhi. New Delhi, capital of the British Empire in the East, was inaugurated in 1931 and in 1947 became independent India's capital.

Agra, a Century of Mughal Magnificence
In 1502, Sultan Sikandar Lodi founded a new city downstream on the Yamuna, 197 kilometres (122 miles) south of Delhi. This was Agra. Twenty-four years later Babur arrived. A Turk of the Burlas tribe, he was poet, diarist, soldier, statesman and adventurer rolled into one. And his conqueror's pedigree was impeccable: Timur (known in the West as Tamburlaine) on his father's side, Jenghis Khan on his mother's. In 1526, on his fifth raid into the sub-continent, he devastated Sikandar's successor, Ibrahim, at Panipat, some 80 kilometres (50 miles) north of Delhi. Then, more significantly, he triumphed over Rana Sanga of Mewar and his confederacy of fierce Rajput rulers at Khanua, about 45 kilometres (28 miles) west of Agra. In addition to clever military tactics, he ensured victory over the enemy's force of 100,000 horse and 100 elephant by a theatrical invocation of divine favour — in front of his flagging soldiers, he forswore liquor, broke wine vessels, poured wine down the wells and gave stirring speeches. The victory of Khanua consolidated his power and marked the foundation of Mughal dominion in India which continued actively until Aurangzeb's death in 1707, and less actively until 1858 when Bahadur Shah II was deposed by the British.

Babur (ruled 1526–30) made Agra, not Delhi, his capital. His grandson Akbar (ruled 1556–1605) expanded and strengthened the empire, using a winning combination of quality soldiering, skilful diplomacy, religious tolerance and alliances sealed with marriage, especially with the fierce Rajput rulers. Rajasthan was perhaps the key part of Akbar's plan to consolidate Mughal power by fusing the two religious communities of Hindustan into one nation. For five centuries the Muslim rulers of Delhi had failed to tame the staunchly Hindu, warrior Rajputs and their inhospitable desert lands. Among the Rajput princes, the Mughals found in the rulers of Amber (later Jaipur) an especially willing ally.

Amber's Agra flourished, despite the 14-year-long (1571–85) sojourn at Fatehpur Sikri, to be further embellished by his son Jahangir (ruled 1605–27) and his grandson Shah Jahan (ruled 1627–58). All the arts were nurtured under royal patronage at the Mughal court, from painting, architecture and music to garden design, jewellery and cooking. To the sophisticated Persian traditions imported by the Mughals were added local characteristics. Hindu carvers put their distinctive designs on Mughal buildings, carpet weavers gave Persian arabesques a new boldness, and painters adopted some of the fresh colours of local courts and were delighted by the realistic European paintings brought by Jesuits and diplomatic visitors. The influences worked both ways: to promote religious tolerance, Akbar had the Hindu epic, the *Mahabharata*, translated into Persian as the *Razmnama*; to emulate the Mughal court, the Amber rulers borrowed craftsmen to decorate their new fort.

But the Delhi siren called again. In 1648 Shah Jahan forsook Agra. Since then, Agra has enjoyed little glory.

Jaipur and the Profitable Mughal Alliance

The Kachchwahas became rulers of Amber, then Jaipur. They are one of the 36 proud and warring Rajput clans of the Hindu Kshatriya caste, second after the Brahmins. Descended from fierce Afghans, Turks, Persians and Mughals, the Rajput clans improved upon their temporal ancestry with claims of direct links to the great Hindu gods of sun, moon and fire. The Kachchwahas traced their descent to the sun via Kusa, the twin son of Rama who is the mythical hero of the *Ramayana*. Legend and reality confuse their story until the 12th century when they won Amber from the Susawat Minas.

Despite Amber's superb location — on a steep rocky hill encircled by protective rugged slopes — it was one of the most eastern Rajput forts and uncomfortably close to Delhi and, later, Agra. So relations with the Muslim invaders began almost immediately. Before the end of the 12th century an Amber prince probably married the Chauhan ruler Prithviraj's sister. But the real alliances began with the Mughals.

After the defeat at Khanua in 1527, the Rajput clans never again rallied under a single leader. One by one they capitulated to Mughal dominance, the notable exception being proud Raja Sanga's Mewar descendants, rulers of Chittaugarh and then Udaipur.

The canny Amber rulers were the first to recognize Mughal power. Raja Bihar Mal (ruled *c* 1548–74) played his hand to the full. Not only was the threat too close for comfort but the road to Ajmer was through Kachchwaha territory. And Ajmer, a drop of Islam in an all-Hindu land, was where the revered saint Khwaja Muin-ud-din Chishti lay buried. Bihar Mal had paid homage to Humayun and led a 5,000-strong Mughal force for him. Then, he was quick to be the first Rajput presented at Akbar's court. And during Akbar's first annual pilgrimage to Ajmer in 1562, he gave his adopted grandson Man Singh into the emperor's service and gave his daughter to be Akbar's wife. Other marriages had been made by Muslim rulers to Hindu princesses, but this was probably the first not made under threat and the first

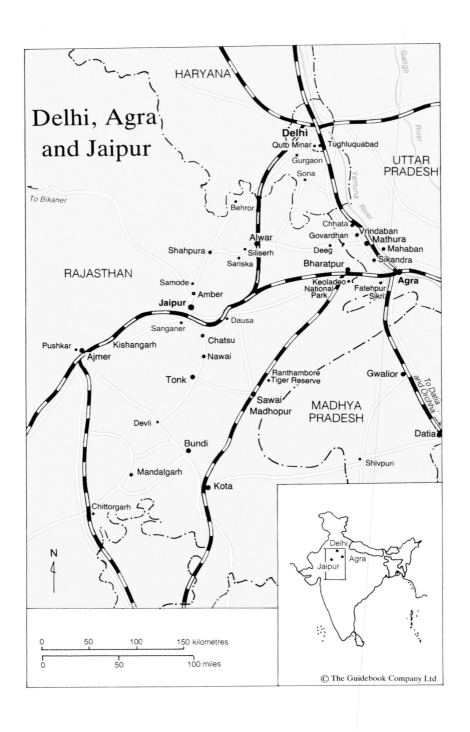

Delhi, Agra and Jaipur

HARYANA

To Bikaner

RAJASTHAN

Delhi
Qutb Minar • • Tughluqabad
Gurgaon
Sona

UTTAR
PRADESH

Ganga

Yamuna River

Behror

Chhata
Govardhan
Alwar
Shahpura • • Siliserh
Sariska

Deeg
Bharatpur

Vrindaban
Mathura
• Mahaban
Sikandra

Samode
Amber
Jaipur

Keoladeo
National
Park

Fatehpur
Sikri
Agra

Sanganer
Chatsu
Dausa

Nawai

Pushkar
Ajmer
Kishangarh

Tonk

Ranthambore
Tiger Reserve

Gwalior

To Datia
and Orchha

Devli

Sawai
Madhopur

MADHYA
PRADESH

Datia

Bundi

Shivpuri

Mandalgarh

Kota

Chittorgarh

N

Delhi
Agra
Jaipur

0   50   100   150 kilometres

0   50   100 miles

© The Guidebook Company Ltd

where the bride was not obliged to convert to Islam; indeed, her own religion had a profound effect on Akbar, and it was she who finally gave the emperor his son, Salim, who became emperor Jahangir.

His successor, Bhagwan Das (ruled 1574–89), cemented the alliance. He was both friend and counsellor to Akbar. As leading general commanding a 5,000-strong Mughal force, he reputedly saved his master's life at the battle of Sarnal, was entrusted with the governorship of the Punjab and gave a daughter to be Jahangir's wife. Next came Man Singh (ruled 1589–1614). He also became one of Akbar's generals, watched over the dubious heir Salim (Man Singh's brother-in-law), was governor of Bengal, and when Salim became emperor Jahangir led Mughal troops in the Deccan for him.

And next but one came Jai Singh I (ruled 1621–67), a military and diplomatic wonder who reached the apogee of Rajput success at the Mughal court. On the throne aged 11, this child prodigy was commanding 3,000 men for Jahangir two years later and then fought all over India for Jahangir's son, Shah Jahan. Later, watching Shah Jahan's sons fight for power, he made his shrewdest move. Jai Singh captured one brother, Dara Shukoh, and handed him to another, Aurangzeb, who murdered him and also won the fight for the throne. Jai Singh was now 48 years old, but all was not done. Aurangzeb created the Rajput ruler 'Mirza Raja' and gave him a command of 7,000, the most permitted to a non-royal Mughal. And Jai Singh dutifully shone yet again when in 1665 he defeated Shivaji, the formidable and god-like Maratha chief of the Deccan, and brought him to Aurangzeb in Agra.

As Mughal power expanded, Kachchwaha power increased and their coffers overflowed. It was Man Singh and Jai Singh I who built the fort-palace at Amber, embellishing it and borrowing ideas and craftsmen from the Mughal court to give it an opulence that outstripped all other Rajput efforts.

Three rulers after Jai Singh I, the 11-year-old Jai Singh II (another child prodigy), came to the Amber throne in 1699. Off he went to pay homage to the 71-year-old emperor Aurangzeb who was in the Deccan. The boy impressed the old man who later awarded him the hereditary title 'Sawai', meaning one-and-a-quarter, putting him firmly above his fellow Rajputs. As a soldier, Jai Singh lived up to expectations, shining at the siege of Khelna at the age of 14 in 1702. But his diplomatic juggling after Aurangzeb's death in 1707 was less skillful. He was ousted by Bahadur Shah I, who installed his brother as puppet ruler. Jai Singh then had to rally the major Rajput forces to win back his throne. That done, he turned from soldiering to indulge his love of science and the arts. Abandoning the rugged hills of Amber, he began laying out his perfect humanist palace-city down on the plains in 1727. He name it Jaipur, a double-edged self-compliment as 'jai' referred to himself and also means victory. It is this city that became the capital of Rajasthan at Independence.

The British and Delhi, Agra and Jaipur

The British came to India as traders, seeking the fabled silks, spices and indigo dye and operating as the East India Company under a charter granted in 1600 by Queen Elizabeth I. During the 17th century they established major ports at Madras and Calcutta on the east coast, and at Surat and Bombay on the west. In 1615 Thomas Roe landed at Surat and early the next year reached the Mughal emperor Jahangir at Ajmer, west of Agra, carrying letters of credence from James I and hoping to make a trading agreement for the East India Company. He was in effect Britain's first ambassador to India. Among his many presents the paintings, especially portrait miniatures, were to influence Jahangir's court atelier.

There followed almost a century of trade and administrative expansion by the Company across the sub-continent, involving battles against both competing European traders, especially the French, and native Indians. In 1774 Warren Hastings became the first Governor-General of British India, with Calcutta as capital of its vast territories. The Company traders had become a solid political force.

For the British in this area 1803 was a crucial year. They were coming under the threat of the stocky, strong Marathas, whose lands stretched from Gujarat to Bengal. As the Marathas plundered the Rajput kingdoms, aided by the French, the British watched and then gave well-timed support to the desperate princes, making treaties whose ultimate goal was to put each prince in the British pocket under the watchful eye of a British Resident. Jaipur made its alliance in 1803, sacrificing independence for British paramountcy and protection but retaining throne and title. Although such very British institutions as a Public Works Department were set up, the best visual testimony to their presence is the Central Museum (see page 171).

The same year, Agra fell to the British after a succession of post-Mughal occupants ending with the Marathas. It then served as the capital of Agra Province, later North West Provinces, 1833−58. The spacious and elegant British cantonment sets the tone for modern Agra, stretching westwards from the riverside Mughal fort, the Taj Mahal and the old city.

Also in 1803, the British won Delhi from the Marathas. Here, the power-less Mughals played out their sunset years with pathetic shows of royalty, their empire restricted to the Red Fort. The last emperor, Bahadur Shah II (ruled 1837−58), was eventually deposed, to die in Burma four years later.

1857 and the War of Independence

Delhi was a focus of this landmark event in Indian history, also known as the Rebellion, the Bengal Uprising or, by the British, the Mutiny. It began at Meerut, 50 kilometres (31 miles) northwest of Delhi. Forty-seven battalions of the Bengal army mutinied on 10 May, their discontent with their masters sparked by two events: the Company's commander ordered Indian sepoys to bite cartridges before putting them into their rifles, and a rumour spread that the cartridge grease was made of pig and cow fat — the first forbidden to Muslims, the second forbidden and sacred to Hindus. The next day the mutineers — or freedom fighters — marched on Delhi. From then until September Delhi was in the hands of the first organized fighters for India's independence. A small British force finally retook Delhi by storm, led by the hero Brigadier-General Nicholson who was mortally wounded during the assault. North of Old Delhi, the cantonment area still has a strong British atmosphere, with several rebellion sites.

The British Empire

The next year, 1858, British India was placed under direct governorship of the Crown instead of through the intermediary East India Company. India was part of the British Empire, the Viceroy was its chief executive, and Indians were subjects of Queen Victoria. In 1875 her eldest son, the Prince of Wales (later Edward VII), made his first visit to India. The next year, Disraeli proclaimed Queen Victoria Empress of India with effect from 1 January 1877. In 1889 the Prince of Wales came again; and in 1905 a new Prince of Wales (later George V) made his first visit.

Finally, in 1911, the ruler of the British Empire, George V, visited his eastern lands. Following Indian tradition, a grand celebratory durbar was held in Delhi's cantonment area on 12 December. To an audience of 562 maharajas and other grandees whose gold, silks, pearls, elephants and Rolls Royces created a dazzling display of pomp and show, the king-emperor announced that the capital of India was to move from Calcutta to Delhi. Delhi had proved irresistible yet again. Another city was built.

New Delhi was inaugurated on 9 February 1931. Designed by Edwin Lutyens, who was assisted by Herbert Baker, it was laid out south of Old Delhi. It reflected the size and power of the British Empire, and options for further expansion were even incorporated into the plan. Just 16 years later India won independence.

The Struggle for Independence

The 1857 War marked the beginning of a ferment of hostility against British rule. It grew gradually, percolating down from the intelligentsia to the masses. In 1885 the Indian National Congress was founded and by 1903 the worried Viceroy Lord Curzon felt the need to hold a Delhi Durbar where, fortunately, the Rajput princes displayed eager loyalty. In 1905 the British attempts to weaken the unified National Movement were answered by a countrywide boycott of British goods; but the All India Muslim League, set up the following year, would disrupt that unity.

When Mohandas Karamchand Gandhi (to become known as the Mahatma, or Great Soul) arrived back in India from South Africa in 1915, India's struggle for freedom entered a new phase. He waged a moral protest against oppression, known as civil disobedience. It meant peacefully defying laws and willingly taking punishment.

On 26 January 1930 the young Jawaharlal Nehru was president of Congress when its resolution demanding complete independence for India was adopted, the pledge being that it was 'a crime against man and God' to submit to British rule. The same year Gandhi launched a second civil disobedience movement, given focus by the mass appeal of his 250-kilometre (155-mile) -long Salt March. This protest against the British monopoly on salt production was a cause that touched every Indian household. After the Round Table Conference in London and more civil disobedience, the Government of India Act was passed in 1935 which gave about 14 percent of Indians a vote to elect representatives. Congress swept the polls. Agitation continued, reaching a climax in the 1942 Congress call for the British to 'Quit India'. Meanwhile the League demanded a separate state for Muslims, to be called Pakistan.

In Britain, the postwar Labour government under Prime Minister Clement Atlee was calling into question Churchill's belief in retaining India. Finally, in 1947, partition and independence came simultaneously, one painfully, one with great joy and optimism.

On 14 August the last Viceroy, Lord Louis Mountbatten, attended the creation of Pakistan. At midnight on 14–15 August, Mountbatten formally transferred power to India's first Prime Minister, Pandit Jawaharlal Nehru. The Union Jack came down, the Tricolour of India went up, and the two leaders went to Viceroy House, soon to be renamed Rastrapati Bhavan, where they generously toasted each other with 'To India' and 'To King George VI'. Meanwhile Mahatma Gandhi wept in Calcutta over the violence, the division of India, and the loss of human compassion. He was assassinated in Delhi on 30 January the following year and cremated on the banks of the Yamuna.

Pagett, M P

agett, MP, was a liar, and a fluent liar therewith,—
He spoke of the heat of India as 'The Asian Solar Myth';
'Came on a four months' visit, to 'study the East' in November,
And I got him to make an agreement vowing to stay till
      September.

March came in with the koïl. *Pagett was cool and gay,*
Called me a 'bloated Brahmin,' talked of my 'princely pay.'
March went out with the roses. 'Where is your heat?' said he.
'Coming,' said I to Pagett. 'Skittles!' said Pagett, MP.

April began with the punkah, coolies, and prickly-heat,—
Pagett was dear to mosquitoes, sandflies found him a treat.
He grew speckled and lumpy—hammered, I grieve to say,
Aryan brothers who fanned him, in an illiberal way.

May set in with a dust-storm,—Pagett went down with the sun.
All the delights of the season tickled him one by one.
Imprimis—*ten days' 'liver'—due to his drinking beer;*
Later, a dose of fever—slight, but he called it severe.

Dysent'ry touched him in June, after the Chota Bursat—
Lowered his portly person—made him yearn to depart.
He didn't call me a 'Brahmin,' or 'bloated,' or 'over-paid,'
But seemed to think it a wonder that any one ever stayed.

July was a trifle unhealthy,—Pagett was ill with fear,
Called it the 'Cholera Morbus,' hinted that life was dear.
He babbled of 'Eastern exile,' and mentioned his home with tears;
But I hadn't seen my *children for close upon seven years.*

We reached a hundred and twenty once in the Court at noon,
(I've mentioned Pagett was portly) Pagett went off in a swoon.
That was an end to the business. Pagett, the perjured, fled
With a pratical, working knowledge of 'Solar Myths' in his head.

And I laughed as I drove from the station, but the mirth died
      out on my lips
As I thought of the fools like Pagett who write of their
      'Eastern trips;'
And the sneers of the travelled idiots who duly misgovern
      the land,
And I prayed to the Lord to deliver another one into my hand.

              Rudyard Kipling

Delhi, Agra and Jaipur Today

Establishing a Democracy with Delhi as Capital

On 26 January 1950 the Constitution came into force; the event is celebrated annually and magnificently in New Delhi as Republic Day (see page 187). Broadly, the Constitution outlines a democracy with a President as Head of State, a Prime Minister as Head of Government and a two-house Parliament elected by universal suffrage: Lok Sabha (House of the People, 542 seats) and Rajya Sabha (Council of States, 250 seats). Based on Westminster's Parliament, the political structure also draws on the 1935 Government of India Act and on the US system, and incorporates a Bill of Rights. The infant democracy inherited its capital, New Delhi, from the British.

Two years after Nehru's death in 1964, his daughter Indira Gandhi became Prime Minister. When the Congress party divided in 1969, she led Congress (I). She remained in power until her authoritarian ways led to the Emergency of 1975, and to her being ousted in 1977. But she won a landslide victory back into power in 1980. There she remained until her assassination on 31 October 1984. Her son, Rajiv Gandhi, was immediately sworn in as Prime Minister, then confirmed in a general election. In the 1989 election he lost power to Vishwanath Pratap Singh whose Janata Dal Party allied with the BJP to form a government. In the November 1990 elections Chandra Shekhar was sworn in as India's new prime minister.

The World's Largest Democracy: Size and Population

Independent India absorbed all the former princely states A new map was drawn. There are now 24 states and seven Union Territories and Special Areas. Its population of 300 million at Independence has shot up to around 800 million, 40 percent of it under 15 years old. After 40 years of rampant urban expansion, which has attracted 25 percent of the population, Delhi and Jaipur are in grave danger of being throttled by too much growth too quick.

Delhi is a Union Territory, with a current population of over six million, the third largest city after Bombay and Calcutta. By comparison, Agra, in Uttar Pradesh state, has a manageable 700,000 inhabitants.

Jaipur is India's 11th largest city, with a population of almost a million. It is the capital of Rajasthan (land of the Rajputs) state, a parched land of 34 million people. Previously there were 23 princely states in Rajputana, whose acknowledged head was Udaipur's Maharana of Mewar. Jaipur's position today fulfils Jai Singh II's dream 250 years ago that his new city should be the capital of a united Rajputana, a centre for government, trade and worship. Indeed, Maharaja Man Singh II became Rajpramukh (head) of the newly formed Rajasthan Union in 1948, when Jaipur became the administrative centre for a collection of democratized, formerly princely, states. The next year it was consolidated as Rajasthan state.

Literacy, Illiteracy and Marriage

India's illiteracy rate is around 64 percent. So in the election run-up for state Members of Parliament, canvassing is a colourful mixture of rousing rallies attended by film stars and the promotion of party symbols by daubing them on any available wall. Congress (I)'s symbol is a raised hand.

Those who do read are voracious newspaper consumers. India prints 1,802 daily newspapers, with the 114 principal dailies totting up a 13-million circulation. English papers provide the visitor with national and local news and an insight into Indian values. In all three cities, *The Times of India*, *The Indian Express*, *The Hindustan Times* and *The Statesman* are available. And the magazine *India Today* provides the best perky round-ups of all current issues.

Sunday papers carry the no-nonsense, serious marriage advertisements listed under classifieds: 'Wanted, convent educated, fair girl from good family for Jat boy age 25 years working in reputed paint company at Jabalpur. Covenanted post four figure salary plus perks. Early marriage.' Thoroughly practical: he knows what he wants, and she can see what she will get. It is a system still favoured even by the university-educated urban middle class who claim that such frankness is a major reason for the low divorce rate. But the marriage deal for poorer women is usually not good: the average marriage age is only 18.3 years, some 75 percent of women are illiterate and the pernicious dowry system means parents pray for a baby to be a boy (abandoned ones are usually girls). Furthermore, dowry deaths, so-called accidents after a girl's in-laws demand extra post-marriage dowry, are back on the increase. So are incidents of *sati*, the practice of a widow's self-immolation on her husband's funeral pyre that was outlawed by the British in 1829.

Language: A Foreign Tongue still Dominates

Despite all efforts, English is still the *lingua franca*. It is even spoken by taxi and auto-rickshaw drivers. But Indian English, like American English, has its own particular accent and idioms, many of them highly imaginative. In 1965 Hindi was proclaimed the national language. This is not fine classical Hindi, a Sanskrit-based language, but a less attractive, simplified version created for administration. It has failed to find approval, and where it is used it is peppered with English words where it lacks Hindi equivalents. Official languages are now both Hindi and English: India's official name is both Bharat and Republic of India. But an erudite Delhi family receiving a wedding invitation in Hindi may still call on their son's schooling to help translate.

There are also 15 recognized national regional languages and another 1,650 or so languages and dialects. Delhi has mainly Hindi, Urdu and Punjabi speakers, whereas Jaipur has Rajasthani and Hindi speakers. However, the visitor to north India, where the nation's 38 percent of Hindi speakers are concentrated, needs English for most occasions and a few Hindi words and phrases for exploring the back streets and villages (see page 195).

Religion: A Tolerance for Gods of Every Kind
India has no official religion. But the breakdown of followers of the six
principal religions is revealing: 82.6 percent Hindu, 11.4 percent Muslim,
2.4 percent Christian, 2 percent Sikh, 0.7 percent Buddhist , 0.5 percent
Jain and 0.3 percent Parsee. India gave birth to two of the world's great
religions, first Hinduism and then Buddhism which developed from it.
The Sikh and Jain movements also grew out of Hinduism. To attend a
major religious festival, see page 187.

Hinduism The astonishing number of Hindu gods and the length and
complexity of the great epics can be approached by the first-time visitor by
starting with the Trinity — Brahma (Creator), Vishnu (Preserver) and Shiva
(Destroyer) — and by reading a good short version of the sacred texts, the
Mahabharata and the *Ramayana* (see page 184). The religion's roots are in the
Indus valley. This early form was disseminated by the Aryan invaders who
arrived in north India around 1500 BC, and given structure by the Vedic
scriptures. Put very simply, Hindus believe that the spirit endures a series of
rebirths ending in *moksha*, when it is freed from the rebirth cycle. The concept
of *karma* is that each person's deeds dictate the soul's progress towards
moksha in the next rebirth: bad deeds lead to lower reincarnation and vice
versa. (See also Glossary, page 199; and bibliography, page 184.) Jaipur
has an all-pervading Hindu atmosphere, especially during *puja* (worship) time
at Govinda Deva Temple, at Amber Fort's Kali Temple and at Hanuman
Temple near Sisodia Rani ka Bagh. For a more intense experience, Vrindaban
and the other villages north of Agra are where the young Krishna played.

Islam Islam came to northern India with the succession of invaders
pouring down over the Hindu Kush, and was consolidated by the long Mughal
rule. The Muslim atmosphere is best seen around mosques on Friday, the holy
day, especially around Old Delhi's Jama Masjid (Friday Mosque), Agra's Jama
Masjid, and at two smaller but intensely Muslim places: Nizamuddin, a
medieval Sufi village that is the oldest living area of Delhi, and Ajmer, an
important pilgrimage centre southwest of Jaipur.

Christianity Although Christianity came to south India very early, possibly
brought by St Thomas the Apostle, it was first brought to the Mughal court at
Agra by the Jesuits in the late 16th century. The Agra cantonment was
serviced by the fine St George's Cathedral, St Patrick's Roman Catholic
Cathedral and an overflowing British Cemetery, all still used by the town's
30,000 faithful. In Delhi, the old cantonment area has the Greek Revival
St James's Church and New Delhi has a clutch of grand churches built for the
empire's subjects.

Sikhism Many Sikhs came from the Punjab to settle in Delhi. Most wear
their distinctive turbans over their uncut hair — although some have now
shorn their locks — and are known for their hard work. They follow a fairly
new religion founded by Guru Nanak in the 15th century. Their five symbols,

introduced by Guru Gobind Singh so they could recognize each other, are the five *kakkars*: *kesha* (uncut hair), *kangha* (comb), *kachha* (shorts), *kara* (steel bracelet) and *kirpan* (sword). Their temples are called *gurdwaras* and the Sisganj Gurdwara in Old Delhi's Chandni Chowk is usually bustling with activity.

Buddhism There are few Buddhists in this area of India. This more contemplative religion was founded by Siddhartha Gautama, a prince who received enlightenment late in the sixth century BC at Bodhgaya in Bihar. As the Buddha (Enlightened One), he preached his first sermon at Sarnath near Varanasi and emphasized *dharma* (religious teachings), *sangha* (monasticism) and *buddhi* (intellectual enlightenment). Bodhisattvas, his close followers, are those who have postponed *nirvana* (release from the cycle of birth) to show others the way.

Jainism This has similarities with Buddhism. It developed early in the sixth century BC when prince Mahavira, the 24th and last Tirthankara (saint), broke away from the prevailing rigid Hinduism to live as an ascetic and attain the highest spiritual knowledge. He then became a *jina* (conqueror), and his followers are called Jains. Emphasizing the monastic life, Jains believe the universe was not created but is infinite so they have no god. But they do believe in reincarnation and salvation, found through such deeds as temple building and *ahimsa* (reverence for life), which demands strict vegetarianism. There are two sects: Digambaras (sky-clad) who possess nothing, not even clothes; and Shvetambaras (white-robed), who are less strict. Jains are concentrated in Gujarat in west India, where they can go in pilgrimage on foot to their sacred hills. In Delhi, Jains go to Digamber Jain Temple and Charity Bird Hospital, at the top of Chandni Chowk, facing the Red Fort.

Zoroastrianism The tiny but exceptional community of Parsees, as the followers of Zoroastrianism are known, has produced some of India's greatest industrialists and scientists, notably the Tata family. Migrating from Muslim persecution in Persia, they arrived in Gujarat in 745 AD and later came to British Bombay as traders, shipbuilders and bankers. Following their prophet, Zarathustra (golden light), they seek knowledge and illumination through worship, fire and sun and follow the path of Asha—good thoughts, words and deeds. As worshippers of fire, they lay their dead in towers of silence for vultures to eat rather than pollute fire or earth.

A Devoted Son

When the results appeared in the morning papers, Rakesh scanned them, barefoot and in his pyjamas, at the garden gate, then went up the steps to the veranda where his father sat sipping his morning tea and bowed down to touch his feet.

'A first division, son?' his father asked, beaming, reaching for the papers.

'At the top of the list, Papa,' Rakesh murmured, as if awed. 'First in the country.'

Bedlam broke loose then. The family whooped and danced. The whole day long visitors streamed into the small yellow house at the end of the road, to congratulate the parents of this Wunderkind, to slap Rakesh on the back and fill the house and garden with the sounds and colours of a festival. There were garlands and halwa, party clothes and gifts (enough fountain pens to last years, even a watch or two), nerves and temper and joy, all in a multicoloured whirl of pride and great shining vistas newly opened: Rakesh was the first son in the family to receive an education, so much had been sacrificed in order to send him to school and then medical college, and at last the fruits of their sacrifice had arrived, golden and glorious.

To everyone who came to him to say, 'Mubarak Varmaji, your son has brought you glory,' the father said, 'Yes, and do you know what is the first thing he did when he saw the results this morning? He came and touched my feet. He bowed down and touched my feet.' This moved many of the women in the crowd so much that they were seen to raise the ends of their saris and dab at their tears while the men reached out for the betel leaves and sweetmeats that were offered around on trays and shook their heads in wonder and approval of such exemplary filial behaviour.

Anita Desai, Games at Twilight and Other Stories

Getting There

Idea to Reality: Vital Decisions

A visit to Delhi, Agra and Jaipur, which make up the Golden Triangle of India, can be the most wonderful journey of your life. It can also be a disaster. Here are three tips to help put you on the road to happiness.

One, the more you inform yourself before you go, working out what you want and then how to get it, the better. It is a very rich, concentrated area. You may wish to travel to see as many places as possible or keep to the highlights, climb up forts or watch skilful craftsmen, explore back streets or relax maharaja-style in a palace-hotel, shop for top quality silk and jewels or attend one of the colourful festivals. To taste a little of everything is perfectly possible, but only *you* know how big a helping of each you want.

Two, have a good spirit of adventure so that the inevitable problem or two is a positive addition rather than an irritation. This is true whether you go solo or take a package tour. The price of freedom is that you do all the bookings, checking-ins and cope with any problems, which then become part of the journey. On a package tour things can go wrong, too. But while someone else sorts it out you can always find something interesting going on, even if it is watching the mysterious ways of how problems are resolved — nothing is boring in India.

Three, this is the top favourite area for tourists, both foreign and Indian. Almost half of all visitors to India will go round the Golden Triangle. Only you know if you mind jostling with the crowd to see the Taj (or doing some careful timing to enjoy it in peace) and having no flexibility to change hotel or air bookings. If you do, and if the heat does not bother you, it is best to avoid the peak season of October–February.

The International Flight

Most major international airlines fly to Delhi. The non-stop flight London—Delhi takes nine hours, increased to more than 12 hours for a one-stop direct flight; from New York it takes another seven hours. Fare structures range enormously and it is well worth ringing several travel agencies; current quotes are as low as £412 return. This competitive market does not exist in the US, so Americans do better to take a cheap NewYork—London flight and then pick up one of the cheap deals for London—Delhi. Air India and British Airways have daily flights from London Heathrow to Delhi's Indira Gandhi International Airport; their fare structure London— Delhi return ranges from £600 (with date and booking restrictions) to Full Economy at £995 non-stop and £1,197 for optional stops; New York—Delhi Full Economy return (no cheap deals) is £1,850 on Air India. From the west coast of the US, the best deal is to take two cheap flights: one to Hong Kong, Singapore or Bangkok, then a second to Delhi.

Internal Flights

Indian Airlines runs the overloaded internal network; domestic flights are bookable with the international flight. Arriving in India with confirmed seats is essential during the high season—wait-listing is thoroughly unsatisfactory; so book as soon as you know your dates and reconfirm the bookings on arrival. Indian Airlines runs various discount deals including Youth Fares and the Discover India Ticket, bookable with the international ticket, but, as this incurs a fee, it is cheaper to buy on site.

Package Holidays versus Going Solo

As India is quite complicated to travel in until you know the tricks, it is well worth taking a package holiday for your first visit. As with the flight, Americans will find the best variety and costs in the UK. Going solo, you can have a more flexible trip. But be warned: you must cope with any problems, and it is essential to arrive in India with a skeleton of confirmed internal flights and hotel bookings, together with written confirmation of each.

Visas

All foreigners entering India need a valid visa. To obtain a tourist one valid for up to 90 days, contact your nearest embassy, consulate or high commission. On the application form, specify a double, triple or multiple-entry visa if you are intending to leave India to visit Nepal and/or another country and return to India. Return the form with three passport photos and the fee, which varies according to the number of entries. Currently UK citizens pay £23 for a single entry, UK citizens with Indian origin pay £7, whereas US citizens pay £7.80 and £3.50. All are payable by cash or Postal Order only, not personal cheques. Visa collection may be the next day, but postal applications take two weeks.

Immunization

Best considered well in advance of departure. Check that the essential jabs are up to date: typhoid, cholera, polio and tetanus. A gamma globulin injection against hepatitis A is advisable immediately before departure. Rabies is widespread among dogs and monkeys; a rabies vaccination means that if a rabid animal bites, the body starts to fight infection immediately but you must still go directly to the nearest hospital for a jab. Taking malaria pills is essential; current advice (constantly updated and changing) is to take two Nivaquine (or Avloclor) weekly starting the week before departure, and two Paludrine daily starting the day before departure, continuing both sets for four weeks after your return. For up-to-date medical centres, see page 205.

Money

It is forbidden to take Indian rupees into or out of India. The best and safest combination is travellers' cheques (US dollars and sterling are the most widely accepted) to change into rupees for day-to-day spending, and credit cards (Visa, Diners Club, American Express are the most widely accepted) to settle larger bills such as in hotels, restaurants, shops. But serious shoppers should bear in mind that even major stores tend to accept only the first £50 worth of a bill on a credit card, the rest to be paid in travellers' cheques or cash. Also, airline tickets bought in India must be paid for in foreign currency, and while Indian Airlines accepts credit cards many travel agents (who are quicker and more convenient to use) do not. They will want either travellers' cheques or rupees, which are accepted only with exchange forms proving the money was changed legally.

Packing

Simply, the less the better. Most essentials are now readily available in Delhi, Agra and Jaipur, but here is a short checklist of things worth taking to avoid paying a premium, risking lower quality or being caught without — or simply to improve your comfort.

Documents Keep all papers, passports, tickets, money, booking confirmations etc. in your hand luggage at all times. Serious photographers claim that film passed through several allegedly film-safe airport x-ray machines can be damaged and they should ask to have it inspected separately.

Clothes Cottons are better than man-made fibres. Unless Delhi embassy dinners are on your circuit, a jacket and tie for smarter hotel restaurants is enough as Indians prefer informal dress; but air-conditioning can be ice-cold, so women may need a jacket or shawl. Hotel laundries have a fast, usually same-day, service but their *dhobis* (clothes washers) are not gentle; the odd button may return broken and favourite garments are best left at home. Essentials include: socks for visiting temples and mosques, to avoid the hot tiles, and slip-on shoes or sandals to go with them; hat for sunny sightseeing; jumper for cool evenings; bathing costume for hotel pools. All three cities have good cheap European clothes and shoe shops.

Medicines In addition to the daily malaria pills, take any regular medicines you need. Nothing else is essential, but these may be useful: a tube of antiseptic cream, Elastoplasts, throat lozenges (against the dust), lip salve (against dust and sun), water purifying pills, anti-mosquito stick or aerosol, soothing cream for mosquito bites, sun lotion and good cosmetics (almost unavailable in India), a course of antibiotics against a bad cold or an inflammation, and a supply of needles and syringes in case you go to hospital.

If the dreaded 'Delly Belly' strikes — usually on the third or fourth day, through exhaustion and lack of acclimatization rather than bad food or drink

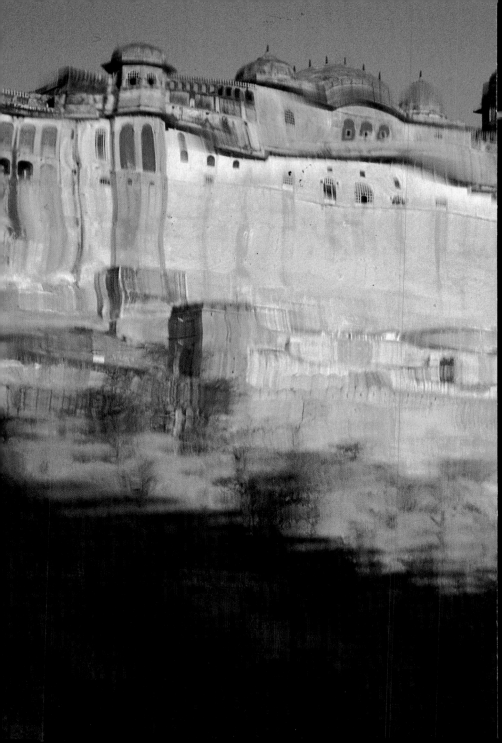

—the current advice is to drink lots of fluids (adding salt and sugar to water or sachets of Rehydrat available at UK chemists) and eat yoghurt and rice (natural sabilizers) for two days; then resort to Imodium or Lomotil if problems persist.

Washing Equipment Indian toothbrushes, toothpaste and soap are not great; if you are fussy, take supplies. An invaluable daily travelling kit is a flannel for freshening up, a plastic water bottle and a roll of lavatory paper.

Sightseeing Equipment Take a full supply of film. Fuji, Kodak and other makes are on sale but prices are high, even away from hotel shops. A small pair of binoculars transforms wildlife- and bird-watching, and homes in on intricate architectural carving.

Gadgets Voltage is 220, with the occasional 230; and a transformer may be necessary. A Walkman with supply of batteries solves the problems of bad hotel radios, long airport waits and less interesting moments on coaches and trains. A travelling iron saves the time and cost of the hotel ironing service. A penknife is useful for peeling fruit and opening bottles, but may be subject to inspection if kept in hand luggage at airports.

Time Zone

India has a single time zone. It is 5.5 hours ahead of London (when on GMT), 10.5 hours ahead of New York and 13.5 hours ahead of San Francisco.

Customs

On arrival in India, visitors are asked if they have anything to declare, implying money and camera equipment above all. For a single person the currency limit is US$1,000 in cash and traveller's cheques; more must be declared. Video cameras etc must also be declared and entered in your passport. Each time you leave India—even for a weekend in Nepal—it is obligatory to take them out, too, and re-declare them on the next entry.

On leaving India, anything that was declared on entry must be declared; if this included currency, then exchange receipts should be available. Rupees may not be taken out of India, but remember to have the Rs300 airport tax ready. Currently, buys in India which may be exported without restrictions are: souvenirs (handicrafts, silk, art, carving, the odd peacock feather, etc.), Rs2,000 worth of gold and Rs10,000 worth of jewellery and precious stones. But there are restrictions on antiques (objects more than 100 years old) and on large amounts of gold, jewellery and precious stones; and it is forbidden to export ivory, skins of animals and snakes, etc. or articles made from them. If in doubt, the local tourist office should have the latest list; for antiques advice, contact the Director, Antiquities, Archaeological Survey of India, Janpath, New Delhi.

General Information for Happy, Hazardless Days

From the moment you first experience that special, exotic Indian smell, everything is different. To help confusion quickly turn into enjoyment, here are some answers to your immediate practical questions. See also Practical Information, page 187.

Inter-city Movement

It saves much time and confusion to make all bookings through a single travel agency, paying a small premium if necessary. Air, train and bus timetables can be tricky to decipher; the booking process, although improving, can be a nightmare; and car hire can be unreliable. See pages 205−8 for tried-and-tested travel agencies.

By Air

Delhi The sparkling new Indira Gandhi International Airport lies a 30-minute drive southwest of central Delhi. The domestic airport is nearby; if you are connecting on to Jaipur or Agra, with only a few hours to wait, it is best to go to the domestic airport (by taxi or bus), check the flight, confirm your ticket if the desk is open, and wait in the excellent, clean restaurant found to the right of the check-in desks.

Connections All three cities have airports. Currently, daily flights connect Delhi with Agra and Jaipur but be warned that morning ones are very often delayed in misty winter weather; late-afternoon flights on Tuesday−Sunday connect Jaipur and Agra.

Buying Tickets The most painless method is to use the in-house travel agency of your hotel (small fee) or a good travel agent (fee small or nothing), see pages 205−8; a visit to Indian Airlines may take several hours.

Departures Each international ticket must be reconfirmed at least 48 hours before departure, otherwise you may be wiped off the airline's computer; check-in time is at least two hours before the flight. Each domestic ticket should be reconfirmed the moment you arrive at the city from where you will be flying out, a job best done for a small fee by the hotel; check-in time is 75 minutes before the flight, but 45 minutes for executive class and for those with hand baggage only.

By Train

Train-rides around the Golden Triangle are all relatively short, much more fun than flying (and sometimes faster), and so full of interest they become part of seeing India. To plan ahead, consult the Tourist Railway Time Table available from Government of India Tourist Offices. To take trains all round the Triangle, diverting to off-beat places and going further afield, an Indrail Pass

might be the best deal. Here are the best daytime connections, all serving
meals and drinks to your seat, but sadly not one pulled by a steam engine:

Delhi—Agra—Delhi The gloriously named Taj Express, fully air-
conditioned, speeds from New Delhi Station (not Delhi Station in Old Delhi)
to Agra in just under three hours, departing 7 am (breakfast on board),
leaving at 6.45 pm to return (supper on board).

A new train runs from New Delhi to Bhopal. The Shatabdi Express leaves
New Delhi at 6.15 am and reaches Agra Cantonment at 8.05 am before going
on to Gwalior at 9.30 am and Jhansi at 10.30 am and Bhopal at 2 pm. The
return trip leaves Bhopal at 2.40 pm, Jhansi at 5.45 pm, Gwalior at 7.00 pm,
Agra at 8.20 pm and reaches New Delhi station at 10.20 pm.

Delhi—Jaipur—Delhi The equally well-named Pink City Express runs
between Delhi Station (in Old Delhi) and Jaipur in five hours, departing at
6.00 am, leaving Jaipur at 5 pm to return.

Jaipur—Agra—Jaipur The super-fast train takes five hours, departing
Jaipur at 5.45 am, leaving Agra late afternoon.

Steam Trains Two good overnight trips, smuts 'n' all, for the train
enthusiast who can be woken with steaming tea and breakfast: Jaipur—Delhi,
leaving 8.30 pm and arriving 7 am, and Jaipur—Agra, leaving 1 am and
arriving 8 am.

Buying Tickets This is not a land where you buy a ticket and seconds later
hop on the train. A ticket is two-tiered: the journey and the seat. Both need to
be booked, preferably a day in advance; again a travel agent saves hours of
queueing. If the budget permits, go for the best class available. When you
arrive at the railway station, a coolie will carry your luggage on his head right
to your seat, which you can locate by finding your name on the checklist
pinned outside each carriage.

By Bus and Coach

Deluxe buses are an excellent way to move around this little area of India.
They are cheap, clean, fast and make drink and lavatory stops at the good
Midway cafés. Pick-up and delivery points are in city centres. The Government
of India Tourist Office in each city holds the latest information on timings and
pick-up points. Current good buses include:

Delhi From the Inter-state Bus Terminal, Kashmiri Gate, in the northern
walls of Old Delhi: buses run almost hourly to Agra (minimum 4½ hours) and
frequently to Jaipur (minimum 5 hours). More convenient for anyone staying
in New Delhi, Rajasthan State Transport Corporation operates buses to Jaipur
from Bikaner House, near India Gate. The Maurya Sheraton Hotel runs the
Sheraton Express bus to and from Agra daily.

Agra From Sheetal Tourist Home near Idgah Bus Stand: three deluxe
morning buses to Delhi (the first at 8.15 am), a 4½-hour run; five deluxe buses
to Jaipur, from 6.30 am, a 5-hour run. For the Sheraton Express bus, see

Delhi, above. ITDC pick up from their office at 7.10 am, then from Taj View
Hotel, then run non-stop to Delhi. Local buses to Fatehpur Sikri leave every
45 minutes from 6.30 am for the 75-minute journey; last bus back leaves 7 pm.

Jaipur From Central Bus Stand, Station Road; deluxe to Delhi hourly
from 5 am to midnight, a 5-hour journey: to Agra about every three hours
from about 8 am (times vary), a 5-hour journey.

By Hired Car

The ideal way to travel, with total freedom to stop for incidental markets,
festivals or just the regular events such as women singing at a village well in
the early morning. It is madness to drive yourself. Hire through a travel agent
(see pages 205 ff.). The car comes with a driver and can be air-conditioned
or not; costs depend upon car type, number of days and distance, with a small
fee for the driver's food and lodging which is often payable daily; a good driver
deserves a good tip put directly into his hand at the end. Hotels will provide
picnics and the essential cold bottled drinks (order the previous day; check
that you have a bottle opener); roadside Midway restaurants are fine; and it is
fun bartering for bananas and oranges in village markets. The essential city
and inter-city maps (some drivers are better than others at orientation) are on
sale in bookshops.

In-city Transport

Airport to Hotel On arrival at Delhi, the airport taxi desk found through
customs organizes a taxi to your hotel at a fixed rate; this avoids jumping into
the deep end with bartering in an unknown city. Alternatively, there are buses.
In Agra and Jaipur, no fixed airport—hotel rates mean visitors should confirm
the price at the airport tourist desk and then with the driver before setting off.

Taxis Taking a taxi for a single journey or keeping it to make several stops
is not as extravagant as it sounds. Drivers can be very good, helpful and speak
good English; the problems start with the young drivers who have a mate and
often have no geography of their own city (this is particularly true of evening
drivers in the capital). In Delhi, the meter should work, the tip is 10 percent
plus waiting time of about Rs10 per hour and an extra tip at night. In Jaipur
and Agra the meters rarely work and hard bargaining is essential. Taking a taxi
from a large hotel naturally costs more; and Jaipur drivers produce an
alarming 'official' rate card (fabricated by their union) with prices higher than
in Delhi.

Auto-rickshaws A two-stroke motorcycle driven by a jolly, often well-
informed man pulls a covered seat big enough for two, although whole Indian
families squeeze into one during the rush hour; good for nipping through busy
streets. Meters may work in Delhi and will not work in Agra or Jaipur where a
fixed sum for the journey or journeys (less than half the taxi rate) needs to be

agreed in advance; tips as for taxis. In the capital, a driver is unlikely to go from Old Delhi down to the hotels in New Delhi; he will go as far as Connaught Place, and you take a second auto-rickshaw for the rest.

Bicycle rickshaws If you can tolerate employing human muscle-power so blatantly, a two-seater drawn by a tricycle makes a pleasant and quiet ride around Agra, parts of Old Delhi and inner Jaipur. Rates should be agreed in advance; big bottoms should pay big tips.

Beware: Drivers of taxis and rickshaws in all three cities are liable to promote shops where they get a rake-off. Take no notice. They will also bad-mouth your choice of shop if their rake-off will be small. The solution is to enter your pre-selected shop alone and announce firmly to the owner that you have come here at your own decision, not your driver's.

City Buses Strictly for the adventurous, especially during rush hour when there seem to be as many people hanging on to the sides as squashed inside.

Hotels

All three cities have a range of good hotels. Advance booking is essential in high season; you compete with other tourists and, increasingly, business conferences. See pages 209–14 for suggestions. Beware: the star-rating system means little, particularly in Delhi.

There are three basic hotel types. Firstly, at the top end of the market, the newly built hotels provide good service, good food, extensive room service, efficient, but often expensive phone, fax and telex systems, swimming pool, well-equipped health club, and a good shopping arcade with chemist, travel agent, bookshop, quality souvenir shop, etc. As most belong to a hotel chain, booking is easy. Secondly, the hotels with distinctive Indian character also offer the full range of facilities but in some cases slightly less glamour. In Delhi these include the older Imperial, Ashok and Oberoi Maidens; in Jaipur the three palace hotels. Thirdly, the less pricy hotels which are central and often family-run, especially the delightful Jaipur homes of the ex-nobles.

Outside the cites, there are several old and relaxing hotels, brimful of character and run by charming locals. They make excellent bases from which to explore the countryside.

Communications

Telephone calls, whether local, long-distance or international, are now direct dial in Delhi's up-market hotels and usually successful. In Jaipur and Agra the hotel operator is crucial; calls often take hours to connect.

The post is rather erratic. Letters and postcards sent by air to Europe or North America take from four to 14 days and parcels follow their own rules; hotels sell stamps, saving post office waiting time. Big buys sent by ship take

about three months to arrive at their destinations; be sure to leave the shop with its full name, address and detailed descriptive receipt (eg. measure the height of an object) in case there is a problem.

Money and Counting

Money is straightforward: 100 paise make one rupee. Coins and smaller notes—for one, two, five and ten rupees—are vital for tips but scarce. It is easiest to change money at your hotel, where you can ensure notes are not torn and ask for small change. The rate may be lower than that offered by a bank, but for a few paise you save hours of queuing. Outside the cities, changing money may be more difficult, so have enough cash in hand for an inter-city journey with overnight stops.

Counting is not straightforward: A *lakh* is a hundred thousand, a *crore* is ten million. Thus, India's 3,166,414 square kilometres (8,203,145 square miles) will have a projected population of 827,152,000 in 1990.

Tipping It is difficult for a Western visitor to adjust to the scale of values and cost of living in India. Rs5 for an airport porter, Rs5 for a hotel porter, Rs10 per hour waiting time for a taxi, and Rs80 for a full-day driver or a trained, full-day guide sound mean. But it is the going rate; to give more upsets the system, unless service is exceptional. Tips are not obligatory in restaurants or hotels.

Taxes These can confuse. Central and/or state (local) taxes may be added to a hotel, restaurant or shop bill, but some are exempt if you settle in foreign currency, e.g . Expenditure Tax (luxury tax) will be added to a hotel room costing more than Rs400, then subtracted on the final bill.

Timings, Holidays and Festivals

Shops open around 10 am. State emporia close at 6 pm, other shops at 7 pm and hotel shopping arcades usually much later. In Delhi, central shops close on Sunday; in Agra most Sadar Bazar shops close on Tuesday (but not Mangalick). On public holidays and for major festivals all bureaucracy closes down, as do services and shops except for the most tourist-orientated. So while it is well worth timing your visit to coincide with a religious festival, it is vital to think ahead a little, otherwise the essential travel agent or chemist may be closed. In Delhi, Agra and Jaipur, major holidays include Republic Day, Holi, Independence Day and Diwali (see page 187).

Climate

In all three cities the most comfortable weather is from October to February. Sunny days turn to chilly evenings and for Delhi nights in December and January a jumper or jacket is necessary. March and April heat up: it is best to start the day early, take a long rest from noon to 3 or 4 pm, then foray out again. With recent monsoons so erratic, the searing heat of May and June (accompanied by dust winds) may or may not be relieved by the life-giving rains of July and August. September can be muggy and humid, with occasional downpours, but it is usually nice and green.

Temperatures in Delhi, Agra and Jaipur

	Jan	Feb	Mar	Apr	May	Jun	Jul	Aug	Sept	Oct	Nov	Dec
Max. °C	21	24	30	36	41	40	35	34	34	35	29·	23
Min. °C	7	10	15	21	27	29	27	26	25	19	12	8
Max. °F	70	75	86	97	106	104	95	93	93	95	84	73
Min. °F	45	50	59	70	81	84	81	79	77	66	54	46

Average Rainfall in Delhi, Agra and Jaipur

Delhi, Agra (mm.)	25	22	17	7	8	65	211	173	150	31	1	5
Jaipur (mm.)	14	8	9	4	10	54	193	239	90	19	3	4
Delhi, Agra (in.)	1.0	0.9	0.7	0.3	0.3	2.5	8.2	6.8	5.9	1.2	0.04	0.2
Jaipur (in.)	0.5	0.3	0.4	0.2	0.4	2.1	7.5	9.3	3.5	0.7	0.1	0.2

Health

To help avoid the dreaded 'Delly Belly' do two things. First, rest on your first day, and eat simple food such as fresh vegetables, yoghurt, rice, eggs and bananas or the south Indian *thali* meal (see page 43) rather than going for a rich Mughlai blow-out. Upset tummies are most often the result of forgetting that the body must acclimatize and that traditional Indian meat dishes are very rich, with lots of spices, cream and *ghee* (clarified butter). Your enthusiasm could be your downfall. Secondly, drink plenty of fluid at all times — a good yardstick is to drink two (if possible three) glasses of liquid whenever you would normally have one. There are also three golden rules: never drink water from the tap (there will be filtered water in the flask in your hotel room); avoid salads; and do not eat fried food cooked on the streets, however tempting it may look. If you *are* smitten, see pages 27—8.

If you are ill in any serious way, insist upon the hotel duty manager telephoning the doctor on call and confirm with him the best private hospital or clinic. Any treatment needs a full receipt for the insurance claim.

Streetwise Tips

Beggars A major worry for first-time visitors. Some points should be clarified. Beggars around tourist areas belong to organized gangs, each with its own beat; if you give, you are perpetuating the pernicious system of gang beggary where the beggar is forced to give a portion of his earnings to the leader and where his opportunities for breaking out of the system are negligible. If, despite this, you wish to give to a beggar, do so with a small amount (a rupee or less) just as you are leaving the area, otherwise an alarming crowd will appear with outstretched arms. If you really want to help the poor of India, give to a reputable charity, either for general aid or for a specific project — there is plenty of choice.

Hawkers Found around any tourist site or shopping area. They offer poor quality goods or try to lure the unsuspecting to an overpriced shop. They can harass and upset. The best solution is to say 'no thank you' very firmly, followed by 'no' even more firmly if necessary.

Manners Indian manners can be embarrassingly thoughtful and charming. Overwhelming and instant personal generosity can be thanked with flowers bought on the spot (which florists make into beautiful bouquets for little or no cost) or a bottle of imported whisky brought in the suitcase. To avoid upsetting local people, low-cut necklines, high-cut hemlines and very short shorts are best worn inside the hotel only, and never in holy places.

Complaints There is an astonishing dichotemy between the laziness in some organizations and the dynamism, speed and efficiency in many others. The all-pervading bureaucracy is often given as an excuse. If your hotel, travel agent or car driver is not up to scratch, it is best to bypass all employees to complain as clearly as possible to the top person. If nothing improves, change companies.

Photography Taking photographs without a special permit is strictly forbidden at airports, bridges and railway stations. While most Indians do not mind being photographed — indeed, many ladies quickly rearrange their *saris* for a picture — some do mind, especially Muslim women in purdah. If in doubt, it is best to ask.

If you need to use a tripod or flash in a museum, permission must be obtained from the director (following a written application). Some museum staff will also try to stop hand-held cameras being used. To use a 16 mm camera, a tripod or video at the Taj Mahal and Fatehpur Sikri prior permission must be obtained from the Director, Archaeological Survey of India, Janpath, New Delhi (behind the National Museum).

Food

Spicy Gourmandising, Refreshing Drinks

There is no single Indian cuisine: eating in India can be gloriously varied for the tastebuds. Roaming around the Golden Triangle, you can try courtly Mughlai dishes simmered in rich sauces or simple north Indian kebabs grilled on charcoal, light street snacks or a rogue *thali* intruding from south India, and sweetmeats coated in real silver or chunks of fresh papaya and mango.

More myths to dispel. There is no single Indian curry and no single 'curry powder' — each dish has its own refined set of ingredients flavoured with its own *masala* (blend) of spices. Indeed, the proper use of spices is the basis of good Indian cooking. The secret is the right selection, blend and quantity. Ingredients may include ginger, cumin, cardamom, mace, cloves, cinnamon, nuts and chillies. In Indian cooking, it is fine for a dish to be hot from a mixture of spices, not so fine for it to be, as locals put it, 'chilli-hot'. As a general guideline to spice explorers, chillies make a dish hot, while yoghurt and coconut keep it mild.

Indians, particularly men, take their food extremely seriously. A man needs only the tiniest hint to effuse poetically about a chicken dish only perfected by his great aunt (could he arrange for her to cook it for you?), the spinach grown in a certain area, the subtle succulence of his mother's *dhal*

(lentils). Jane Fonda aerobics may have penetrated a few homes, but a showy stomach is still an accepted sign of well-being. As one woman candidly remarked: 'The sari is no incentive to slimming; it can expand as I do with no alterations.'

Western visitors have often been frustrated in their efforts to find good food. This is because until recently Indians preferred to eat at home, and home cooking is still the best. The change began in the 1970s in Delhi, when the growing middle class began to eat out and a new generation of foreign visitors arrived with more discerning and adventurous palates than their Raj forebears. The Punjabi hotel-owners who moved to New Delhi after Independence could no longer serve up *tandoori* chicken (spices removed in case memsahib gets the hiccups) and nursery Raj food in flock wallpapered rooms. The food revolution began. Out went brown soup, spiceless tandoor chicken and caramel custard. Old chefs were consulted; authentic recipes revived. And in came the speciality restaurant. Now restaurant eating is part of fashionable New Delhi life. The local clientele is enticed with new decor, regional cuisines and a string of food festivals — French, Italian, Thai, even Japanese.

In essence, whatever the tastebuds demand is available in Delhi; there is even an American Pie and a Wimpy for fast-food addicts. In Jaipur, capital of Rajasthan, there is a fair range of cuisines, but almost no distinctive Rajasthani food unless you make a special request. And Agra offers little of its great Mughal past. For general tips and specific restaurant suggestions, see pages 215 ff.

Ordering a meal is not as difficult as the long menus imply. Try a lamb (*gosht*) and chicken (*murg*) dish with a seasonal vegetable — cauliflower (*gobi*), spinach (*saag*) and potato (*aloo*) are delicious in winter. The huge variety of Indian breads taste best hot and fresh, so it is best to order one, then more (perhaps of a different type) after the food arrives — in an Indian home the breads are cooked throughout the meal. Among the pickles (called chutneys in the West), mango is likely to pep up a dish enough and chilli is likely to blow the roof of your mouth off, although some Indians start their day with a palate-cleansing raw chilli before breakfast. Chutney (a Hindi word, meaning relish) is, confusingly, a fresh sauce, such as the mint, spice and yoghurt mixture served with *samosas*. To cool off any unwelcome heat and to keep the tummy happy, yoghurt (*dahi*) eaten plain or mixed with cucumber, tomato, etc., works better than water.

As for eating, to really enter the spirit follow the old proverb: 'Eating with a knife and fork is like making love through an interpreter.' Using your right hand, never the left, mix mouthfuls of rice with meats and vegetables or nimbly tear off pieces of bread and wrap them around the drier foods, using a spoon for more liquid dishes.

Being adventurous and trying the different cuisines on offer is part of visiting India. In Delhi a rich and royal Mughlai feast complements a day exploring Old Delhi. Agra has few Mughlai restaurants, although it was to this city that the first emperor, Babur, brought his taste for exotic Persian food. In his diary he constantly refers to food and feasting: the transport of 'excellent' almonds by camel merits a large picture, the gini-cow is 'very tender and savoury' and the citron is a 'deliciously acid fruit, making a very pleasant and wholesome sherbet'.

Babur set the tone for Mughal feasting, a combination of present-giving, entertainment and gourmandising. Later, Akbar claimed that 500 different dishes were essential for a regular royal meal, let alone what would be expected at a feast.

Today, a Mughlai meal still sits heavily. Try rich *shami* or *seekh kebabs* to start, then a *biryani* (meat tenderized in herbs, spices, nuts, raisins, coconut and cream, then cooked with rice), *raan-i-mirza* (leg of lamb cooked in curd, cardamoms and cumin) or *murg massalam* (chicken stuffed with ginger, eggs, pistachios, cashew nuts and other goodies). Scoop it up with rich Mughlai breads such as the flaky, butter-oozing *paratha*, a *sheermal*, a *bakarkani* or a *kabuli naan*; or order a pile of rice given royal status with saffron and cardamom. *Nav-ratan* (nine gems) is the specially good chutney. The brave can finish with the immobilizing, sweeter-than-sweet rice dish, *muzafar*; the less brave with a sherbet. Hotel and Connaught Place restaurants can provide sumptuous food and settings; Old Delhi restaurants such as Karim (see page 73) have equally good food but in simpler surroundings and with good local atmosphere.

Regular north Indian food, of the kind eaten by the hungry Muslim armies sweeping down the Himalayan passes to conquer Hindustan, traces its origins to the Northwest Frontier and western Punjab. Like the Mughlai cuisine, it focuses on meat, but it is simpler and less rich. Kebabs of spiced meat on long skewers are plunged into the red-hot clay or iron tandoor ovens. Unlike Mughlai dishes, the meat is usually cooked on the bone in its own juices and a few spices. It is not tenderized too much so it keeps a good chew to it, and the gravy is left unstrained and slightly nutty compared to Mughlai smoothness. For breads, there are plain *naan*, *parathas*, the *makai-ki-roti* (made of cornflour) and the *roomali* (handkerchief) *roti* which the chef tosses and twirls high in the air to stretch it to transparent thinness. Northerners like vegetables, especially potato (*aloo*), spinach (*saag*) and peas (*matar*). A pulse, perhaps chickpeas (*chenna*) or lentils (*dhal*), and mango pickle complete the meal. The favourite winter Punjabi pudding is *gajar* (carrot) *halwa*.

After those Indian spices, you could try chewing a *paan* to cleanse the palate and aid digestion. There are paan-sellers on street corners, and several restaurants keep paan boxes. To concoct a paan, a sliced, woody betel nut is laid on a betel leaf with lime, *catechu* paste and as many other ingredients as you wish, both sweet and sour. The leaf is then deftly wrapped into a tidy parcel. You pop it in, chew, swallow the juices, and spit out what is left when you have had enough — only the most tender ones can be swallowed.

For a light meal, south Indian is the answer. A thali has the advantage of being easy to order: just one word brings a complete meal, usually only lightly spiced, easy to digest in the heat and gentle on a stomach new to India. It is all vegetarian, the dishes selected by the chef from an almost infinite list of vegetable combinations cooked with gentle spices. (Some northern restaurants serve a 'non-veg', i.e. meat thali, to pander to locals.)

The thali (platter) is delivered with a ring of *katoris* (little dishes), each containing a different dish and usually arranged in order so you progress round the circle through complementary flavours ending with *payasham* (rich rice pudding). The centre is filled with rice and breads, replenished whenever you wish. Another good south Indian meal is a *masala dosa*, a large paper-thin rice pancake wrapped around a dryish potato filling and served with a more liquid vegetable dish and some fresh coconut chutney. As it is often eaten in the morning in the south, masala dosa is on some hotel breakfast menus. And the steaming south Indian coffee is excellent, like Italian espresso.

Then to fruits. North Delhi's Sabzi Mandi, the largest vegetable market in Asia, ensures a constant flow of fresh vegetables and fruits. Without importing, India can produce fruits from cool hills and burning plains. And India is so big that some fruits are available all year by being grown in different places. Papayas, pineapples and coconuts are always around, as are delicious bananas. Then there are limes, custard apples, guavas, five-star fruits, apples from Kashmir, *chickoos* (like kiwi fruit), *kinos* (a man-made hybrid of sweet lime and orange which ripens in January) and the divine mangoes which make their first appearance in April. One special fruit is found in the Agra backstreets. It is *petha*, a huge green-skinned pumpkin whose white flesh is cut up, pricked, washed in soda and then cooked in sugar syrup until it turns transparent. If you like pumpkin pie, you may well like petha. The place to taste the best is Panchi Petha Store on Bhagat Singh Road.

Snacks are an important part of Indian life. And the delicious-looking dishes prepared at roadside stalls and in tiny shops are too tempting to resist. To try these is not as dangerous as many people believe, for while it is sheer madness ever to drink unboiled water, freshly cooked food should not upset a good constitution.

Snacks start at the pavement *chaat* stalls. Chaat is a spicy mixture which tingles the tastebuds. Everyone eats it including suited office workers, and it is also a favourite with pregnant women. Found all over India, with infinite local variations, it is always eaten cold. Delhi chaats usually include dry mango and fresh mint chutneys (and raw mango in season). Try one based on *chole* (chickpeas in gravy) or on seasonal fruits and topped with coriander and ginger. In Agra, *pani puri* is the chaat speciality. A watery liquid (*pani* means water) spiced with

tamarind, lime, mint paste and hot chillies is poured into a crisp fried shell (a puri), to be popped into the mouth in one, quickly, before it collapses. Another is *sank*, a boat-shaped *poppadum* filled with a spicy fresh chutney, often on sale in the main market street behind the Jama Masjid.

After the savoury, the sweet. In India, gods and humans alike have a very sweet tooth. If you enjoy the sweetmeat shops (see page 68) and the hot *gulab jamun* served in restaurants, try a roadside special. In Old Delhi, moving down Chandni Chowk main street from the fort, you can find Naim Chand Jain on the left, a kiosk where the founder's grandsons cook huge, golden-brown, calorie-laden *jalebis* day and night, soaking the fried twirly shapes in cauldrons of bubbling syrup. Around Fatehpuri Mosque, fresh nuts and dried fruits are sold straight from the sack. Although these ones are intended to further enrich the Mughlai dishes, Mahatma Gandhi believed that man's diet 'should consist of nothing but sunbaked fruits and nuts'. In old Agra, they are sold on roadside carts together with a winter local favourite, *gujak*, a nutty-textured biscuit made of caramelized sugar and sesame seed. As for freshly-made ice-cream, the fruit or nut ones such as mango and pistachio are delicious, especially at LMB on Johari Bazar in Jaipur and at Giani Ice-Cream found a few yards along the road to the right of Fatehpuri Mosque in Old Delhi; Giani also has mountains of irresistible hot *halwa*.

Hotel snacks offer none of this fun. Best is to loll beside the hotel pool or sink into a wicker chair for teatime *samosas* (a fried, pyramid-shaped envelope with a meat or vegetable stuffing) or *pakoras* (deep-fried vegetables) with fresh mint chutney, washed down with strong Indian tea.

For drinks, the most thirst-quenching is fresh lime juice mixed with water (*nimbu pani*) or soda (*nimbu* soda) and drunk plain or with sugar or salt. *Lassi*, a drink of fresh yoghurt, is also taken plain, sugared or salted and is both refreshing and tummy-settling. (In the heat, salted drinks help keep the body's fluids in balance.) Then there are the many fizzy sweet drinks, the safest if you want a drink from a street café or kiosk. Pure fruit juices such as fresh mango or pineapple are delicious, especially at Nathu's in Delhi; but be careful where you order them. For something stronger, Indian beers are similar to lager and the Indian-made spirits are considerably cheaper than imported brands. Indian rum is particularly good and Indian gin makes a perky Tom Collins cocktail, a sort of alcoholic nimbu soda.

Postscript: In any restaurant, smart or modest, if you think the hygiene is dubious, order freshly cooked hot food, avoid lingering buffets and resort to an omelette if necessary. For drink, use purifiers if you think the water has not been filtered or boiled, see that bottled drinks are opened in front of you and do not take ice unless you are confident the water is OK. And remember, alcohol is not a sterilizer.

Shopping
Irresistible, Exotic, Quality Craftsmanship

India offers sensational handicrafts at affordable prices. To watch an Indian craftsman at work is to begin to understand the years of patient practice needed to become master of his craft. The range of quality craftsmanship is vast, from sweet-smelling carved sandalwood and exotic silk weaves to pricy jewellery and intricately inlaid marble using precious and semi-precious stones. Delhi is the place for top-quality shopping for all India's crafts; Agra and Jaipur have the best range of their own specialities, with craftsmen to watch so you can really appreciate the skill.

There are three ways of shopping: in government-run emporia, in private shops including hotel arcades, and in the bazaars.

In the government-run emporia, particularly in Delhi, the prices are fixed, the goods specially commissioned for the shop by good buyers who know their subject, and the payment and shipping systems work. These are the best places for big buys that need shipping, for speedy mass present buying, and for browsing to get an idea of the standard of craftsmanship, the range and the prices before taking the plunge into the smaller shops or the bazaars.

In the private shops fixed prices are rarely fixed and a more sophisticated form of bartering takes place, especially for pricier goods. If your buys include precious metals or stones, it is essential to have a fully detailed receipt. It is always best to check up comparative prices in competitive shops. It is never wise to be led to a shop by a tout, rickshaw driver, taxi or coach driver, charming young lad or excellent local guide — even one provided as part of a package holiday booked from home; the price you pay includes a cut for them. And beware of private shops which have a title remarkably like a government-run emporium, or who boast 'government approved' on the facade.

In the colourful, bustling bazaars bartering is the game. This is the fun way to buy small items, especially in the evenings when locals come to shop. Fairy lights brighten the twilight and men at little stalls fry up delicious-smelling snacks to compete with the sweet perfumes of the piles of garlands on the flower stalls. There is no clear yardstick for price reduction — everyone acquires a triumphant tale of bashing a trader down from Rs100 to Rs5 — but it is worth remembering that the trader is never going to sell below the price he paid, never.

For basic tips, see below; for practical shopping, see page 218.

Delhi

The best place in the Golden Triangle for quality and variety, with plenty of opportunities to buy at fair prices. The government-run **Central Cottage Industries Emporium** on Janpath is the perfect all-India craft department store with everything from picnic hampers and Kashmiri lacquerware to furnishing fabrics and inlaid chess boards. Departments are devoted to different states; a rainbow of fabrics dazzles upstairs; ordering goods to be specially made or shipped is quick. For more in-depth buying, go to the **Crafts Museum** (see page 84) to watch the skills and buy the objects; or to the individual **state emporia** in Baba Kharak Singh Marg off Connaught Place (so-called government approved shops elsewhere are suspect). Ones for **Gujarat, Bihar, Andra Pradesh, Orissa, Rajasthan** and **Tamil Nadu** are all excellent.

For fine silk and cotton weaves, the government emporia are hard to beat. But for *khadi*, the rough hand-spun and hand-woven cloth promoted by Mahatma Gandhi, **Khadi Gramodyog Bhawan** at 24 Regal Building is the place. The fine *chikan* (white embroidery on white muslin) made by the **Tandon** family of Lucknow are sold at their shop in the rabbit warren Palika Bazar under Connaught Place. Antiques abound in Sundar Nagar Square, where shops such as **Bharany** and **Kumar** sell wood, brass, bronze, silver etc. and will supply certificates for objects less than 100 years old. This is also the place for contemporary silver.

To buy something made in Delhi, go to Old Delhi. Traditional gold and silver jewellery is found in **Dariba Kalan** off Chandni Chowk as is **Gulab Singh Jahrinal** the attar (perfume shop) and the den-like shops of nearby **Kinari Bazaar** stock every accessory for an Indian celebration.

Delhi is the place to find Western designs at a fraction of Western prices.

The deluxe hotels stock quality goods which range from clothes and shoes to briefcases and jewellery. The **Taj Mahal, Maurya Sheraton, Taj Palace** and **Ashok** shops are so good that discerning locals patronize them. In town, Connaught Circus has **The Shop** in Regal Building (household goods and clothes), shoe shops with fashionable Western designs, **Ravissant** in Hansalya Building on Barakhamba Road, and bargain rejects or fashion copies at the stalls along Janapth, either side of the Cottage Industries Emporium entrance (check carefully for faults). Further out, **Fab India**, 14-N Greater Kailash I was the pioneer in quality Western goods, now joined by many others including **Haveli** on the outer Ring Road and the wacky **Once Upon a Time**, opposite the Qutb Minar in south Delhi—an outpost of this is in a cluster of village houses in romantic Haus Khas. These mushrooming shops are run by Delhi's stylish women; *City Scan* magazine and weekend newspapers carry articles on the latest ones to open.

Agra

Agra is rip-off-ville. Unless you are very, very careful, the euphoria of a special buy can dissolve into the realization that good money was spent on rubbish. Quantities of rip-off shops slip words such as 'government', 'official', 'emporium' and 'cottage industry' into their titles but bear no

A New Jaipur Queen

In 1940 Maharaj Man Singh II of Jaipur, known as Jai, married the beautiful and emancipated Gayatri Devi from Cooch Behar in north-east India. After a visit to the Amber temple and "eight or ten nights" of parties, Devi was finally taken to the City Palace and into the zenana.

When we reached the outer gates of the City Palace, I was transferred into a palanquin and carried through a labyrinth of corridors and courtyards. Then I was set down and, as a new bride, had to perform a prayer ceremony at the threshold to mark my entry into my husband's home for the first time. After this there was a women's durbar, when one by one the ladies of the zenana and of the aristocratic families filed past me, parting my veil to look at the bride's face and, following the Rajputana custom, leaving a gift in my lap after their first glimpse of me. The older ones made assorted comments, such as 'What a lovely bride!' 'How fair her skin is!' 'She's got a small nose.' 'Let me look at your eyes,' but the remarks weren't all complimentary.

The zenana quarters were divided into a series of self-contained apartments. Mine, decorated in blues and greens, was much like the others, with a little square courtyard and a private durbar hall hung with blue glass lamps, and inner rooms opening off it. There were a hundred women living in the zenana. Presiding over them was the only one of the late Maharaja's wives who was still alive. As one of Jai's wives, I could almost never uncover my face in her presence and always had to be seated a few paces to her left.

She instructed her ladies to devise and act out plays for me to watch. During the war I remember struggling between giggles and tears of gratitude as the ladies, dressed up as soldiers, performed scenes in which Jai, victoriously and apparently single-handedly, triumphed over the German forces in the Middle East. Even apart from such naive theatricals, Jai's activities were closely followed with extreme and affectionate attention in the zenana, and any achievement was promptly celebrated. When Jai's team won the All-India polo championship, for instance, skirts and shawls were embroidered with polo sticks; when he gained his flying license, the ladies, who never had—and were never likely to—set foot in a plane themselves, loyally decorated their clothes with aeroplane motifs.

Gayatri Devi and Santha Rama Rau, A Princess Remembers

relation to the reliable, government-run emporia in Delhi (see above). Trust no-one for advice, least of all those who lurk in hotel lobbies.

Here are a handful of safe shops. First, inlaid marble, perhaps the most tempting buy (but not to be confused with soapstone, a cheap soft stone that resembles marble but will scratch and stain unlike marble and has none of its luminosity). Prettily inlaid soapstone boxes sold outside the Taj and Fort should cost only a few rupees. To buy the real thing, it is safest to shop at the best marble inlay store, **Subhash**, at 18/1 Gwalior Road, where you get top-quality materials and craftsmanship but at surprisingly high prices.

Next, dhurries and pile carpets. One reliable shop is **Mangalick** at 5 Taj Road, Sadar Bazar where the owners employ craftsmen in and around the city working to the highest standards (see page 114).

Of the jewellers, **Ganeshi Lall & Son** at 13 Mahatma Gandhi Road has good and reliable jewellery and stones, will make to order and issues fully descriptive receipts. They have a shop in the Mughal Sheraton Hotel and an associated shop in the Maurya Sheraton, Delhi, so there is often time to have a piece altered while touring elsewhere and then collect it before leaving Delhi. Lall also stocks another Agra craft, velvet decorated with gold embroidery and. semi-precious stones. He sells it made up into evening belts, handbags and pictures. But do look at Lall's showpieces — a magnificent replica of the Peacock Throne and his Pride of India tapestry — justifying the shop's proud title 'By appointment to Late Queen Mary'. Please note that not all stones are genuine.

For cheap and cheerful dhurries, wedding tinsel and saris, go to the market behind Jama Masjid in Old Agra, or forge through narrower streets to find Sando and his fellow *patang wallahs* (kite makers) in **Mal-ka-Bazar**.

Jaipur

Shopping in the old bazaars at twilight, in the shadows of the City Palace, can be magical in this most romantic city. But shopping in private shops can be another story. Suffice to recount that when Delhi's Central Cottage Industries Emporium set up a branch here, the local guides and drivers ensured it received no publicity, got no trade and finally had to close down. There is a **Rajasthan Government Handicrafts Emporium** on M.I. Road but its stock is disappointing.

Best buys are the local crafts. Jaipur and nearby Sanganer's best-known export to the world is block-printing (see page 172). There are several good shops. **Anokhi** on Tilak Marg, south of the Pink City, uses some of the best printers available to produce fine Western garments (they also have a shop in Delhi at Santushti, opposite the Samrat Hotel); **Kin Fabrics** is on Station Road; **Saadh Textiles** and **J K Arts** are both on Sanganer's main road; and **Maharaja Textile Printers** is conveniently on the road to Amber. For the offshoot of Sanganer printing, coloured or gold-speckled handmade paper, go to **Khadi Ghar** on M.I. Road.

Still on fabric, the bright plain cottons worn by locals are sold by the metre

in **Johari Bazar**. Here also is the *bandhani* (tie-dye) work, often sold still crinkled up and unironed. Some is worked in Jaipur, some in western Rajasthan in and around Jodhpur. This cloth of intricate patterns of many thousands of dots, tied by nimble fingers and then dyed in great vats, can be made to order, the customer choosing colours and design. To see the craft, seek out Neel Garo ka Mohla off Ramganj Bazar where young Mohammed Ramzan is already an award-winning craftsman; to buy his work, go to **Rana Sari Emporium** or **Rajasthan Sari Emporium**, both in Johari Bazar. Still off Ramganj Bazar, **Marudhara Enterprise** at 1677 Khawas ji ka Rasta is piled ceiling-high with pieces of appliqué and embroidery including white *kanas* (shawls) made in Barmer.

. Jaipur blue pottery is undergoing a revival. **Kripal Singh** (see page 168) sells his beautiful pots from his Jaipur **studio**, B-18a Siva Marg, Bani Park (and in Delhi at **The Shop** and the **Rajasthan Government Emporium**). **Anokhi** stocks pots, doorknobs, jewellery and other ceramics from Leela Dordia's workshops in Jaipur and Sanganer.

Another Jaipur craft is the tricky art of lacquering and engraving brassware. To see some of the skill and possibly invest in a piece, go to **P M Allah Buksh & Son** on M.I. Road (closed on Friday). The dish, bowl or tray is made first. Then the craftsman applies the delicate pattern by repoussé (raising parts), embossing (indenting parts) and engraving fine arabesques, finally colouring some areas and then polishing the whole piece to show off a glittering and complex design.

As in Agra, jewellery is a tempting but dangerous buy. For semi-precious stones, bargain hard in Gopalji-ka-Rasta which runs west off Johari Bazar; here live jewellers skilled in Jaipur's traditional *meenakari* work (combinations of gold, stones and delicate floral enamel designs). For precious stones, bargain equally hard in Haldion-ka-Rasta on the opposite side of Johari Bazar. Not far along, **Bhuramal Rajmal Surana** is at Lal Katra, found upstairs through a painted archway. One of the finest (and one of the few reliable) jewellers in town, Surana stocks both the traditional meenakari pieces and regular Indian and European designs. It is here that old Jaipur families come, not to the clutch of jewellers on M.I. Road who should be approached with the greatest caution.

The most enjoyable Jaipur shopping is in the bazaars. In addition to the fabric, bandhani work and stones, you can find splendid puppets opposite the Hawa Mahal, near the **Famous Nagra Shoe Store** which stocks local shoes from all over Rajasthan. There are more shoe shops in Ramganj where Mr Nizamuddin's **Fancy Nagra Shoe Store** has camel-skin shoes and the Jaipur black and silver embroidered slippers. Back at the Badi Chaupar crossroads, local girls giggle as they select yet more treats from walls of coloured glass bangles, while old silver jewellery is sold diagonally opposite, in kiosks behind the flower carts. At the bottom of Johari Bazar find kites by Sanganer Gate and cheap 'n' cheerful costume meenakari jewellery in Bapu Bazar at shops such as **Beauty Palace** at no. 35.

Delhi

New Delhi is the political nerve-centre of India. Purpose-built as the Eastern capital for the British Empire, it now operates under different management as the capital of independent India. Corridors and leafy gardens buzz with political gossip and intrigue. Bungalows, hotels and public buildings are settings for an endless flow of news-exchange and contact-making by diplomats, politicians, international traders, entrepreneurs and journalists, whose public socializing is glamourized by silk sari-clad beauties and turbaned servants and oiled with an astounding consumption of whisky and tray upon tray of chicken *tikka*.

The wide avenues lined with blossoming trees clog up with an assortment of traffic including the Indian-built Maruti (it is said that 500 new cars hit the capital's tarmac every month). Painted and overloaded lorries, lolloping old Ambassador cars and nippy auto-rickshaws belch fumes into the air. In the midst of the hubbub, locals calmly stroll, chat and take naps in the lush parks and on the many roundabouts ablaze with competitive municipal planting — a Delhi gardener's dream is to win an annual award and adorn his mound of flowerbeds with, perhaps, the sign 'First Prize Middle-sized Roundabout'.

The flat plains have encouraged many past Delhi rulers to indulge in large-scale rebuilding. But even by their standards, where to abandon a conquered city and start entirely afresh was normal, the twisting tentacles of the modern capital have a rampant appetite for infinite expansion. Hungrily they gobble up acre after acre, sometimes bending with good grace to include an old building from an older Delhi, sometimes bulldozing the past in favour of concrete and, of course, highrises. To the north, the Mughal emperor Shah Jahan's Old Delhi presents a barrier; but to the south, smart New Delhi estates known as colonies have eased themselves around Delhi's old cities; and to the east and west more colonies sprawl over the plains into the distance.

Getting to know any big capital is bewildering, and Delhi is no exception. To cope with its size and complexity, the most rewarding way to begin exploring is to take one area at a time. For transport, an auto-rickshaw is ideal for the centre, and the driver will wait if you want to hop down for a few minutes; walking is best for Old Delhi lanes; but take a taxi for the old British area to the north and for southern New Delhi's old cities. The vital accessory is a map, available free from the tourist office or for a few rupees at a bookshop.

New Delhi

A good starting place, right at the heart of the capital. The announcement by king-emperor George V and Queen Mary 'to Our People' at the 1911 Delhi Durbar that the capital of British India was to move from Calcutta to 'the ancient Capital of Delhi' was a total surprise, to be remembered as the best-kept secret in the history of India. The words, as Robert Irving later remarked,

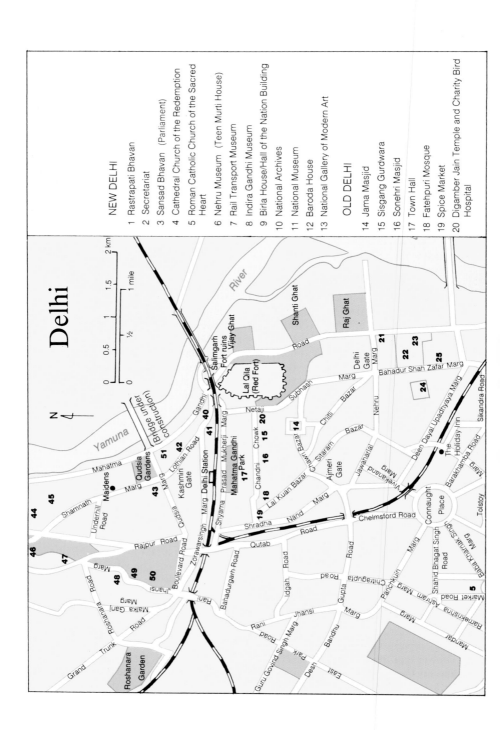

Delhi

0 0.5 1 1.5 2 km
0   ½   1   1 mile

NEW DELHI

1 Rastrapati Bhavan
2 Secretariat
3 Sansad Bhavan (Parliament)
4 Cathedral Church of the Redemption
5 Roman Catholic Church of the Sacred Heart
6 Nehru Museum (Teen Murti House)
7 Rail Transport Museum
8 Indira Gandhi Museum
9 Birla House/Hall of the Nation Building
10 National Archives
11 National Museum
12 Baroda House
13 National Gallery of Modern Art

OLD DELHI

14 Jama Masjid
15 Sisgang Gurdwara
16 Sonehri Masjid
17 Town Hall
18 Fatehpuri Mosque
19 Spice Market
20 Digamber Jain Temple and Charity Bird Hospital

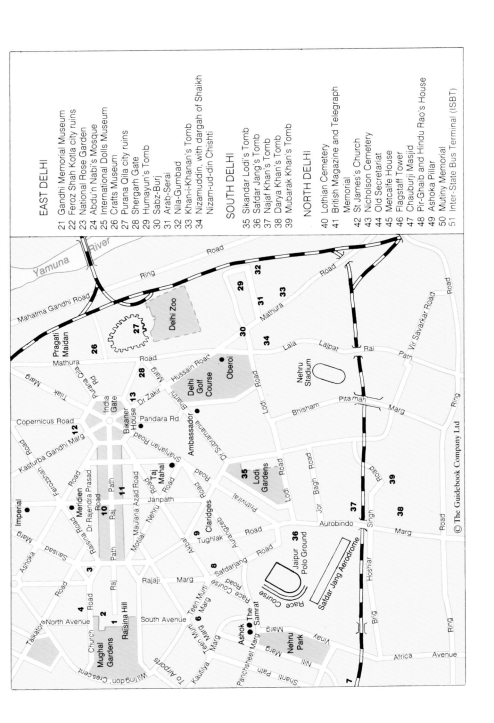

EAST DELHI

21 Gandhi Memorial Museum
22 Feroz Shah Kotla city ruins
23 National Rose Garden
24 Abdu'n Nabi's Mosque
25 International Dolls Museum
26 Crafts Museum
27 Purana Qila city ruins
28 Shergarh Gate
29 Humayun's Tomb
30 Sabz-Burj
31 Arab-Serai
32 Nila-Gumbad
33 Khan-i-Khanan's Tomb
34 Nizamuddin, with dargah of Shaikh
   Nizam-ud-din Chishti

SOUTH DELHI

35 Sikandar Lodi's Tomb
36 Safdar Jang's Tomb
37 Najaf Khan's Tomb
38 Darya Khan's Tomb
39 Mubarak Khan's Tomb

NORTH DELHI

40 Lothian Cemetery
41 British Magazine and Telegraph
   Memorial
42 St James's Church
43 Nicholson Cemetery
44 Old Secretariat
45 Metcalfe House
46 Flagstaff Tower
47 Chauburji Masjid
48 Pir-Ghaib and Hindu Rao's House
49 Ashoka Pillar
50 Mutiny Memorial
51 Inter-State Bus Terminal (ISBT)

© The Guidebook Company Ltd

'burst over Delhi like tropical sun through the dark rain clouds of a monsoon'. In one stroke, Delhi changed status from provincial town to imperial capital of the sub-continent.

Plans were launched for the last and arguably the finest of Delhi's cities. Work was fast. By 1929, when journalist and architectural historian Robert Byron arrived, he could proclaim excitedly: 'That New Delhi exists, and that, twenty years ago it did not exist, are facts known to anyone who is at all aware of the British connection with India.' But that it 'marks, besides an advance in the political unification of India, a notable artistic event, has scarcely been realized . . . in the darkness of contemporary standards, the event shines with a Periclean importance.'

Standing on Raisina Hill, you get an idea of what he meant. This is the core of **Sir Edwin Lutyens**'s triumphant plan. When he and the rest of the Planning Commission — Herbert Baker, J A Brodie, G S C Swinton and others — first arrived from England, the royals had already laid a foundation stone north of Old Delhi. The team plodded about the Delhi plains on elephants, got very hot and decided otherwise. One night, in 1913, they acted: the foundation stone was unearthed, put on a bullock cart and pulled southwards to Raisina Hill.

The great work began. First the style. Lutyens, who had made a tour of inspection of north Indian buildings, was impressed by the Buddhist monuments of Sanchi (seen in Rastrapati Bhavan domes) but by little Hindu architecture apart from the fairytale Datia Palace (south of Agra); and he apparently wrote off Fatehpur Sikri as 'the work of monkeys'. So Western classical won, with additional Indian elements which lent themselves to his imagination, wit and attention to detail. Lutyens was to describe the building 'as an Englishman dressed for the climate'. Next, the overall design. Raisina Hill was to be the focus of a large triangle. On its summit the Viceroy's palatial home (now Rastrapati Bhavan) looked down between the Secretariats (the two principal administrative buildings, now North Block and South Block) and the broad green vista of Raj Path (road of those who govern) right along to India Gate. The view should have been closed by the magnificent ruins of Purana Qila, but Lord Willingdon (Viceroy 1931–6) permitted an ugly new stadium to block it out. A road either end of Raj Path and one bisecting it in the middle, Janpath, led northwards up to Connaught Place, the top of the triangle. A mirror-image residential triangle stretched south of Raj Path.

New Delhi was Lutyens's crowning achievement. A largely self-taught man of humble origins who married the daughter of the previous viceroy, Lord Lytton (Viceroy 1865–80), he won the New Delhi job and a cluster of honours — including a knighthood in 1918 — by the imperial scale and character of his work. Lutyens was responsible for the overall design and the viceregal estate at its centre, plus some monuments and buildings along Raj Path; a bevy of architects filled the honeycomb of roads north and south of Raj Path. While

Baker did some landmark buildings, the almost-forgotten R T Russell and his team designed more than 4,000 flat-roofed residences of stuccoed brick, ranging from quarters for menials and clerks to bungalows for senior officers, plus hospitals, post offices, etc.

Next, the building. Thirty thousand labourers — both men and women, just as you see on the building sites today — were enlisted from Agra, nearby Bharatpur and Mirzapur (near Varanasi) to level land, build roads, install water pipes and electricity, transport stone from Dholpur (south of Agra) and erect buildings. For planting the arid soil, Lutyens consulted William Robertson Mustoe whose knowledge was gained at Kew Gardens and Punjab Horticultural Department. Together with W S George, they landscaped the dry plain into unimagined lushness which has reached maturity today.

Costs and controversy soared. When the official buildings were up, 10,000 trees planted and £15 million spent, plans were firmly modified. When Baker, Lutyens's assistant, made the gradient up Raisina Hill too steep and transformed the view of Rastrapati Bhavan from power symbol hovering over the new capital to one in which only the dome was visible, the furious Lutyens said he had 'met his Bakerloo'. And when Baker's bungalow on Akbar Road failed to catch much-needed breezes, it was dubbed 'Baker's Oven'.

The vistas in the central core of this 20th-century city are breathtaking. And several buildings are open to the public. To see a little, start on **Raisina Hill**, looking along Raj Path to India Gate. In the foreground, Vijay Chowk at the bottom of the slope is where the magical, sunset Beating Retreat is held every January (see page 187). Up the slope, Baker's Secretariats decorated with Indian elephants, pavilions and balconies stand to left and right.

Behind rises **Rastrapati Bhavan**, built as the Viceroy's house with a facade 192 metres (630 feet) wide and a plan covering 18,580 square metres (200,000 square feet) — larger than Versailles — and set in a Viceregal Estate which took an army of 2,000 staff to run it. It was here in the huge Durbar Hall that Britain's last Viceroy, Lord Mountbatten, handed over power to India's first Prime Minister, Pandit Jawaharlal Nehru. Now the home of India's President, the palace can be visited sometimes when he is out of town. Arrange the visit through the Tourist Office or your country's mission and marvel at Lutyens's crisp architectural details, his witty imperial lion doorknobs, his cooling internal grottos and the huge teak-lined dining-room's colour-coded lights to tell the two wine and food butlers behind each chair when to serve and clear. A visitor in Lord Linlithgow's time (Viceroy 1936–42) recalled how at a banquet 'every other guest at the long table was the ruler of a State' and how each night the band played diners in with 'The Roast Beef of Old England'. When there were no official guests, the Linlithgow family sang along 'in a rousing chorus'.

In the forecourt, the **Jaipur Column** reflects the close ties between the princely state which had wisely made diplomatic ties with first the powerful

Mughal, then the British. Given by Maharaja Madho Singh to commemorate
the new city, the 44-metre (145-foot) -high sandstone column topped by a
lotus and star finial soon became a symbol of dominion and victory, as public
columns have been throughout history. One face of the plinth is inscribed with
an interesting early plan of New Delhi.

The Viceroy's back garden is the **Mughal Gardens**, open to the public in
February and March and not to be missed if you are in Delhi. Inspired by Lady
Willingdon's trip to the real Mughal Gardens of Kashmir, they were designed
by Lutyens with helpful breakfast-time hints from Mustoe. Today, 150
gardeners tend the perfect blossoms, tinkling fountains, velvet lawns, and
stone pergola leading to a circular secret garden. Originally the gardens were
merely part of the 101-hectare (250-acre) estate which had swimming pool,
cricket ground, golf course and tennis courts, kept immaculate for the Viceroy
by 418 gardeners, of whom 50 were employed just to scare off unwanted birds
and 20 to do the palace flower arrangements.

Today, Rastrapati Bhavan is still a host's dream, used by the President to
entertain at the highest level. Banquets are given in the dining-room; and
those Raj tea parties with starched suits, flower-patterned dresses and delicate
sandwiches are still held in the Mughal Gardens.

A core of temporal and spiritual buildings encircled the Viceroy's palace.
Domed, circular **Sansad Bhavan** (Parliament House) stands to the north. The
colonnaded building has a central hall and three semi-circular halls, designed
by Baker to house the Chamber of Princes, the Council of State and the
Legislative Assembly. It now houses the Rajya Sabha (Council of States) and
Lok Sabha (House of the People); the princes' magnificent hall is the library.
Members of the Rajya Sabha are elected, a third of the 244 members retiring
every two years; the 544 elected members of Lok Sabha provide the ruling
party with Prime Minister and Cabinet. MPs provide good theatre as they
argue out the day's issues with tremendous gusto, often lapsing out of English
into an assortment of languages as debate hots up (again, the Tourist Office or
your country's mission can arrange a visit). To the left of Sansad Bhavan is
H A N Medd's **Cathedral Church of the Redemption** (completed in 1935), for
which money was raised by the pious Anglo-Catholic Lord Irwin (Viceroy
1926−31). It is a bold building 'infused with the spirit of Palladio and Lutyens'
(Philip Davies). Medd's other Delhi cathedral, the Roman Catholic Church of
the Sacred Heart (completed in 1934), stands directly north at the top of
Pandit Pant Marg.

Three fascinating New Delhi houses are nearby, connected by wide
boulevards. Curved Willingdon Crescent, which runs round the back of
Raisina Hill, is lined with Staff Quarters and elegant bungalows, one of which
(no. 1) was used by Lutyens during his 1923−8 visits. At the southern end it
meets Teen Murti Road. Here Nehru lived on the corner at **Teen Murti House**,
set amid large gardens with a rose walk where he plucked his buttonhole each

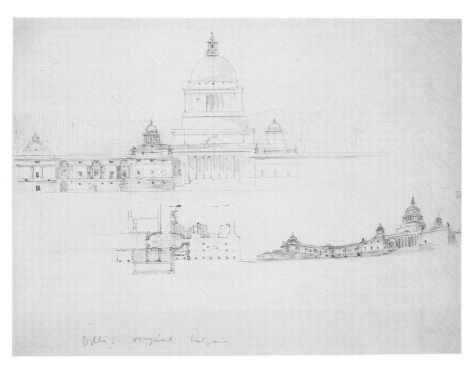

Delhi: original design

morning. Designed by R T Russell for the Commander-in-Chief, second only to the Viceroy, the palatial house (completed in 1930) suited the Anglo-Indian taste of the Harrow-educated Prime Minister who lived there from 1948 until his death in 1964. House and garden are now a museum devoted to him, with furnishings, desk, library and bedroom as he left them.

A detour southwest from here reaches **Chanakyapuri** (diplomatic enclave) whose central Shanti Path runs past modern palatial embassies including the beautiful blue-domed one for Pakistan. Satish Gujral's Belgian Embassy (1980−3), with exciting bold brick shapes, is more difficult to spot. At the end, the **Rail Transport Museum** is a train buff's delight and one of Delhi's best museums. And for the really keen, a foray west into Church Road in the Cantonment Area reaches A G Shoosmith's remarkable **St Martin's Church** (1928−30), built of three-and-a-half million bricks; to architectural writer Gavin Stamp it is 'one of the most remarkable of 20th-century churches; a

---

Flowers and Flowering Trees

The Indian light makes the brightly coloured blossoms glow even brighter. From February to May, New Delhi is a public flower garden: yellow and crimson blossoming trees line the avenues, each roundabout is a nurtured riot of colour, the Nehru and Indira Gandhi museum gardens and the public parks are at their best, and the magnificent Rastrapati Bhavan gardens are open (but for February and March only) (see page 58). Here are some flowers to spot, with their local names in brackets. See pages 62−3 for illustrations.

Indian laburnum (amaltas) Deciduous tree with large, perfumed, bright yellow blossoms hanging in bunches of drooping tails. Durable wood used for carts, wheels, bowls, good furniture, etc.

Babul (kikar/babul) One of several acacias in India, this variety has bright yellow flowers. Many practical uses for villagers: saplings for poles, young branches for fencing, leaves and pods for cattle fodder. Excellent hardwood used for beams, door frames, agricultural implements, oil presses, blocks for cloth dyeing, etc. Bark and root-bark used for making rum, country alcohol and brown dye; pods for toothpaste and buff dye; gum for sweets and printing, dyeing and sizing fabric; twigs for cleaning teeth and making baskets.

Bougainvillea Named after Louis Antoine de Bougainville (1729−1811), the first Frenchman to circumnavigate the world. A mature plant coats a building or clambers up a large tree to transform it with vivid clouds of mauve, crimson and cerise paper-like blossoms.

Rose (gulab) A favourite Mughal flower. Emperors from Babur onwards laid out gardens with rosebeds; Mughal miniature paintings

sublime mass of brick', to others merely 'Lego in Indis'.

Teen Murti Road leads to Race Course Road where Nehru's grandson, Prime Minister Rajiv Gandhi, lives, and Safdarjung Road where his mother, Indira Gandhi, lived at no. 1, now the **Indira Gandhi Museum**. The modest bungalow is utterly different from the palatial splendour of her father's residence. Furnished simply and hung with photographs recounting her life, from childhood days with the Mahatma to later off-duty relaxation with her grandchildren, it stands in a mature garden where visitors are assailed with Mrs Gandhi's speeches proclaimed from megaphones hidden in the bushes. It was here in her garden early on the morning of 31 October 1984 that she was assassinated.

The third New Delhi museum-house in this area is **Birla House** on Tees January Road, now called the **Hall of the Nation Building**. Mahatma Gandhi was often guest of the Birla family and would stroll round to talk with Muslim

---

include roses; and Shah Jahan's favourite sweetmeat was the rose-flavoured gulab jamun. Jahangir is said to have given the huge stone bath in Agra Fort to Nur Jahan on their marriage, and she or her mother is credited with discovering gulab attar (rose perfume, see page 107).

Marigold (genda) The deep orange blossoms seen everywhere from municipal gardens to hotel room vases contain the gendia shade of yellow which is used in home dyeing to create dull green and brownish-yellow cloth; it is also used for colouring butter.

Crape jasmine (chandni; tagara) 'Chandni' means moonshine, and the evergreen shrub's deceptively small white flowers are pungently fragrant at night. Flowers are used for garlands, the hard white wood for incense and perfumes, and the red pulp of the follicles for fabric dye.

Coral jasmine (harsinghar; parijattaka) Another jasmine, this one a small deciduous tree whose fragrant white flowers have orange tubes. Flowers produce a beautiful golden-orange dye used to colour alcohol; the rough leaves are used as sandpaper.

Yellow champa (champa; champaca) An evergreen tree with large fragrant yellow-centred flowers. The mottled wood is used for cabinet-making, veneers and ornamental carving, etc.; the flowers produce the highly valued *champaca* oil used in perfumery and as fabric dye.

Butea gum tree or **Flame of the forest** (tessu; dhak; palasha) Deciduous with a crooked, gnarled trunk and large deep orange flowers that hang in grape-like clusters. They produce brilliant yellow cotton and carpet dyes of three shades — saffron, yellow and lemon yellow. The trunk produces gum butea used for tanning and as a blue dye; bark fibre used for caulking boats, root fibre for rustic sandals.

Bougainvillea

Babul

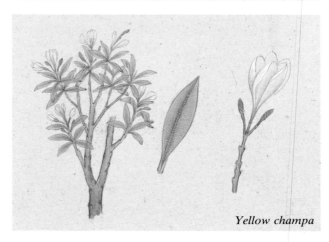

Yellow champa

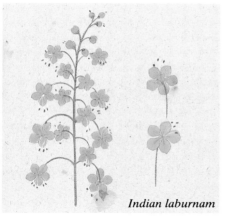

Indian laburnam

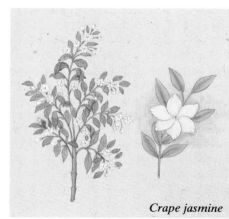

Crape jasmine

Butea gum tree

Rose

Marigold

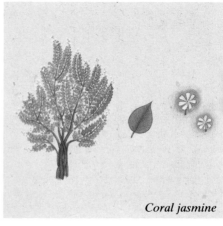

Coral jasmine

League leader Muhammad Ali Jinnah who lived nearby. After Independence in 1947, amid the turmoil of partition, Gandhi returned here from Calcutta. Bravely he campaigned for the plight of the persecuted Muslims waiting to be expatriated, an act considered by historian Percival Spear to have been 'the noblest and most courageous moment of his life'. On 30 January 1948, 12 days after he had completed a successful fast for their sake, he was shot by a Hindu fanatic as he went to his daily prayer meeting in the garden. This is a most moving place to visit, where the atmosphere is usually heightened by Indian pilgrims bearing garlands as offerings.

Janpath (the people's road, originally called Queen's Way) runs north from here right up to Connaught Place. Lutyens's grand plan was to make the crossing with Raj Path a cultural focus, with museums of Eastern and Western cultures. All that was built was his columned National Archives of India on the north side, with R T Russell's Eastern and Western Court beyond. Later, the **National Museum** was added on the south side. It holds a magnificent collection established only in 1950 and is the easiest way to taste the richness of Indian art. Before you even buy your ticket, you will see the sensual, exquisite sculptures from ancient temples displayed in the lobby. Beyond, India's ancient treasures fill a corridor room around the courtyard. Upstairs, the painting gallery is hung with detailed miniatures painted in jewel-bright colours to celebrate Mughal and Rajasthan court and battle life. Here, too, is half of Sir Marc Aurel Stein's collection found along the Silk Route (the other half is in the British Museum, London). Weird and wonderful musical instruments fill the new wing.

Pausing at **Raj Path**, you are now far enough back from Raisina Hill to look left and see almost all of Rastrapati Bhavan, a magnificent view as the sun sets and the skies glow coal red. To the right is **India Gate**. Lutyens designed it as the All-India War Memorial Arch, extracting from Lord Hardinge (Viceroy 1910–16) 'a bountiful crop of lakhs' to pay for it. The king's uncle, the Duke of Connaught, laid the foundation stone in 1921. The memorial, honouring the 90,000 Indian soldiers who died in the First World War, was completed in 1931. Lutyens wanted (but did not get) a flame glowing by night on top, and a column of smoke by day, to express the eternal nature of sacrifice. Today an eternal flame burns to honour the Unknown Soldier.

Lutyens also designed the monument to George V just beyond. The white marble statue of the king-emperor, who had announced the conception of New Delhi and who died in 1935, used to look out from the graceful sandstone *baldachini* set in a reflecting pool; it can now be seen, along with other imperial relics, at the site of the 1911 Durbar (see page 53) between Kingsway camp, in north Delhi, and the river (see pages 53, 97 and 99).

This area, Princes' Place, was to be surrounded by town palaces for India's top royals, loyal allies of the British. But only a handful were built, to be occupied each February for the Chamber of Princes meetings and the climax of the Delhi season, when India's social elite decked themselves in diamonds and flitted between horse shows, polo playing, the Delhi Hunt Ball, the Viceregal Ball and the Viceregal garden party. In 1930, Aldous Huxley noted that 'for a week Rolls Royces were far more plentiful in the streets than Fords. The hotels pullulated with despots and their viziers. At the Viceroy's evening parties the pearls were so large that they looked like stage gems; it was impossible to believe that [they] were the genuine excrement of oysters.'

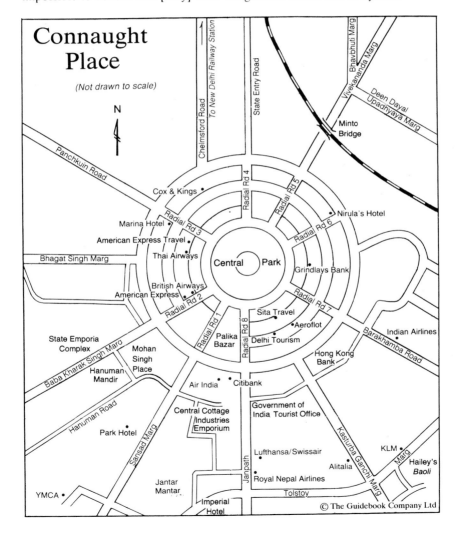

Connaught Place

(Not drawn to scale)

© The Guidebook Company Ltd

Each palace looks to the Viceroy's House to blend classical and Indian ideas from Western colonnades to exotic *jalis* (carved screens). On the north side Lutyens designed the grandest, **Hyderabad House**, for the grand Nizam of Hyderabad, believed then to be the richest man in the world; today, newly restored, it is the Prime Minister's principal place for top-notch entertainment. Next door stands Lutyens's **Baroda House**, which had American plumbing, Irish linen, French cooks and a dinner service from Aspreys in London's Bond Street. The furnishings are gone, but the building, now headquarters for Indian Railways, is still worth a visit. Sir Reginald Blomfield's quieter Jaipur House on the south side is now the **National Gallery of Modern Art.** The ground-floor galleries host temporary exhibitions, while the first-floor rooms house Indian scenes by the British brothers Thomas and William Daniell and canvasses by the strong Bengali School which includes Jamini Roy and Nandalal Bose. The garden round the back is gloriously peaceful.

On the way up to Connaught Place along Kasturba Gandhi Marg, there is a relic of an older Delhi to seek out. This is **Hailey's Baoli** (step-well), found by taking Hailey Road on the right (one before Tolstoy Marg), then the first lane on the left. It was possibly built in the 14th century under the Tughluqs, and traditionally built by Raja Ugrasen. A tiny mosque sits at the top of the steep steps. At the bottom of them, the second to last arch on either side leads to more steps which reach the roof and another well opening. Young Delhi lads daringly dive into the water from here.

Connaught Place, bustling with traders, businessmen and restaurants, is the link between Old and New Delhi. Here, in and around R T Russell's huge amphitheatre of stuccoed colonnades, some of Old Delhi's lively hubbub spills into New Delhi's calm order. Named after George V's uncle, the monumental plaza ringed by shops, hotels and commerce was created to symbolize British progress in India.

It took time to catch on. Early houses stood amid haunts of jackals and wild pigs, the Regal Cinema could only attract a dozen patrons, and plum sites were sold off at a bargain two rupees a square yard. Eventually, it worked. The airy colonnades punctuated by Palladian arches gave shade from the fierce sun and were compared to Bath and Cheltenham; the stylish shops stole custom from Old Delhi's Chandni Chowk. Today, despite Delhi's mushrooming shopping and commercial centres, such big fish as the international airlines, travel agents and the principal political magazine *India Today* are all here; and land prices are so ferociously high that ugly skyscapers are wickedly permitted to replace gentler proportions.

Of the eight radial roads, Barakhamba is the next round anti-clockwise from Kasturba Gandhi Marg. Its eastern end is Delhi's cultural campus: dance, drama, music, puppets, café, etc. in Shivnath Prasad's **Sri Ram Centre for Art and Culture** (1966–72), one of New Delhi's better modern buildings; drama, galleries and the Lalit Kala Academy in Habib Rahman's **Rabindra Bhavan**

Nathu's Sweet Shop
Delhi's Top Mithai Wallah

The sweet-toothed gourmet finds paradise at Nathu's. In Bengali Market, east of Connaught Place, the corner site buzzes with activity all day as locals come for their favourite milk-based *mithai* (sweets), flavoured with pistachio, coconut, carrot, cashew nut or almond. *Gulab jamun* and other concoctions steeped in syrup are carefully packed in an earthen pot; drier sweets go into boxes. But the caviar of sweetmeats, green and nutty *pista* (pistachio) *barfi*, is so precious that it is kept in a back room.

These delicacies were traditionally made by Hindus, since they kept the cows and made milk products. Sweets play a vital part in Indian life. They are both presents for a host and snacks offered when a guest arrives. They are given at festival time, especially Diwali in October. And *ladhu*, a very pure sweet made from gram-flour and sugar, is *prashad* (worship gift) for the Hindu gods in temples.

Clearly, it is a good business to be in. Arun and Vipen Gupta run the firm started by their grandfather, Nathu Ram Gupta, who set up as a milk supplier in 1952. The shop is open every day from 7 am to 11 pm. In the spotless kitchens upstairs, 70 cooks work in three shifts and use 1,000 litres (220 gallons) of milk and 600 kilos (1,320 pounds) of sugar each day. To avoid monotony, their tasks are regularly changed. Some stir bubbling mixtures in enormous black pans; others skilfully drip batter through a sieve into boiling oil to make the beads for jelabies. Some heave spade-sized paddles through thick reduced milk; others squat on the floor stuffing sweets or adding leaves of real silver — and occasionally gold — to special sweets.

Every town has its speciality. *Sohan halwa* is a Delhi one, a flour-based calorie-concentrate cooked in syrup and soaked overnight in full fat. *Patisa* is another, a sweet mixture cooked in ghee (clarified butter), then folded over and over to create *mille feuilles* layers. Arun Gupta's favourite is *gulab jamun*, originally a Bengali sweet of fresh cheese cooked in rose-scented sugar-syrup but given its heavier Delhi character by being fried and then sugar-soaked. (It is said a royal cook first made it by mistake; certainly it was Shah Jahan's favourite.)

There is more to Nathu's than sweets. In the large café behind the counters, locals enjoy one of the nicest informal atmospheres in town. The savoury cooking is all on view. At the snack counter, *pani puri* and *papri* are good ones to try. The south Indian chef makes *idlies* (rice cakes) and *dosas* (huge rice pancakes); the Chinese fries up noodles; and the North Indian makes puffed-up *puris*. To drink, there is *lassi* (fresh yoghurt) or pint mugs of freshly-squeezed juice. Then pudding. Perhaps a piece of *badam* (almond) *barfi* or a creamy light Bengali *rasmalai*, or both. And if you are homesick, Nathu's Western cakes and bread shop is almost next door.

(1959−61), another interesting building; and art, dance, drama and café at the **Triveni Kala Sangram**. Bengali Market is just north of here, an atmospheric haunt whose heart is Nathu's café-restaurant (see page 68).

Janpath, one move clockwise from Kasturba Gandhi Marg, is the north−south nerve of New Delhi. The Tourist Office and Central Cottage Industries Emporium, both essential stops for visitors, uphold Connaught Place's commercial function. Further down, the **Imperial Hotel** (1933−5) was, according to Lutyens's son Robert, 'jerry-built by Blomfield, patronized by Lady W and frightful'. But, furnished with London silver and Italian marble, it opened with a glamorous banquet where Lady Willingdon was guest of honour, ensuring its place as a social and political centre. Today, with palm trees swaying majestically, its tranquil lawns are still a gathering place for locals; most of the interior is fortunately untouched or renewed to '30s designs.

Just before the Imperial, Tolstoy Marg leads on clockwise to Sansad Marg (Parliament Street) and to **Jantar Mantar**, another relic of earlier Delhi and another Jaipur link. These huge, salmon-pink, abstract shapes are not exhibits in a modern sculpture park. They are brick and plaster versions of astronomical instruments for a giant observatory built in 1724 by Maharaja Jai Singh II. A keen astrologer, he revised the calendar and astronomical tables for the Mughal emperor Muhammad Shah and provided him with an on-site observatory, the first of five he built (see also page 166). Hanuman Road on the left leads round to Baba Kharak Singh Marg where the Hindu monkey god, Hanuman, is given extra pujas (worship) on his special day, Tuesday, and local women and children seek bargains at the toy and bangle bazaar. The unassuming buildings opposite are the state emporia (see page 47).

On 9 February 1931, New Delhi was inaugurated by the Viceroy, Lord Irwin. Ten million pounds had been spent on the city and visitors were suitably impressed: Edward Hudson, owner of the English magazine *Country Life*, proclaimed 'Poor old Christopher Wren could never have done this!' During a fortnight of festivities, celebrations included the gathering of 5,000 guests to watch massed bands, fanfare trumpets and a 31-gun salute to accompany the unveiling of Baker's Asokan columns. Up in Old Delhi, an extraordinary People's Fete included extracts from 'Madame Butterfly' in the Red Fort's marble halls, broadsword dancing by the Scottish Highlanders, and the Viceroy watching a pageant of painted elephants, camels and other Indian transport from the very window where the Mughal emperor Shah Jahan had daily shown himself to the people.

But astute contemporaries recognized the 'gilded phantom'. One was Aldous Huxley, who found the new imperial city 'no less rich in social comedy than Paris; its soul is as fertile in snobberies, dissimulations, prejudices, hatreds, envies. The dispute of races, the reciprocal hatred of colours, the subjection of one people to another — these things lie behind its snobberies, conventions, and deceits, are implicit in every ludicrous antic of the comedians. The clouds against which imperial Delhi appears so brilliantly comical, are ... black, huge and menacing.'

The freedom movement was accelerating. Sixteen years later, New Delhi was perhaps the most glorious legacy the British gave to India.

Old Delhi

Shajahanabad was the splendidly egoistic and exotic-sounding name given by its creator, Shah Jahan, to Delhi's penultimate city, now known mundanely as Old Delhi. In 1648, the emperor triumphantly entered his new city, bringing with him the Mughal empire's vast administration, a treasury overflowing with gold and jewels, and his Peacock Throne which symbolized his untold wealth. Shahjahanabad fizzed into life. Princes, princesses, courtiers and their attendant servants and hangers-on paraded in the fort-palace, attended the emperor and jostled in the markets for jewels, exotic foods and attar. Merchants hurried to serve them; top craftsmen created masterpieces for them; chefs brewed up delicacies to delight them; entertainers amused them. Today the fort-palace is deserted and lifeless; but a little of the Mughal lifestyle is played out in the Old Delhi streets — women choosing gold jewellery, Muslims trading spices, and the faithful hurrying to prayer at the Jama Masjid.

Shah Jahan (ruled 1627–58) was the fifth Mughal emperor and the greatest Mughal builder. He channelled his considerable executive ability, his unimaginable wealth, his love of magnificence and his refined aesthetic sense into architecture. Born in 1592 in Lahore and named Khurram (joyous) by his grandfather, he ascended the throne at Agra as Shah Jahan (Ruler of the World) to play the lead part in an enactment of stultifyingly precise court etiquette that would make the Sun King's Versailles lifestyle look liberal. His passion for building found expression in projects to beautify the forts at Lahore and Agra and, after the death of his beloved Mumtaz (see page 110), the construction of her mausoleum, the Taj Mahal. In 1638 he decided to bring the court back to the traditional capital and to lay out yet another new city, Shahjahanabad.

The site Shah Jahan chose was beside the Yamuna — the waters have since moved further eastwards, leaving muddy flats — and north of all previous Delhis except the ruins of Salimgarh fortress. With the royal astrologers' approval, the foundation stone was laid during Muharram in 1639. A string of marble palace rooms was built overlooking the waters and enclosed by a protective fort with high, red sandstone battlements modelled on Akbar's at Agra. The great gateways were Lahore on the west side, Agra on the south, leading to the two other great Mughal cities. To the west, an adjoining model city served his courtiers and soldiers and was encircled by another wall pierced by 14 gates. Chandni Chowk was its east–west thoroughfare; a magnificent

mosque, the Jama Masjid, was its southern and religious focus. According to his courtier Inayat Khan, these 'edifices resembling Paradise' were built to the 'promptings of his generous heart', employed 'multitudes of common labourers' from all over the empire, and were completed in just 'nine years three months and some days'.

To taste the flavour of Shah Jahan's city, start from the Jama Masjid, reaching it by going up into Old Delhi past Delhi Gate where you can see a good stretch of the city wall on the right. After the mosque, wander through the narrow lanes to Chandni Chowk. You will then have some images to help bring the fort, a deserted mini-city of its own, to life.

The **Jama Masjid** (1650–6), meaning Friday Mosque, was Shah Jahan's last building. Standing on a mound called Bhojla Pahar, the great royal mosque — one of the largest of Islam—was designed by Ustad Khlil who placed it on a high plinth to show off its glowing red sandstone inlaid with marble and brass. It was at first named Masjid-i-Jahan Nama (mosque with a view of the world). Certainly, its two slender minarets flanking the three black-and-white striped, marble, onion domes of the prayer-hall dominate Old Delhi. The faithful ceaselessly stream up and down the steep north steps to the courtyard. Here they wash, study the Qur'an, pray and join visitors to gaze at the fort through the arcades, which are especially beautiful under soft morning sunlight. When pious Aurangzeb came to prayer riding a decorated elephant or carried in a golden throne, the streets from fort to mosque were doused with water to reduce heat and dust and were lined with 300 musketeers. (It is sometimes possible to go up a minaret, worth the climb for a bird's-eye view of the city.)

The area around Jama Masjid seethes with Muslim life. On the south side, the air is scented with spices from the cluster of tiny restaurants where Karim, found down the central lane, is worth a look at any hour (see next page). Further round, the markets sell baskets of clucking white chickens and an assortment of weird-shaped fish. Shah Jahan's daughter, Jahanara Begum, built Urdu Bazar which runs off to the east. Back on the west side, every conceivable car part and size of tyre spills out from busy workshops. In sharp contrast, Delhi ivory work is patiently carved behind Ivory Mart's shopfront on the north side. Then come the fireworks shops, supplemented by roadside stalls at festival time. Fireworks displays are an old Indian tradition (paintings show princesses playing with fireworks on palace terraces). Huge wooden elephants or gods dissolve into a mass of crackers at Hindu festivals; and one current favourite rocket has a plastic mini Ganesh (the elephant-headed god) who descends in a parachute.

The lane running north from the mosque's north steps leads to **Dariba Kalan**, a turning on the left, which emerges into Chandni Chowk (to avoid getting lost, it is best to check by asking). The narrow paths twist between the high walls of ancient *havelis* (courtyard houses) with carved wooden doorways, some still home for descendants of Mughal traders, others still owned by

Karim
Meaty Treats in a Corner of Old Delhi

On the south side of the Jama Masjid, you can almost smell the kebabs of Karim's restaurant. It lurks down the first narrow alley on the left along Motia Mahal, a busy lane lined with Muslim café-restaurants. The alley opens into a courtyard of humming activity, where every surrounding room is a kitchen or dining-room. So loved is Karim's that loyal customers from New Delhi's smartest boulevards will send their chauffeurs to collect *nahar* (morning lamb curry) for breakfast. And one of India's top artists, Hussein, designed its visiting card, adding the motto 'Secret of good mood, taste of Karim's food'.

Karim's is an all-day theatre run by the grandsons and great-grandsons of the founder, Hafiz Karim Uddin. Doors open at 7 am for hearty breakfasts, when the alternative to nahar is *paye* (lamb's trotters) and *khameeri roti*, a special bread left to ferment overnight. Vegetarians would be horrified, for this is just the beginning. When the show ends, around midnight, the day's 3,000 customers will have chewed their way through more than 300 kilos (660 pounds) of mutton and 150 chickens.

As business hots up, a portly chef squats on the stage-like stone platform of the courtyard to stir his brews of kidneys, mutton, beans, potatoes and brains, each potion bubbling in a huge bulbous pot. On the other side of the courtyard, a boy kneads spiced and minced meat onto thick kebab sticks and lays them over glowing coals. The five dining-rooms include one overlooking the courtyard and another at the far end decorated with tiles and patronized by locals. They may start with some *seekh* or *shami* kebabs before tucking in to a plate of *firdausi qorma* (lamb curry) and *sheermal*, an unusual leavened bread. Others go for the *badam pasanda*, a very aromatic lamb dish, and a *rogani naan*. But for offal lovers, the most succulent dish is the soft sheep's brains curry.

Then there are the breads. Out in the courtyard, a young lad confidently performs his trick of hurling *roomali* (handkerchief) *roti* dough into the air, then nimbly lays the transparent skin on a large, circular convex hot griddle, flipping it over after a few second and then quickly folding it up ready for delivery. In one dark room behind, strong-armed men knead dough. In another, younger men skilfully flip and stretch pieces into oblongs, slapping each onto the side of a red hot clay *tandoor* oven built down into the ground. In another kitchen a special iron tandoor, found only in Muslim kitchens and even trickier to control than a clay one, gives the *naan* and *kulcha* breads an extra crispness and dark colour.

Each chef is fascinating to watch. Little has changed since the time of Hafiz Karim Uddin. The only sop to the 20th century is the electric paging system for the waiters to give orders and to be notified when the food is ready. And no-one minds if you poke your nose into all the rooms before deciding where to sit and what to order.

families who now live in the air-conditioned comfort of south Delhi colonies. Tiny, polychrome temples are jammed between them, goldsmiths sit cross-legged working miracles with nimble fingers, cows laze about nonchalantly and a paan seller trundles his box of ingredients from one customer to the next.

Not far down Dariba Kalan, **Kinari** (braid) **Bazar** is a lane on the left lined with tiny shops glittering with all kinds of essential equipment for weddings and festivals: gold-embroidered shoes, fancy braid, glitzy saries, gold-lamé turbans, tinsel, plumes and magnificent papier-mâché masks of Durga, Hanuman and other favourite gods, with extra Ravana heads, swords, bows and arrows on sale in the run-up to the Dussera festival in October. The next lane is Paratha Walan (alley of paratha sellers), formerly lined with cooks frying up delicious flat paratha breads on their griddles; today, Kusha Rai is the best of the three remaining cafés.

Back on Dariba Kalan, Gulab Singh's attar shop has tiny bottles of strong-smelling Lotus and Moonlight perfumes, much used by Muslim men and women. Further down, the old silver and gold shops glisten with traditional jewellery. On the left, the basement of Sri Ram Hari Ram is like a non-stop market; women debate over which piece to buy, shop assistants pop them on the scales as cost is by weight, not design. And at the end, on the corner of Chandni Chowk, a perpetual crowd hovers around the sweet aroma of Naim Chand Jain's jalebi kiosk, customers greedily gobbling up the hot, sweet and crisp twirly shapes, licking their fingers and lips with delight.

Chandni Chowk (moonlit crossroads) is the centrepiece of Old Delhi. When the wide avenue was laid out by Jahanara Begum, refreshing water ran down the centre between shady trees; merchants' shops and noblemen's homes set in lush gardens lined the sides; and the lanes leading off it stocked a rich assortment of goods and fine foods, from dried fruits and roasted meats to partridges and *singala* fish. Indeed, in 1663 the traveller François Bernier thought it the biggest commercial centre in the East and ruminated 'whether a lover of good cheer ought to quit Paris for the sake of visiting Delhi'. Later, Robert B Minturn declared Chandni Chowk 'the handsomest street' and 'the gayest scene in India'. Today, its lacklustre appearance belies a rich history and, if you watch carefully, some amusing commercial entrepreneurship.

To the left, the flower-stalls of Phul-ki-Mandi (flower market) trade outside the **Sisgang Gurdwara**, now being grandly enlarged. It is dedicated to the ninth Sikh guru, Tegh Bahadur, whom emperor Aurangzeb (ruled 1618-1707) had beheaded in 1675. This was also when in 1659 Aurangzeb, to underline his absolute power as new emperor, exhibited the corpse of his older brother Dara Shukoh, having paraded him down the street dressed as a beggar on a dirty elephant—a warning to locals who had supported this popular heir apparent. Further along is the *kotwali* (police station) in front of which the British exhibited the corpses of three Mughal princes and hanged the freedom fighters after they retook Delhi in 1857.

A Special Favour

The first thing she saw on her desk was a letter from Ajaib Singh, lying on top of other papers in obedience to her instruction that any matter concerning any of her staff must be brought to her immediate attention. 'Respected Sir: Deeply moved always of your noble and kind remembrance of me in matters large and small I am bold to write this epistle. Only to noble high and mighty soul such as your sweet self would I write. Sadly Sir our country is passing through bad days when sons do not so much listen to fathers. I write Sir with bowed head and shame surpassing of my third son who did not obey his mother and me failing many examinations at school. Now he has barely passed Matriculate and what future for him honoured Sir without degree. Therefore only your great name and high office will gain him admission to college and I humbly request this no-good worthless may be admitted to Jammu College near my land and home. Where if he does not succeed in first year I will put him out and train him in drivery and put him in taxi service but always preferring him to be educated and above me. May God keep my noble and delightful Sir, your obedient servant Ajaib Singh.' The signature was scratched in spidery Urdu with a very thin nib under Ajaib Singh's letter writer's smudgy black typewriter ribbon. Devi read it all over again for sheer pleasure. No acquaintance of her own social position had ever offered to remove a lazy offspring if he did not make the grade after the first year. Quite a number of them, Devi recalled, might be better suited to 'drivery' than a B. A. degree. However, she knew Ajaib Singh would do exactly as he said, remove his third-born 'no-good worthless' without further ado, and that either the republic of India would have a successful B. A. with a horizon wider than Ajaib Singh's or else a cracking good taxi driver. It pleased her to think that one of her last acts in the Ministry might be a service for Ajaib Singh.

Nayantara Sahgal, A Situation in New Delhi

Sonehri Masjid (golden mosque) comes next, with even darker memories. Built in 1722, this was where the Persian king Nadir Shah stood on 11 March 1739 to watch his soldiers massacre most of Delhi's inhabitants (20,000– 150,000, depending on whom you believe) and devastate the city in six hours flat. At first all had gone well. The defeated Mughal emperor, Muhammad Shah, laid on feasting and fireworks to welcome Nadir Shah and his 200 servants and 4,000 horsemen, whom he controlled with threats to chop off noses and ears if they caused trouble. But when the Delhi mob reacted violently to the soldiers' demands for free wheat and mutton, the conqueror took his revenge.

A contemporary recorded: 'The inhabitants, one and all, were slaughtered. The Persians laid violent hands on everything and everybody; cloth, jewels, dishes of gold and silver ... for a long time the streets remained strewn with corpses ... the town was reduced to ashes, and had the appearance of a plain consumed with fire.' Two months later, Nadir Shah left Delhi for Persia laden with the royal jewels, the treasury and more, including the Koh-i-Nur diamond and the Peacock Throne. The poet Mirza Mohammed Rafi Sauda wrote movingly of the desolation: 'In the once-beautiful gardens where the nightingale sang his love songs to the rose the grass grows waist-high around the fallen pillars and ruined arches. Shahjahanabad, you never deserved this terrible fate! You who were once vibrant with life and love and hope, like the heart of a young lover.'

Ghantewalla's sweet shop is on the same side. Its name means 'bell' because, one story goes, the royal elephant in Mughal processions would stop here and jingle his bell to ask for a sweet.

Across the road, the handsome Town Hall (1860–5) fronts a drop of British Old Delhi and an airy oasis. The roads either side lead to tall, swaying palms surrounding the circular **Mahatma Gandhi Park**. Built as Queen's Gardens, it is now a great meeting place for pink-robed *sadhus* (ascetics) — find them right at the back offering flowers and incense to shrines, massaging one another and listening to musicians. The keen can forge further back, crossing what was elegant Queen's Road to the turreted castle of Old Delhi Railway Station, where teams of red-coated porters serve the always-overloaded crowds of passengers.

Back on Chandni Chowk, the western end has a more exotic flavour. **Fatehpuri Mosque** (1650), paid for by Begum Fatehpuri, one of Shah Jahan's wives, closes the vista. The little kiosks in its outside walls are piled high with dried fruits and nuts, some in sacks, some heaped on trays. A portly merchant, dressed in fine white muslin, presides over each, portable telephone and calculator at the ready. Just before the mosque, Dr Vasdevabbot the sex specialist has his huge billboard to attract customers to his thriving and competitive trade.

Turning right at the mosque, make a detour to Giani's Ice-Cream shop straight ahead. Even if you are wary of the ice-cream, the succulent hot cashews and the two sorts of hot halwa, nutty dhal (lentil) and gajar (carrot), are safe and utterly delicious. Back and right, along the mosque's north wall, Delhi's **wholesale spice market** is hidden through an archway on the left. Clues to finding it are first the mosque kiosks displaying fewer fresh walnuts and

Lal Qila (Red Fort)

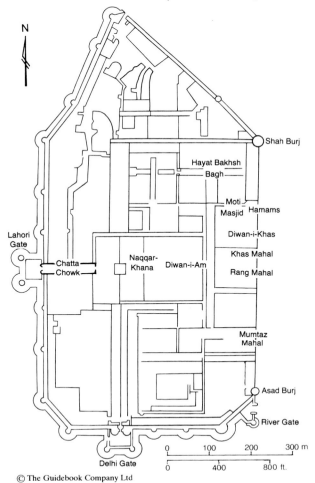

© The Guidebook Company Ltd

more trays of nutmeg, peppercorns, chillies, ginger and turmeric, then the increasingly spice-scented air and the crowds of coolies loading heavy sacks onto carts blocking up the road. The market is pandemonium. Spice dust fills the air and brings on incessant sneezing. Merchants sit beside outsize weighing scales, eyeing buyers who test a sackful of costly spice by prodding in a knife at random and tasting the contents. The splashes of colour are piles of blood-red chillies, and a confused hubbub of coolies load and unload their strained backs and whistle to warn people in their path to get out of the way, quick.

The relaxing way to reach the fort from here is by bicycle rickshaw to its entrance, Lahore Gate. Tickets are at the kiosk; avoid freelance guides.

Shah Jahan reaped treble the income of Akbar and Jahangir and spent four times as much. The greatest Mughal builder, his Delhi fort, known as **Lal Qila** (red fort), is twice the size of Agra's . Designed by Ustad (master) Ahmed Lahori, the building was probably overseen by two mastermasons, Ustad Hamid and Ustad Hira. On completion, it enjoyed its glory under Shah Jahan who lived within a precise court ritual. The best way to see it is through the eyes of his courtiers; for today, despite past glory and being built to a single design, it lacks the essential magic of the Agra Fort. Furthermore, the British tore down two thirds of it when they ousted the last Mughal emperor in 1858.

Lahori Gate from where the Prime Minister speaks on Independence Day, August 15 (it was here the Indian flag was first raised), leads into Chatta Chowk, a covered bazaar for the elite. Here the courtiers jostled for fine gold, jewels and silks. Today, Goel and Mehra, the last shops on the right, are worth a look, but few others.

The **Naqqar-Khana** (royal drum house), the official gateway, was where the formalities began. Musicians, seated above, played in an important arrival with huge, deafening cymbals, drums and trumpets, while guards removed his weapons and announced his name.

Ahead is the **Diwan-i-Am** (public audience hall), a raised, colonnaded plinth. Here the emperor and his princes, ministers and courtiers assembled in strict rank for the day's public business, while the royal women watched through jalis (latticed windows), and the public filled the courtyard to bring their requests and complaints before their ruler. An important visitor approached with deep salaams and presented offerings of gold coin and jewels or perhaps elephants and horses. He was then dressed in plush robes and took his allotted place. The business of the day took about two hours and might include reading aloud reports from the empire's outposts or hearing criminal cases and proclaiming sentences (executioners with hatchets and whips stood on hand to carry them out on the spot). Throughout there was constant music to accompany acrobatic shows, dancing girls and parades of tigers, elephants and rhinoceros.

The more private palace area lies behind, across gardens that were planted

with roses and crisscrossed with cooling water-channels. A string of six palaces runs along the east wall of the fort overlooking the now-distant Yamuna waters. Today's acrobats and an ingenious 'levitating man' performing below the walls have succeeded the Mughal entertainment of elephant fights staged exclusively for the emperors.

Starting on the right, the first palace is **Mumtaz Mahal** (Mumtaz palace). It is now the fort's museum and worth a visit, although some of its fine paintings are on loan to the National Museum. **Rang Mahal** (painted palace) had a silver ceiling, stripped off by the Jals. Here the **Naher-i-Bahisht** (stream of paradise) flowed from the other palaces into the marble, lotus-shaped pool, cooling the stifling Delhi air and making dancing reflections in the jewelled and mirrored interiors.

Khas Mahal (house palace) follows, three marble rooms where the emperor ate, slept and worshipped. It was on the decorated balcony that the royal day began, observed by Sir Thomas Roe to run 'as regular as the clock that strikes at set hours'. As the morning star appeared, the royal musicians played appropriate morning music and the muezzins of all the Delhi mosques called the faithful to prayer. By sunrise, a crowd of citizens had gathered beneath the balcony and the emperor presented himself to show he was alive and well, a ritual called Jhuroka-i-Darshan. Mid-morning was public business in the Diwan-i-Am, then private business in the Diwan-i-Khas, then the most private business. Whacked out, the emperor retired to his harem for a four-hour lunch break, when 50 or more dishes were served on gold and silver by eunuchs via favourite ladies, the morsels eaten to the soothing tones of music and poetry readings. After a siesta, he dealt with the extensive harem business — many women did charity work or ran estates and trading businesses — and then gave public proof of his existence again before, perhaps, watching an elephant fight. The day ended with prayers, family dinner and a return to the harem.

The **Diwan-i-Khas** (private audience hall) is conveniently next door. This is the heart of the fort, the inner sanctum for top meetings, vital decisions, the best parties and the most tragic events. Here Shah Jahan sat on his Peacock Throne or relaxed on silk rugs and cushions, while candlelight danced on the jewel-encrusted silver ceiling. Here he apparently said: 'If on earth there be a paradise of bliss, It is this, it is this, it is this', inscribed in fading gold above the arches. Less blissfully, it was there that Muhammad Shah surrendered to Nadir Shah in 1739. Affairs of state were also discussed in the next rooms, the more informal *hamam* (baths), now closed but their carpets of marble inlay have miraculously survived and can be glimpsed by peeping through the window.

Shah Jahan's blissful Delhi life ended in sadness after nine years. In 1657 he became ill. His four sons quickly began plotting for the throne. Dara Shukoh, the heir apparent and the favourite, went with his father to Agra and sent armies to quell the other brothers. The next, Shah Suja, was defeated and fled to Burma. The third, **Aurangzeb**, allied with the youngest, Murad Bakhsh, and defeated Dara Shukoh. He then imprisoned his father in Agra Fort (where he died in 1666), tricked Murad and had him murdered, proclaimed himself emperor in 1658, captured Dara Shukoh and his son and had both executed in 1659, and then again proclaimed himself emperor. It was a bloody beginning to the long rule of the last Great Mughal.

The same year the orthodox (and perhaps penitent) Aurangzeb added the tiny marble **Moti Mahal** (pearl mosque) to the fort, for on-site prayers five times a day rather than journey to the Jama Masjid. It is set back from the hamams. Beyond lies the peaceful Hayat Bakhsh Bagh (life-bestowing garden), where blossoms and water-channels surround the central Zafar Mahal.

East Delhi
Riverside Cities and Monuments

Modern Delhi has turned its back on the River Yamuna. But the waters played a crucial role in the siting of some earlier cities. Landlocked now after the waters changed their course eastwards, these ruined forts stand amid offices, stadia and modern memorials. The main thoroughfare, Mahatma Gandhi Road, is a major dual-carriageway, so it is worth setting off early to explore the north end first.

Start outside the back walls of Lal Qila — this was where the public congregated to check on Shah Jahan's well-being each morning; the emperor's balcony juts out from the marble palace facades. North of it, the ramparts and bastions of **Salimgarh Fort** (1545–54) were built by Sher Shah's son, Islam Shah Sur, who failed to consolidate his able father's achievements (see Purana Qila, below).

Lal Qila has lost its riverside views to a large tract of new land where some of India's recent heroes are remembered. It is an oasis of peace. First of the memorials is **Vijay Ghat** dedicated to Lal Bahadur Shastri, India's second prime minister (died 11 January 1966); then **Shanti Vana** (forest of peace) where Jawaharlal Nehru (died 27 May 1964) and his daughter Indira Gandhi (assassinated 31 October 1984) were cremated, and where her son Sanjay is remembered. Finally, **Raj Ghat** is at the south end, a serenely peaceful place. This is where Mahatma Gandhi was cremated (31 January 1948) on the memorial platform which is now set in a sunken square garden surrounded by caves and high ramps, the design of Vanu G Bhuta. The **Gandhi Memorial Museum** is nearby, where the Mahatma's life and achievements are movingly remembered with photographs, descriptions and quotes such as 'I shall work for an India in which the poorest shall feel that it is their country in whose making they have an effective voice.' (Plenty of literature to buy and, on alternate Sundays, films in English.)

The next city is **Feroz Shah Kotla**, really just the riverside citadel of **Feroz**

Shah Tughluq's vast and wealthy city that stretched from the North Ridge of Old Delhi down to Haus Khas in south Delhi. In its heyday the palaces, mosques, hunting-lodges, reservoirs, hospitals and colleges buzzed with princely and intellectual life. Then, in 1398, Timur (Tamburlaine), ancestor of the Mughal conqueror Babur, sacked and laid waste this fifth great Delhi city, leaving with elephants, stonemasons and such booty that, according to one account, 'they could scarcely march four miles a day'. Today, hoopoes hop about the blossoming gardens which link the ruins of a mosque, palace, living quarters and baoli (step-well); the entrance is on the west side, in Bahadur Shah Zafar Marg.

Feroz Shah (ruled 1351–88) was the third sultan of the Tughluqs (1320–1413). Son of a Rajput princess and cousin of the previous, madcap ruler Muhammad, he was politically weak but a great builder, intellectual and antique collector. He had translations made of Sanskrit texts into Persian and Arabic. And here, on top of his Kushk-i-Firuz (Feroz's place) he put one of the two remarkable **Ashoka pillars** (273–236 BC) he found, transporting them from Meerut and Topla to Delhi down the Yamuna (the other is up on the North Ridge). When the Mauryan emperor Ashoka's ancient Brahmi script, a forerunner of modern Devnagari, could not be unravelled (that was James Princep's feat in 1837), Feroz Shah was told it was a magic charm used in religious ritual. In fact, it bears Ashoka's messages and promotes dharma (the Buddhist teachings) and the welfare and happiness of the people.

The **National Rose Garden**, glorious in February–March, is in the southeast corner of Feroz Shah Kotla, while by the entrance stands Khuni-Darwaza (bloody gate), possibly a gate to Sher Shah's city, the next to see downriver. Mathura Road, the royal route to Mughal Agra, leads down to it and has several good buildings either side. Not far along, the **Abdu'n Nabi's Mosque** (1575–6) on the right was built by Akbar's ecclesiastical registrar who went to Mecca to distribute money to the poor but failed to account for it on his return, for which he was finally murdered. On the left, a parade of concrete newspaper offices ends with the charming **International Dolls Museum**. Under Tilak Railway Bridge, modern Pragati Maidan opens on the left. Here is the **Crafts Museum**, an essential stop if you are interested in India's cultural, village and craft life (see page 84). Charles Correa designed the museum buildings; Raj Rewal's pyramidal engineering feat, the Hall of Nations (1970–2), rises behind.

To the south there are splendid views of **Purana Qila**. Closer to it, the great walls belie a chequered history. This is not one city site but several. The earliest may well have been the sacred site of **Indraprastha** (city of Indra, Hindu god of rain and thunder), founded by Arjuna, one of the Pandava brother heroes in the epic *Mahabharata*. Excavations on the southern slopes are now revealing the reality behind the myth. Next, the second Mughal emperor, **Humayun** (ruled 1530–40, 1555–6), returned from Agra to the traditional capital and in 1533 founded **Dinpanah** (shelter of the faith), Delhi's sixth city. Its surviving two kilometres (1.2 miles) of walls pierced by three giant, double-storey gateways were surrounded by a wide moat opening into the Yamuna. Although he dreamt of ruling a liberal empire with Dinpanah as a cultural capital to rival Samarkand, the aesthete Humayun was too self-indulgent and politically indecisive to consolidate Mughal power. After crushing defeats at Chausa (1539) and Kanauj (1540), he was ousted by **Sher Shah Sur**.

This remarkable Afghan was a talented organizer and skilful general who, before his death in 1545, was encouraged by Persian renaissance thought to set up an administration which was in effect the blueprint for Akbar's Mughal government. He enlarged Purana Qila and extended his prosperous city northwards, calling it **Shergarh**; one gate is up by Feroz Shah Kotla. Two buildings inside Purana Qila survive: **Qal'a-i-Kuhna-Masjid** (old fort mosque, 1541) whose five great arches, decorated mihrabs and marble-inlaid sandstone facade mark the change from Lodi to Mughal architecture; and the octagonal **Sher Mandal**, possibly built as a pleasure house but soon to witness tragedy.

Humayun had wandered India and then taken refuge at Shah Tahmasp's court in Persia for ten years, paying for his keep with the Koh-i-Nur diamond and other jewels. In 1555, when Sher Shah's followers were split into warring factions, he won Delhi back. The next year, having made the Sher Mandal his library, he was standing at the top of its steps directing his astrologers to watch

The Crafts Museum
Village Serenity in the Busy Capital

On Pragati Maidan, locals meet at the National Handicrafts and Handlooms Museum to take a break from the city hubbub. This is an exceptional museum in every way. The concept is an all-India village: 15 open-fronted villagers' huts grouped around a core of exhibition halls, offices and demonstration areas.

Each hut is typical of an area of India, and each is splendidly decorated inside and out. Some have elaborate plasterwork around windows and fireplaces. Others have huge wall-paintings crammed with warring kings and soldiers, parading elephants, royal lion hunts and favourite Hindu gods. One wall may be Rajasthani, another south-Indian, another painted by wandering Bhils. Together, they make a gallery of folk art.

Near the halls and offices, tea is sold in traditional throwaway clay cups. Lifesize terracotta horses welcome visitors up steps to the exhibition hall whose floors and walls are totally changed to create a sympathetic environment for each new show. A recent one was a crowd of giant wooden figures and animals, 175-year-old *bhutas* (folk deities) from Karnataka. A Tulsi tree and deep eaves give a nearby courtyard the character of an Indian *haveli* (courtyard house); a reference library, publications area and offices surround it. A larger courtyard houses a permanent display of beautiful vessels. Behind the courtyard, architect Charles Correa has added to his earlier buildings here with another gallery and a restaurant, incorporating an 18th-century carved wooden house from Ahmedabad. The museum's rich growing collection of 25,000 items ranges from icons, lamps and wood carvings to toys, masks, ivories and a cross-section of traditional textiles.

Finally, the demonstration area. Here craftsmen from all over India come to work for a period (except July–September). At any one time there may be a Varanasi weaver making fine silk brocade, a Rajasthani puppet-maker who also gives impromptu shows, a Bihari woman from Mithila creating bright and bold folk paintings, a potter from Orissa and a man from Bangalore casting brass deities. Although the museum buys craftsmen's work, some pieces are on sale or can be made to order.

The energy, imagination and sparkle behind this achievement is Jyotindra Jain. Although the museum was founded in 1951, his arrival in 1984 brought the vital dynamism. An anthropologist with a deep interest in ritual art, he has contributed to the great folk-art exhibitions for the Festivals of India around the world. He wants his museum to relate to the villages throughout India and to save and improve traditions that are being lost. In addition to film shows and lectures, workshops with the craftsmen are open to anyone — about 20,000 people a year try their hand at moulding clay, casting metal and other skills.

for the transit of Venus, an especially auspicious moment, when he heard the muezzin's call. He tripped on his robe, fell and died three days later. Looking past the south gate of Purana Qila, you can see his tomb in the distance.

Between Humayun's city and tomb there are several good things to see. **Delhi Zoo** fills most of the space, its entrance right beside the Purana Qila gateway. This is India's biggest and most important zoo. Beautifully landscaped grounds house a few of the world's 70 rare white tigers as well as one-horned rhinoceroses from Assam, Asiatic lion from Gujarat, crocodiles, a ravishing assortment of exotic birds, storks, elephants and a rogue Mughal pavilion perfect for picnicking in and enjoying the squawks, squeaks and soaring views up to Purana Qila. As you go back onto Mathura Road, you will espy a Shergarh gate opposite. Next to it is **Khairu'l-Manazi-Masjid** (the most auspicious of houses, 1561), built for Maham Anga who, as wet-nurse to Akbar, became head of the harem and achieved almost royal stature and influence — her son became an army general (see page 93). Steps lead up to good rooftop views. On the way down to Humayun's tomb the Sundar Nagar antique shops are on the left.

Humayun's tomb (1565−71) is the first great Mughal garden tomb. This is the blueprint which reached maturity in the Taj Mahal at Agra. His senior widow Bega Begum, known as Haji Begam, built it to the designs of a Persian, Mirak Mirza Ghiyas, who took local materials and forms and arranged them to Persian spatial concepts. He also added a new element: a double dome whose two skins made possible a lofty exterior and a well-proportioned interior. Together, widow and architect achieved 'one of the most arresting examples of the building art in India' and 'an outstanding landmark in the development of the Mughal style ... the synthesis of two of the great building styles of Asia — the Persian and the Indian' (Percy Brown). Successive gateways finally open into a *char-bagh* (four garden, see page 117) where the domed memorial sits on a high plinth. Clamber up onto it for more good views back to Purana Qila and to more monuments scattered nearby.

Inside the mausoleum, the emperor is not alone. Other Mughals here include Bega Begam, Shah Jahan's son Dara Shukoh and Mughal emperors Farrukhshiyar (ruled 1713−19) and Alamgir II (ruled 1754−9). The last emperor, Bahadur Shah II (ruled 1837−58), was found hiding here during the Mutiny. Outside the gateway, the aptly named **Sabz-Burj** (green dome) on the roundabout gives an idea of how luxurious the Mughal buildings looked when first built, as does the tiled **Nila-Gumbad** (blue dome, 1625), at the southeast corner of the tomb walls. On the way there, you will pass Bega Begam's so-called **Arab-Serai**, which probably housed the Persian craftsmen working on the tomb. Near here is another Mathura Road monument, the massive square tomb of **Khan-i-Khanan** (died 1627). It has lost its exterior decoration to Safdar Jang's tomb (see below), but held onto its delicate incised and painted plasterwork inside.

Nizamuddin is opposite, a medieval Sufi village replete with Muslim atmosphere living on quietly in the bustle of India's capital. Stalls lining the lanes sell kebabs, Qur'ans, rose petals, lace caps and the latest cassette tapes of *qawwalis* to the visiting faithful. The village heart is the *dargah* (shrine) of the Sufi saint Shaikh Nizam-ud-din Chishti (1236–1325), whose royal followers included two Tughluqs, Muhammad and Feroz Shah, and several Mughals. (The *Akbarnama* recounts how, after Akbar's visit, an assassin's arrow failed to kill the king 'as the Divine protection and the prayers of the saints were guarding him'.) The sacred land surrounding the shrine attracted other important tombs including those of court poet Amir Khusrau (died 1325), who contributed much to the qawwali form of singing; Shah Jahan's daughter Jahanara, who laid out Chandni Chowk; and emperor Muhammad Shah (ruled 1719–48). The daily qawwalis at the dargah continue all night during the Urs festivals (see page 192).

South Delhi
Spotting Survivors of Early Cities

Delhi's first cities lie in the south. Remnants of energetic building by successive rulers pop up in the most unlikely places — a chic New Delhi bungalow has a Mughal tomb in its back garden; the way to a concrete block of flats is around the rubble of a Lodi mosque. Indeed, New Delhi's fashionable housing estates, known as colonies, have beaten their way around, into and even on top of the old monuments.

Here are just a few groups that are easy to find, with hints for the adventurous to seek out more treats; even so, you will need a map and a willing driver. To plot your way to others, invest in the Archaeological Survey of India map of their protected Delhi monuments. To make a pleasant day trip, take a picnic to enjoy on the grassy hillocks behind Qutb Minar.

A magical start to the day is a stroll in **Lodi Gardens**, just south of Lutyens's boulevards. Here, amid scented jasmine, blossoming shrubs, ponds and lawns stand the majestic domed tombs of several sultans, saved from New Delhi expansion by Lady Willingdon who laid out the park in the 1930s. The Sayyids (1414–51) and the Lodis (1451–1526) continued the Delhi Sultanate after the Tughluqs (1320–1413), but as a shadow of its former self: the Lodi sultans had little power over their nobles' confederacy and in 1502 moved off to Agra. You can spot the octagonal tomb (1445) of the third Sayyid sultan, Muhammad Shah and the two square tombs of high-ranking Lodis, Bara-Gumbad-Masjid (large dome mosque, 1494) and Shish-Gumbad (glass dome, retains some blue tiles). The octagonal tomb of Sikandar Lodi (ruled 1488–1516), the second Lodi sultan, is on the north side, with its newly imported Persian double dome and good views from the roof (steps in the right-hand corner of the courtyard).

The ten-kilometre (six-mile) drive from here south down Sri Aurobindo Marg to the Qutb Minar, Delhi's Eiffel Tower, passes roadside monuments, with more down the byroads. Here are a few to look out for.

Safdar Jang's tomb (1753–74) comes first, built for the Nawab of Oudh, minister to Mughal emperor Ahmad Shah (ruled 1748–54) who came to the throne a 'vicious, dissipated, perfidious, pusillanimous and utterly worthless young man', preferring as advisers 'those least worthy'. His is the last of the great Mughal garden tombs, still following the format of the first, Humayun's, but lacking its style. Still, it is worth exploring the gateway, interior plasterwork, rooftop views and well-kept garden. Down the road, by Safdarjang Airport, Najaf Khan's less pristine tomb (1782) stands on the left.

A kilometre (0.6 mile) further, a detour left to Kidwai Nagar leads to the **tomb of Darya Khan**, who served all the Lodi sultans: a grand affair of tiered platform, central tomb and surrounding domed *chhatris*. Beyond it and past a cluster of tombs in South Extension I stands the octagonal tomb of the second Sayyid ruler, Mubarak Shah (1434); more good plasterwork. The keen can detour south, over Ring Road and into Haus Khas, to find **Moth-ki-Masjid** (lentil mosque). It was built by Miyan Bhuwa with money, so the story goes, earned from healthy yields of lentils which began when a single grain was picked up and handed to him by his master, Sultan Sikandar Lodi.

Along Khel Gaon Marg, the scanty **remains of Siri**, Delhi's second major city, are on the left. It was built by Ala-ud-din (ruled 1296–1316), the third and popular sultan of the Khaljis (1290–1320), who preceded the Tughluqs. The ablest of all Delhi sultans, he conquered the main Rajput forts and all of Gujarat, reduced to vassalage the principal Hindu kingdoms of south India, kept a standing army for his expanding empire and built up a firm administration. In his capital, water came from a huge reservoir in Haus Khas and markets were inspected daily for fair prices. When Timur sacked Feroz Shah Kotla in 1398, old Siri impressed him with its 'lofty' buildings and 'very strong' fortifications. South of Siri, just after Palam Marg or Outer Ring Road, lie the insubstantial remains of Jahanpanah city, Delhi's third city, begun in 1325 by the second Tughluq sultan. However, the fascinating **Museum of Everyday Art** housed in collector O P Jain's house is worth a visit and is found along Palam Marg to the right (Sanskriti, C-6/53 Safdarjang Development Area).

For a final detour, a left turn by Aurobindo Ashram leads towards Sarodaya Enclave to **Begampur** village where the splendid **mosque** is said to be one of seven built by Feroz Shah Tughluq's prime minister, Khan-i-Jahan Junan Shah; again, worth clambering onto the roof for views.

And so to the first Delhis at **Lal Kot**. Little survives of the citadel built around 1060, extended and renamed **Qila Rai Pithora** by Prithviraj III, the Chauhan Rajput ruler. In 1192 he was thoroughly defeated by **Qutb-ud-din Aibak**, a Turkish lieutenant of Mohammad of Ghor, who proclaimed himself Sultan in 1206. The Delhi Sultanate began, to end in 1526 when Babur's triumph marked the beginning of the Mughal empire.

A former slave, Aibak (ruled 1206–10), became the first sultan of the so-called Slave dynasty (1206–90). He was a keen, if religiously intolerant, builder. Having destroyed two dozen temples here, he built India's first mosque, the **Quwwat-ul-Islam Masjid** (might of Islam mosque), economically re-using delicately carved Hindu temple columns in the strictly Islamic structure; see especially the soaring, five-arched *maqsura* (screen) coated in deeply-incised Qur'an verses. Aibak also built the **Qutb Minar** (begun 1191), the intricately carved, red sandstone, five-storey, 72.5-metre (278-foot) -high minaret that was both the muezzin's minaret to call the faithful to prayer and a symbol of justice, sovereignty and Islam. As with the mosque, Indian craftsmen built it to an Islamic design.

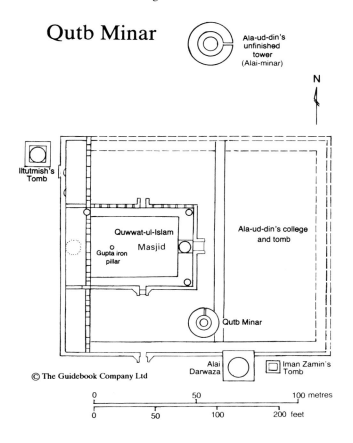

Qutb Minar

Ala-ud-din's
unfinished
tower
(Alai-minar)

N

Iltutmish's
Tomb

Quwwat-ul-Islam

Gupta iron
pillar

Masjid

Ala-ud-din's college
and tomb

Qutb Minar

© The Guidebook Company Ltd

Alai
Darwaza

Iman Zamin's
Tomb

0   50   100 metres

0   50   100   200 feet

Other monuments are scattered around. Inside the complex are the fourth-to fifth-century **Gupta iron pillar** with Sanskrit inscriptions, a mystery of origins and casting, carrying the legend that anyone who can encircle it with his arms will have his wish granted; the richly carved **tomb of Iltutmish** (ruled 1211−36), Aibak's son-in-law and successor, who was equally able and made Delhi the permanent capital, consolidated power and kept the Rajput chiefs in check; and the outposts of the builder of Siri, Ala-ud-din, comprising an unfinished giant rival tower and a college for Islamic studies incorporating his tomb. Outside the complex and after a right turn through the car park and left past the rest-house, a wander onto the Delhi plains finds **Metcalfe's Folly** — an old building adapted as a country retreat — on a hillock, and **Jamali-Kamali's mosque** and the domed tomb (begun 1528−9) of the poet-saint Jamali.

Trees

Among the huge variety of Indian trees, here are a handful to spot in this area, despite rampant deforestation. Leaves, fruits, wood, sap and bark are used in all sorts of ways, from medicines and furniture to dyes and toothbrushes; and spreading branches give welcome shade in the searing heat. Local names are in brackets. See also pages 94−5.

Banyan or **Indian fig** (bar; vata) Aerial roots of this magnificent tree dangle from spreading branches, some embedding themselves as accessory trunks to make huge natural umbrellas for a roadside café or bus stop. Ripe figs turn scarlet; wood from accessory trunks (stronger than main trunk) is used for cart yokes, etc; bark and aerial root fibre makes coarse ropes.

Neem (limbe; neem) Large and rough-barked with serrated leaves, white flowers and yellow ripe fruits. Twigs make a shockingly bitter toothbrush for locals; leaves double as culinary herb and insect repellent, while seeds yield margosa oil used to make soaps, cosmetics and insecticides; the aromatic wood makes good furniture, carved images, drums, etc.

Ashok (Ashok) Named after the great Mauryan Empire ruler, Emperor Ashoka (reigned c 273−236 BC), the tree has dark, shining, pendulous leaves and is often trimmed to a bulging cigar shape, as in the avenue of ashoks leading to Humayun's tomb in Delhi.

Pipal (ashvatha; pipal) Large deciduous tree whose young pendulous leaves are flushed pink. Ripe figs turn purple-black; the bark's tannin is used for dyeing and leather tanning, the low-quality wood for packing cases, matchboxes, fuel, etc. The Buddha received enlightenment under a pipal tree at Bodhgaya.

Kadamb (kaim; kadamb) Deciduous with fluted trunk, fragrant

Finally, outside the complex and left, **Mahrauli** village is a kilometre (0.6 mile) away. As you enter it, Adham Khan's tomb is on the right, known as **Bhul-Bhulaiyan** (labyrinth) for the confusing passages in its thick walls. It is the burial place of both Adham Khan and his powerful mother, Maham Anga, wet-nurse to Akbar, whose house is opposite Purana Qila (see page 85). As foster brother to Akbar, Khan was part of the royal family. Impetuous and ambitious, in 1562 he murdered Akbar's chief minister in the private palace quarters at Agra. The emperor discovered him, knocked him unconscious, and had him thrown down from the fort ramparts. When this failed to finish him off, he was tossed over a second time. At the end of a lane found on the left just after Adham Khan's tomb, a cluster of mosques and a splendid baoli (step-well) stand unvisited in the countryside.

greenish-yellow flowers and winged seedpods. The blue-skinned god Krishna climbed into a kadamb tree at Mathura to play his flute and tease the bathing maidens. Strong, durable wood used for planks, rafters, furniture, carving, combs, etc.

Jambul or **Black plumb** (jaman; jambul) Evergreen with scaly bark, shining aromatic leaves and heads of scented, whitish-green flowers. Juicy, sweet fruits make a port-like wine, a distilled spirit and vinegar. Seeds, equal to cereals in protein and carbohydrate content, are fed to cattle; tough wood used for house-building, cart wheels, etc.; tassar silkworms gobble the leaves.

Sissoo or **South Indian redwood** (sissoo; shisham) Deciduous, usually with a crooked, peeling trunk; cream flowers, long pod. Much-prized wood used for quality furniture and cabinet-making, musical instruments, railway sleepers, hookah tubes, shoe heels, sports equipment such as skis, etc.

Mango (amb) Evergreen with dark elliptical leaves and pinkish or greenish flowers. The juicy, orange-yellow fruit with large fibrous stone is such a delicacy that in May boxes of Alfonsos (considered the best variety, grown south of Bombay) are sent to favoured business clients and loved ones throughout India and the world. It may be eaten raw, ripe or as chutney, juice, ice-cream, etc. Distilled flowers produce amb attar (perfume); the urine of cattle fed on mango leaves makes a yellow dye, as does the bark.

Siris or **Indian walnut** (siris) Deciduous with brown-grey bark and fragrant white flowers. Lustrous, durable wood with decorative burrs used for classy furniture, panelling, veneers and parquet floors, as well as for toys and carving, etc.; bark used as dye and detergent. (The fruiting walnut is another tree.)

Banyan

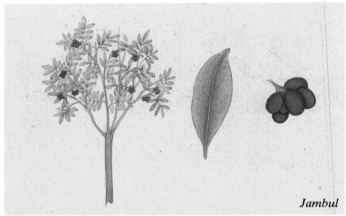

Jambul

Kadamb

Sissoo

Ashok

Pipal

Mango

Neem

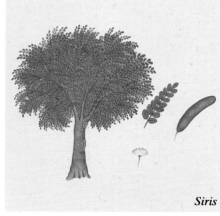

Siris

If you get this far, it is well worth taking the eastwards Mahrauli Badarpur Road back past the Qutb Minar and through countryside dotted with sultanate remains. Eight kilometres (five miles) on, **Tughluqabad** rises on the left. Clambering up the steps and through the ramparts, you reach the colonnades, corridors, steps and soaring arches that are the magnificent ruins of Delhi's third great city, a Piranesi paradise. The citadel was to the right, palaces to the left, and grid-plan walled city straight ahead, all served by a huge reservoir to the south built by joining up the gaps between surrounding hills.

Ghiyas-ud-din Tughluq (ruled 1320–5), first of the Tughluq sultans (1320–1413), built his octagonal, 13-gate fort before his son Muhammad (ruled 1325–51) committed patricide. Muhammad began Jahapanah (south of Siri), then in 1327 forced his citizens to abandon Delhi for Daulatabad more than 1,500 kilometres (930 miles) away in the Deccan, only to return a few years later. Ghiyas-ud-din's nephew, Feroz Shah, would build another great Delhi, Feroz Shah Kotla. The first Tughluq's handsome tomb stands south of the road, originally surrounded by water, hence the causeway to reach it. When Edward Lear came to sketch the ruins in 1874 he drew two views 'characteristic of the eternal squash and harry this land has been devoted to' and then sat under a mimosa full of turtledoves and parrots to tuck into his usual noontime breakfast of 'bread and cold mutton, eggs, sherry and soda water, little and good'.

North of Old Delhi
A Trip into Raj Land

A jaunt up north into the old British area passes several interesting British sights and a few much older ones. It is best to explore by car, forging on right up to North Ridge which at dusk feels hauntingly Raj. Here are a few places worth seeking out; to guide your driver, you will need a map.

Netaji Subhash Marg runs up past the fort, down a hill and under Lothian Bridge, a railway bridge. Just after it, **Lothian Cemetery** lurks on the right, its gate beneath a grey crenellated tower, its assortment of gravestones including a grand sandstone one to Thomas Dunn, erected by James Skinner. Back on what is now Lothian Road, you find an arched ruin in the middle of it. This is the remains of the **British Magazine**, with a bit more further along. The huge ammunition storehouse was deliberately blown up on 11 May 1857 to prevent the freedom fighters, who had mutinied in Meerut the previous day, ever getting hold of it. The bang was said to have been heard at Meerut, 50 kilometres (31 miles) away. The grey obelisk beyond is the **Telegraph Memorial** from which the Anglo-Indian operator warned the British army of what was going on, concluding in fine Indian English 'We must shut up' ('We are off'). And the dilapidated, columned building on the right was the first **British Residency** in Delhi, first occupied by Sir David Ochterlony in 1803.

Further along the road, the pastel yellow, domed, Greek Revival **St**

James's Church (consecrated in 1836) stands in an immaculate churchyard with pots of flowers and a cluster of Skinner family tombs. This was Delhi's first church, built by **Colonel James Skinner** (c 1778–1841), the son of a Scotsman and a Rajput. As a half-caste, he was at first refused by the British army and served a Maratha chief. Later accepted by the British, he founded Skinner's Horse, cavalry regiments distinguished by their yellow uniforms. Inside the church, the Skinner family pew is at the front and Skinner's tomb is by the altar, while monuments to William Fraser, Thomas Metcalfe and others coat the floors and walls. As Philip Davies (see Recommended Reading) acutely observes, the church is 'a resplendent monument to that curious mixture of martial and pious qualities that pervaded Anglo-India and which reached its most distasteful extremes during the Mutiny.'

Kashmiri Gate is a little further on, just after one splendid survival of the smart shops that served the Raj. The facade of **Varma's leather shop**, on the left, proudly lists its patrons, from Queen Mary and Lord Willingdon to the Lord Mayor of London; and if you go in and ask, you can see the treasured album of the shop's illustrious history.

Kashmiri Gate is the only surviving double-arched entrance to Shahjahanabad. It was through here that royal processions set off to escape Delhi summers for the cool gardens of Kashmir. And it was here in September 1857 that 5,000 British came down from the Ridge, breached the walls and, after six days of fighting an estimated 20,000 Indians, retook Delhi. The hero was the legendary **Brigadier-General John Nicholson**, whose devoted Indian followers included some who believed 'Nikkul Seyn' was the reincarnation of Brahma. He died at the gate as victory approached, to be buried in **Nicholson Cemetery** found further up the road on the left, by the Qudsia Road crossing. Peacocks and striped squirrels lend an exoticism to the eery Victorian graves. Further back in history, in 1748, pretty **Qudsia Gardens** on the right side of the road were laid out by Qudsia Begum, a rags-to-riches dancing girl who became emperor Muhammad Shah's favourite wife and mother of the next emperor. Of the garden buildings, just the west gateway and mosque survive.

Still on the same road, by now called Sham Nath Marg, the **Oberoi Maidens Hotel** is on the right, built with Raj spaciousness by Mr Maiden in 1900 and later one of Lutyens's homes while he watched his new city being built. (If you go on north from here, the Old Secretariat is on the right, with Metcalfe House at the end of the lane just before it. Metcalfe's riverside home had one room dug out under the Yamuna to beat the summer heat. Both buildings are interesting but difficult to visit.)

Turning left opposite the Maidens into Underhill Road, you come to an area reeking of the Raj, with grand colonial houses set in leafy gardens. A turn right at the end into Rajpur Road leads into scrubland. At the top, a sharp left turn into Rani Jhansi Marg leads back onto **North Ridge**.

Flagstaff Tower is on the crest, a circular tower where British women and children gathered on the fateful 11 May 1857 before fleeing to Karnal. The remains of **Chauburji Masjid** are further along, on the right, probably part of Feroz Shah Tughluq's Kuskh-i-Shikar (hunting palace) built in 1356; and **Pir-Ghaib**, in the compound of Hindu Rao Hospital, is part of it, too. William Fraser's country retreat, known as **Hindu Rao's House**, is just beyond, on the same side, built in 1830 with obligatory verandas and pilasters. (Fraser was assassinated in 1835 at point blank range by a Nawab who suspected him of having designs on his beautiful sister.) Next, on the left, is one of emperor Ashoka's extraordinary pillars (273−236 BC, see also page 82).

Finally, the **Mutiny Memorial** on the way down from the Ridge is an octagonal, tapering tower similar to the Gothic memorial Eleanor crosses in England. Built to commemorate the British who died in 1857, it was renamed **Ajitgarh** on the 25th anniversary of India's freedom and aptly converted into a memorial for the Indian martyrs who rose against colonial rule. At the crossroads, a left turn leads back along Boulevard Road to Kashmiri Gate.

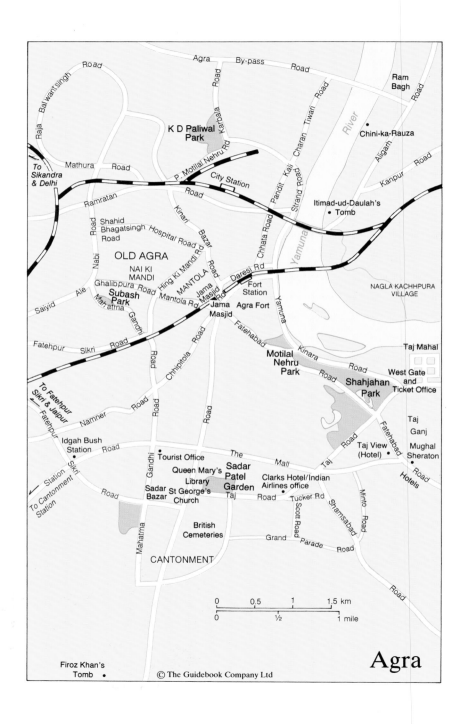

Agra

Agra

In the chilly mauve light of dawn, a sleepy-eyed couple tap on the shoulders of a bicycle rickshaw driver curled up in a blanket asleep on the seat. A yawn or so later, the boy is peddling the couple through the silent streets. As he freewheels down Shahjahan Park, the pale dome of the Taj Mahal floats in the misty sky ahead. The great wooden doors of the west entrance are ajar. The precinct is quiet: not a hawker in sight. Behind it rises the pale grey dome, closer now but still undefined. At the towering inner gateway, dozy ticket collectors chatter and a boy sweeps. Ahead, all is white at first. Then the full quiet majesty of the Taj comes into focus. A few other visitors arrive, but the atmosphere is totally serene, almost private. Blowing cupped hands for warmth, some sit gazing at the Taj head on, others wander the dew-coated lawns or stroll up the side avenues watching the changing light on the Taj. Slowly, it turns from pale mauve through cream and pink to a warm yellow. The sun's first rays touch the top of the dome, then creep down over this white marble mausoleum, the supreme monument to love.

This is the best way to start a day in Agra. And it is why a day trip is crazy unless there is no option. The Taj is Agra's magnet — even the most regular India visitor returns again and again, to be lost in wonder each time.

But there is more to Agra than the Taj. The great Mughal emperors made the whole city splendid. The Hindu epic, the *Mahabharata*, had called the city Agrabana, meaning paradise. Later, in the 16th and 17th centuries, the sumptuous Mughal courts of Akbar, Jahangir and Shah Jahan made myth a reality. Agra became a sophisticated, utterly luxurious, man-made paradise.

It was a court where a favourite fish might be fitted with a gold nose-ring, where a queen discovered how to distil and capture the heavy scent of rose petals, where a prince's dress was decorated with pearls and where a single giant ruby was fashioned into a ring. It was a court where twice a year the emperor was weighed in gold and silver which was then distributed to his people. As for food, humble rice was served with membrane-thin sheets of real gold and chefs were given the title 'maharaj', great king.

The dazzling fame of this fairytale court travelled as far as Europe, where François Bernier's account of his visit to unimaginable pomp and luxury was a bestseller. Envoys hurried eastwards to verify the fabled 'gold of Ind' and to strike up lucrative trading deals. Later, it was these Mughal rulers who gave the West the word 'mogul' to describe the fantasy-rich barons of commerce and kings of Hollywood.

Today, it needs only a jot of imagination to bring the magnificent riverside fort alive. Behind it, old Agra city bustles with the descendants of those who served the Mughal courtiers: thousands of craftsmen still inlay marble as their forefathers did on the Taj. On the same bank but downriver and round a bend sits the Taj, while upriver on the far bank a nobleman's tomb is the Taj's precursor. And Akbar's idealistic city of victory, Fatehpur Sikri, where he lived for 14 years, is just 37 kilometres (23 miles) away and not to be missed.

Despite the tourist boom since the 17th century, seeing Agra's monuments is peaceful and hawker-free since they are run by the Archaeological Survey. Bicycle rickshaws ride between Fort and Taj and around old Agra and the interesting British cantonment. But you will need a car to visit treasures on the far bank and Akbar's tomb at Sikandra; and a car or bus (see page 34) for Fatehpur Sikri.

The Fort

The best place to begin. Here Agra's Mughal life began and ended. Here the three great Mughals associated with Agra's most splendid period lived and built (they built outside the fort as well). And here is the most magical first view of the Taj.

After **Babur**'s triumph over Sultan Ibrahim Lodi at Panipat in 1526, he sent his son Humayun to secure the Lodi treasury at Agra. Humayun found the local Maharaja of Gwalior's family cowering in a corner of Lodi Fort, clutching their jewels. To placate Humayun, they gave him the best: a golf-ball-sized diamond. This was probably the **Koh-i-Nur** (mountain of light) which Babur valued at 'two and a half days' food for the whole world' and which Humayun later gave to Shah Tahmasp of Persia in thanks for ten years of hospitality when Mughal power in India temporarily lapsed. The stone seems to have been mined at Golconda in the Deccan, then glittered on various eastern rulers' heads before being claimed by the British from the Lahore treasury as compensation for war losses. Today, kept safe with the Crown Jewels in the Tower of London and worn only at coronations, it is still one of the world's great diamonds and weighs 108.93 carats even though Queen Victoria (and possibly others) cut it down.

Babur next needed to defeat the Rajput chieftains to consolidate Mughal power. This he did the following year, at Khanua. With justification he could now call himself Badshah, a Persian title meaning emperor. As his daughter, Gulbadan, wrote: 'The treasure of five kings fell into his hands'. The next year, 1528, he celebrated at Agra, initiating the pomp and splendour that would flow until the fifth emperor, Shah Jahan, moved back to the traditional capital, Delhi, in 1648. Even though his successor, Aurangzeb, sometimes held court at Agra, the Mughal show was already closing.

Babur's feast was magnificent, attended by all his loyal servants who arrived over some months from distant lands. It contained the three ingredients for a successful Mughal feast: presents, entertainment and, of course, food. Babur sat beneath a special pavilion, his important guests in a vast semicircle around him. Each guest heaped piles of gold and silver on to a special carpet laid before the new emperor. Babur returned the largesse with such favourites as jewel-encrusted sword-belts and ceremonial dresses woven of silk and gold. Meanwhile, musicians, dancers, acrobats, jugglers, gladiators, wrestlers and fighting animals amused the guests.

To Jawaharlal Nehru, India's first Prime Minister, Babur was 'a typical Renaissance prince, bold and adventurous, fond of art and literature and good living.' But his four years as emperor were mostly occupied with battle. He kept a diary in which he recorded with acute observation and wit his battles and feasts. And although he missed the stimuli and comforts of the Timurid Renaissance he had left behind beyond the Hindu Kush, as well as the cool climate there, he also noted in his diary the birds, animals, flowers and fruits of his new homeland. It is called the *Baburnama*; and this diary tradition, leaving a minute record of every aspect of Mughal court life, was kept up by his descendants.

Babur set the character for Mughal rule, although he had little time for building. His only legacy at Agra is Ram Bagh, a forgotten garden on the east bank (see page 122). His son Humayun (ruled 1530–40 and 1555–6) returned to Delhi in 1533 to build his Dinpanah city (see page 83) before being chased off the throne in 1540, only winning it back in 1555, the year before his death.

It is Humayun's son **Akbar** (ruled 1556–1605) who developed Agra's glory. Aged 14 and virtually illiterate, he ascended the throne for half a century of rule, providing the glamour and magnetic leadership that inspired the next two emperors, Jahangir and Shah Jahan.

Akbar built his Agra Fort (1567–75) beside the then wide and fast-flowing Yamuna whose waters lapped the walls (so much water is now diverted from the Yamuna at Delhi that most of the gentler flow here is the accumulation of streams emptying into it below the capital). Qasim Khan was his Superintendent of Riverine Works who put up the sandstone walls and buildings over an earlier Hindu fort. It is one of the largest riverside forts in India, quite different from the traditional hilltop forts such as Amber, Jaipur's precursor. Inside, a substantial army with its artillery and treasure could withstand a long siege with no water shortage; outside lived the common citizens. To get an idea of its scale, take a stroll in the gardens along the Yamuna Kinara Road, where the river ran, and spot Akbar's great ramparts and sandstone buildings and then, further along, the row of marble palaces added by his grandson. The walls are magnificent, with a moat between inner and outer walls. Where the space between the two walls is bigger at the left end, Akbar would look down from the octagonal tower at his favourite spectator sport, elephant fights.

Amar Singh Gate is the main entrance, across the drawbridge over smelly moat waters. Shah Jahan built this gate in 1665 to commemorate the daring of Rao Amar Singh, brother of the Rajput ruler of Jodhpur and a top court noble. When Rao Amar took offence at remarks made by the court treasurer in the emperor's presence, he slew the treasurer, realized his unpardonable breach of court etiquette, jumped on his horse and leapt the fort walls.

Too Many Cooks

"This is the third time you have phoned me this month about Jayanthi's health, Ma," said Bhola crossly. "I don't think there's anything at all wrong with her apart from wedding nerves. But if you are worried you should get the doctor. What can I do from here? Also I am not a doctor, but a scientist, so I would not be able to advise you about anything medical."

"The ten-rupee is at a wedding and the four-rupee can't be found," Mama told him. "And she is really ill, unconscious like someone sleeping."

"How do you know she isn't sleeping?" asked Bhola, but promised to send a good doctor from Calcutta at once. "He'll cost you a hundred rupees though, Ma," Bhola warned her. And Mama said she would pay rupees a thousand to have her baby restored to health.

Mama laid down the phone and together Ayah and she prepared a brass cup of warm buffalo milk sweetened with palm sugar and spiced with ginger.

Kneeling by the side of the unconscious girl, Ayah held the cup to her lips whispering. "Nice milk for Baba. Baba drink lovely milk," while Mama watched, her hand on her breast to keep down the palpitations. And, to their enormous joy and relief, after a few moments Jayanthi's eye-lids fluttered, and a smile came on her lips. Then she sat up, took the cup from Ayah and said, "Thank you, Ayah!"

"Oh my goodness, you gave us such a fright!" gasped Mama, cross again with relief. Then catching sight of Jayanthi's tummy would have started all over again if Ayah had not said firmly, "She is not pregnant, Ma. She is only tubby, that's all. She always was a tubby one ever since a baby. But now she has become even more so after all those Calcutta curds and sweeties and the like!"

Then Mama Mandel, laughing with happiness, took her daughter in her arms, and planted wet kisses all over her face while hugging her so hard Jayanthi was almost suffocated. "We will be having the wedding after all!" laughed Mama Mandel, who had really been much looking forward to the good pilaus and biryanis laced with ghee and spiced with cardamoms from Malabar.

At this moment the four-rupee doctor arrived, puffing and panting as though he had been running, which indeed he had.

"Oh, a thousand pardons, Madam!" he gasped. He had read a lot of classical literature from books owned by Papa Mandel. "I am come even now!"

But before he had time to examine the patient the ten-rupee doctor arrived, his face grave, having been fetched from the wedding by Mama Mandel's little servant boy. This servant had given the doctor the impression that Jayanthi Mandel was almost, if not entirely dead. "Blood everywhere," the boy had told the doctor, "and half her bones broken. The robbers snatched her gold chain from her neck, and broke her eye glasses. . . ."

"Does Jayanthi Mandel wear glasses?" asked the ten-rupee doctor in some surprise.

"Well they would have broken if she had worn them," amended the child hurriedly.

And then the hundred-rupee doctor from Calcutta arrived.

Mama, if she had had time, would have ordered Jayanthi to feign illness. However as it was too late to do this she made up by angrily upbraiding everyone in sight, the four-and ten-rupee doctors for not having been available when she wanted them, the servants for not having found them fast enough, and the rickshaw wallah who had pulled the hundred-rupee doctor from the station for having run so slowly. "If you had run quicker she would still have been unconscious when the Doctor Sahib arrived," shouted Mama Mandel. And most of all she blamed Jayanthi for having got ill in the first place, and said that perhaps it would have been better after all if Jayanthi had been pregnant, for then the three doctors would have something to examine her for.

"Anyway now you are here," Mama told the three men of medicine, "you might as well look her all over, for she is to be married soon, and it is as well to make sure she is in good health before the great occasion." The three doctors looked at one another questioningly.

"Examine in order of price," said Mama. "Hundred first, then ten, then four."

The two cheaper doctors sat down side by side, while the august man from Calcutta rolled up his sleeves.

Sara Banerji, The Wedding of Jayanthi Mandel

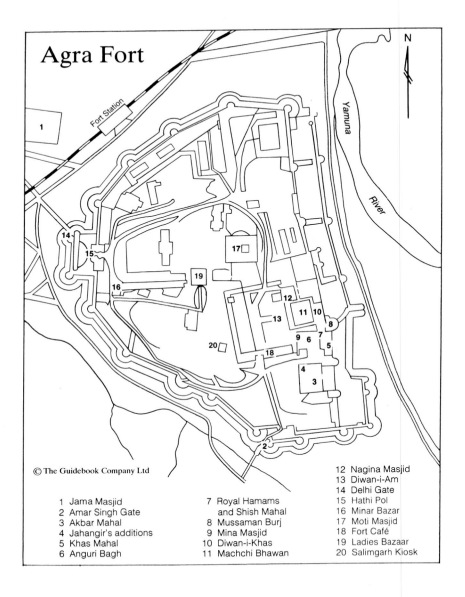

Agra Fort

N

Fort Station

Yamuna

River

1

14

15

16

19

17

20

12

11 10

13

8

9 6 7

18 5

4

3

2

© The Guidebook Company Ltd

1 Jama Masjid
2 Amar Singh Gate
3 Akbar Mahal
4 Jahangir's additions
5 Khas Mahal
6 Anguri Bagh

7 Royal Hamams
  and Shish Mahal
8 Mussaman Burj
9 Mina Masjid
10 Diwan-i-Khas
11 Machchi Bhawan

12 Nagina Masjid
13 Diwan-i-Am
14 Delhi Gate
15 Hathi Pol
16 Minar Bazar
17 Moti Masjid
18 Fort Café
19 Ladies Bazaar
20 Salimgarh Kiosk

The horse died and Rao Amar was put to death; but the emperor admired his courage.

At the top of the ramp, the gardens on the right lead to **Akbar Mahal** (palace). The great bath (1611) in front dates back to Jahangir's love-match wedding to Nur Jahan and was possibly one of his presents. When the queen bathed it was filled with rose petals to scent the hot water sprayed from above. The ritual was the origin, so one story goes, of the queen's discovery of rose attar which became the fashionable court perfume. (Other stories credit her mother with this breakthrough.) The facade (1605−15) of marble in the densely decorated pattern is also a Jahangir addition.

Through the archway lie Akbar's rooms. Since they are thoroughly Hindu in character, Akbar must surely have looked at local buildings for inspiration and used local craftsmen. The central courtyard has square arches, a roof supported on decorative brackets and extravagant carving which even includes delightful parrots, a Hindu favourite but banned from pure Islamic buildings. The rooms around it have richly carved surfaces. There is a living room to the right, his Rajput princess's quarters behind (with niches for her Hindu gods), his harem to the left and three rooms straight ahead which included his library in the centre.

Here Akbar lived when not on campaign. He was a soldier of genius and daring, an empire builder who turned a foothold in India into control of the whole of Hindustan. He was a diplomat who pacified the Rajput chiefs, most usefully the Jaipur chief who became his general and whose daughter, Jodhai Bai, gave him his son. He was a true liberal who showed such religious tolerance that he created din-i-Ilani (religion of God, see also page 122). He was a great builder, administrator and idealist, seen best in his purpose-built capital, Fatehpur Sikri. He promoted all the arts: his cultural circle, nicknamed his 'nine jewels', included the musician Tansen. He had a mesmerizing personality: visiting Jesuits who joined the emperor's theosophical discussions described his compelling eyes as 'vibrant like the sea in sunshine'. And he must have had tender feelings towards some of his many wives: Jodhai Bai's charm could persuade her king-lover to forsake both onions and garlic because, apparently, they were 'inconvenient in kissing', to shave off his beard and to give up eating a Muslim favourite, beef, forbidden to cow-worshipping Hindus.

From the pavilions in the courtyard ahead, Akbar watched his elephant fights below, including one fateful fight the year of his death, between his son and grandson.

His first son, Salim (who became emperor Jahangir), was finally born in 1569 to jubilant celebrations (see also page 131). But during the prince's long wait for the throne he descended into debauchery via over-indulgence in drink and opium, while his two younger brothers died of drink. Disappointed Akbar, who had given them plenty of military and administrative training and experience, became estranged from Salim and began openly to favour

Khusrau, Salim's son, as heir. Salim responded with a half-hearted rebellion and had Akbar's favourite, Abu'l Fazl, assassinated, a foretaste of the atrocities the royal family would mete out to one another (see page 81 for its culmination under Aurangzeb). After several reconciliations organized by the court women, Akbar staged an elephant fight in September 1605 between Salim and Khusrau's strongest elephants, hoping to find an omen for the future. Salim's elephant won. A month later Akbar died and Salim inherited the stable empire and made a surprisingly undisastrous emperor.

Salim chose the name **Jahangir** (seizer of the world) when he became emperor (ruled 1605−27) aged 36. Brought up in the idealistic and creative environment of Fatehpur Sikri, he lifted Mughal court culture to new heights. His diary displays his interest in everything from cranes to meteorites, and especially painting and coins. It is illustrated by top artists, including the great Mansur who painted a turkey and falcon for him. But when one coin depicted him holding a wine-cup, such frankness shocked the more orthodox courtiers. Here in the fort, he decorated Akbar's palace with polished and gold-painted stucco and added equally fancy rooms to the north, behind his long facade. The British-restored gilded plasterwork in the central room gives an idea of this launch into richer Mughal decoration.

In 1609 William Hawkins arrived in quest of trade. He noted the emperor's lifestyle and the precision that ruled his day, from morning prayers to afternoon public audiences, after which he 'eateth a bit to stay his stomache, drinking once of his strong drinke.' He then retired to a private room where 'he drinketh other five cupfuls, which is the portion that the physicians alot him. This done, he eateth opium, and then ariseth; and being in the height of his drinke he layeth him downe to sleepe.' After two hours 'they awake him and bring his supper ... at which time he is not able to feed himself, but it is thrust into his mouth by others ... Now in the space of these five cups, whatsoever he doth, either without or within, drunken or sober, he hath writers who by turnes set downe everything in writing, so that there is nothing passeth in his lifetime which is not noted, no, not so much as his going to the necessary, and how often he lieth with his women, and with whom.' Certainly, it makes today's newspapers seem less intrusive into royal life.

It was while Jahangir was at Ajmer in 1615 that **Sir Thomas Roe** arrived from James I to discuss trade deals; he was later regarded as Britain's first, unofficial, ambassador to India. He brought trunkloads of diplomatic gifts, but the only ones to impress the emperor were paintings. The portrait miniatures stimulated his painters towards a new freshness and realism, and the pictures of Christ inspired him to add a celestial nimbus to his portraits.

Meanwhile, one ambitious family became the powerful extension of the emperor. A Persian adventurer, Ghiyas Beg, rose under Akbar. On Jahangir's accession he became chief minister with the title **Itimad-ud-Daulah** (pillar of the government) and helped keep Khusrau in check. His beautiful daughter

Mehrunissa married Jahangir in 1611 and took the name Nur Mahal (light of the palace), soon upgraded to Nur Jahan (light of the world). As Jahangir weakened, this ambitious beauty, poet and keen hunter effectively ruled from inside the harem and even rode into battle carried in a litter slung between two elephants. Her brother Asaf Khan became deputy chief minister; and his daughter married (1612) the next emperor, Shah Jahan. The two great mausolea in Agra are built to Itimad-ud-Daula and Shah Jahan's wife, not to Mughal emperors.

Despite leaving the plains for the solace, beauty and gentle climate of his Kashmir gardens, Jahangir died in 1627, to be buried outside Lahore. And it was not Khusrau but a younger son Khurram who now, after years of intrigue and rebellion, became emperor (ruled 1627−58) aged 35, awarding himself the title **Shah Jahan** (ruler of the world). His father had been half Rajput, but Shah Jahan was three-quarters Rajput as his mother was another Jaipur princess.

Shah Jahan's rule began happily. He lived in style here at Agra, beginning his palace improvements; and he campaigned with his beloved wife, Asaf Khan's daughter Arjumand Banu, who as queen was called **Mumtaz Mahal** (chosen one of the palace). Mumtaz was a constant companion and valued adviser. But tragedy struck in June 1631 when she died giving birth to their 14th child. A blissful marriage of 17 years ended. Shah Jahan was heartbroken. He mourned for two years, giving up music, feasting and glamorous garments. Then, putting his campaigns into the hands of his sons, he threw his energy into architecture. In addition to the Taj Mahal for Mumtaz, he added to palaces in Lahore and Agra and then built a whole new city at Delhi.

Here he added his string of **river palaces** (1628−37), plundering the overflowing royal coffers to build in gleaming white marble which he then had decorated with the most sophisticated carving: vases of identifiable flowers surrounded by colourful and perfectly balanced floral arabesques made of inlaid precious and semi-precious stones. Yet more similar but less tip-top work was done at Lahore and Delhi.

Step out of Jahangir's Agra Fort rooms onto characteristic Shah Jahan marble and you come to three white marble pavilions on the right. The central, five-arched **Khas Mahal** was Shah Jahan's private palace which he called his *aramgah* (place of rest) and where he gathered with his painters, musicians and books. The two flanking pavilions were for his two favourite daughters, Jahanara (who laid out New Delhi's Chandni Chowk) and Roshanara. Curved and elongated roofs follow Rajput tradition; translucent marble over the riverside screens filter light but not heat; ceilings were painted gold and blue (see the 1875 restoration for an idea of how they appeared); and walls were hung with portraits and tapestries. Outside, the air was cooled with playing fountains and perfumed with flowers. Around the sunken Anguri Bagh (grape garden) lived the women of the imperial household, their sandstone rooms built by Akbar. The royal hamams (baths) were in the northeast corner, complete with two antechambers known as Shish Mahal (mirror palace), for their ceilings were set with glass which glittered in the candlelight.

The next cluster of buildings on the marble platform epitomizes Shah Jahan's refined taste and tells of his love for Mumtaz and of his sad old age. This is **Mussaman Burj** (octagonal tower). The exquisite and gloriously inlaid chambers form a self-contained mini-palace intended for Mumtaz, with courtyard, baths, living room and breeze-catching terrace. While emperor, Shah Jahan would leave his Khas Mahal and pass through here to business in the Diwan-i-Khas (private audience hall). Later, having moved up to Delhi in 1648, he was deposed by his third son, Aurangzeb, in 1658. Kept prisoner here, he was tended by Jahanara and would gaze across the Yamuna bend to his wife's mausoleum, the Taj Mahal. When Aurangzeb decided his father was not to be trusted even to go to the mosque, he possibly built the tiny Mina Masjid here (others say it was already part of the mini-palace). Finally, captive for eight years, Shah Jahan died here in 1666. Every view of the Taj from here has a romantic poignancy, but perhaps the most ravishing is when it emerges out of morning mist or glows under late-afternoon sun.

The beautiful and spacious **Diwan-i-Khas** (private audience hall, 1637), with especially fine *pietra dura* columns close to Taj Mahal designs, is found beyond, upstairs and overlooking the large riverside platform with two thrones. The white one was where emperors received visitors on summer nights. The black one was used when Jahangir assumed his emperorship at Allahabad four years before Akbar died, and then moved here for watching elephant fights 'sometimes twice a week, in the afternoone', according to traveller Peter Mundy. There would be one, two or three couples, 'of the fairest bignesse and strongest, whose teeth are sawen off in the midle and then bound about with iron or Brass ... Running one against the other with their Truncks aloft they meete head to head. There they with their Teeth lye Thrustinge and forceinge', their keepers parting them with 'fireworks on long Bamboes, whose cracks and noyse, fire and smoake doe sever them, soe lett them joyne againe' until one wins, 'thrusting att him with his teeth, tramplinge and overlyeing him.'

Below the Diwan-i-Khas the fabulous royal treasury was stored. Below the platform are the river rooms of Akbar's Malchchi Bhavan (fish house) whose large garden courtyard was where the courtesans held their special bazaars, rare chances for public flirting and, according to legends, the place where Jahangir met Nur Jahan and Shah Jahan his Mumtaz. Aurangzeb put a stop to such fun and dug fishponds, hence the name. Along the north side is the tiny, triple-domed, marble Nagina Masjid built by Shah Jahan for his ladies.

Nearby, narrow steps lead down to the large, sandstone **Diwan-i-Am** (public audience hall), probably built by Akbar but with new marble columns added by Shah Jahan or Aurangzeb, and best seen in the afternoon when the sandstone glows and the shadows lengthen. To the roar of drums and trumpets, Shah Jahan would arrive to sit on the balcony on his Peacock Throne glittering with diamonds, sapphires and rubies. Sons and close attendants stood in rank here, women peered through the screens of rooms behind, and the emperor spent two hours or more listening to an odd range of reports which might even include a courtier's dream. Then to complaints, requests and accusations with — according to Hawkins who sat in pride of place on the balcony — his master hangman and 40 helpers at the ready. The public stood where there are now lawns, arriving through the northwestern Delhi Gate and the fort's Minar Bazar in which Mundy found everything from partridge, turtle doves, geese and ducks to mangoes, almonds, walnuts, oranges and musk melons.

Finally, the magnificent **Moti Masjid** (pearl mosque, 1643–53) built by Shah Jahan. To reach it (which sometimes needs determination), go through the north wall of Diwan-i-Am square, across a courtyard, through a door in the left corner and up a majestic flight of internal steps. To see the vast yet serene white marble courtyard, with mosque proper to the north and inscription along the east wall likening it to a precious pearl, is worth every effort. Back at the south end of the Diwan-i-Am, there is a nice café (the Agra Fort is one of the few historic monuments in India to have one) and, in the gateway of the southern wall, excellent postcards are on sale.

Old Agra City

The citizens of Agra lived hard by the fort, outside Delhi Gate (now closed) on the north side. Court patronage abounded, crafts flourished and Agra became a major centre for textiles and jewellery as well as banking and trade. Although starved of court patronage when the Mughals declined, the city continued to thrive at a quieter level and still does today. A stroll around these lanes brings alive the atmosphere of Mughal Agra. If you get lost, it does not much matter as the area is quite small; but enlist some local help to seek out specific craftsmen.

The **Jama Masjid** (Friday mosque, 1648) is the heart of the old city, in Mantola area, its zigzag red and white domes rising above the lanes. It was built by Shah Jahan in the name of his favourite and loyal daughter, Jahanara. Beside its main entrance stands Agra's one forgivable tourist shop, Mughal Marble Emporium, which stocks splendidly gaudy replicas of the Taj made of soapstone with red and yellow plastic trees, fairy lights and glass baubles, each scene enclosed in a glass box. Opposite, the pot-seller's kiosk overflows onto the road. These beautiful spherical water-pots are natural fridges which keep water cool and fresh but apparently only do their job for a few weeks, keeping their sellers in good business.

The cloth market runs round behind the mosque, bustling with ladies

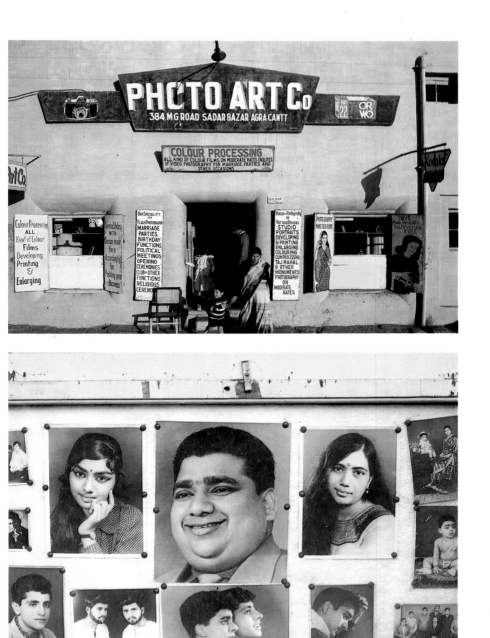

Dhurrie Weaving

From Prison Occupation to Chic Floor Covering

The family goat tethered to the doorpost may be the only sign of life in the sun-beaten lane of an old Agra Muslim quarter. But behind at least one firmly-closed door the women will be busy weaving at a huge loom which almost covers the floor of the dimly-lit living area. Whenever they are free from housework they weave, gossiping and chewing *paan* as they work, disturbed by the occasional visits of the dhurrie-merchant's supervisor, the only non-family man permitted to enter the house.

The Mughal emperor Akbar probably introduced pile carpet weaving into India. But the flat dhurrie — a Hindi word for flat-weave rug — seems to have been an indigenous craft. Although the Agra city weavers are Muslim, those in the nearby villages are mostly Hindu.

Last century, in the more enlightened princely states including Jaipur, prison inmates were taught to weave dhurries to relieve the boredom. Finished rugs furnished the maharaja's many palaces or were sold in the bazaar, with proceeds going to the prisoners' families. The period of top workmanship and design was the 1880s to 1920s.

Today, the traditional cotton Agra dhurries with red or blue pointed stripes on a plain field are loosely woven with cheap yarn. In the bazaars they fetch just Rs40 a pair. Damodar Das Mammo Mal is Agra's biggest manufacturer. In his shop on Johri Bazar (found on the left side if the Jama Masjid is behind you), dhurries are stacked up to the roof.

Quality craftsmanship has been revived for the lucrative Western market. Traditional geometric design elements of stars, diamonds, crosses, chevrons and diagonal patterns have been kept, but the strong, traditional vegetable dyes of indigo, red and saffron have been abandoned to cater to the Western taste of ice-cream'pink, peppermint green and baby blue.

Mr Mangalick, a reliable dhurrie and carpet merchant, sells his dhurries according to yarn quality, design complexity and tightness of weave. And he exercises quality control through supervisors who visit his hundred or so weaving families inside and outside Agra. In town, the men of a Muslim household build the wooden loom and go to the local supervisor for cotton or wool, specially dyed with colour-fast dyes. (Despite this, dhurries should only be dry-cleaned.) Mr Mangalick also dictates the design. It then takes two women 15−20 days to weave a 6 × 8 foot cotton dhurrie with a good tight finish, but just ten to weave a wool one. Unless it is a new or special design, they weave from memory, beating down the threads of each completed row with a comb and chopping off the ends with an iron knife.

If you take measurements and colour swatches with you to India, you can discuss designs and sizes with Mr Mangalick and even visit the weavers who will make your dhurrie. A few months later, it will arrive through the post.

bargaining for silks and cottons; the main street, **Johri Bazar**, runs off to the right. Along here are local dhurrie shops such as Damodar Das Mammo Mal's on the left (see previous page), men's cloth shops where locals meet to gossip over tea, photographers to hire for special occasions, shops selling glitzy braid and other essential wedding accessories, carts loaded with fresh walnuts or crispy gujak, shoe shops (a major Agra trade) and, on the right, a wonderful shop packed with fancy walking sticks. Further on, **Kinari Bazar** has the jewellery shops, while Panni Gali off it (found with difficulty via Fulati Guli) has Agra's top master of *zari* (gold) embroidery work, Shams Uddin. He and his craftsmen work in his family haveli (his name is on the door) with the family pigeons strutting about the roof. Back towards the Jama Masjid, a lane to the left leads eventually to **Malka Bazar**, street of the great kite-makers, such as Sando and Allo Jamalo, whose creations are flown by children from the flat roofs, fluttering until they are trapped in a tree.

Another good area to explore is **Nai ki Mandi**, found northwest of Jama Masjid and across Hing ki Mandi Road. Here shoemakers work in tiny kiosks, women pile up water-pots to dry beside the canal, cows stand motionless mid-lane, and marble craftsmen work quietly behind the old carved doors piercing the whitewashed walls of the narrow lanes (see page 118).

Taj Mahal

The world's greatest monument to love always surpasses expectation. No reproduction on a badly-coloured postcard or faded cake-tin top can cheapen its perfection and romance. Bathed in dawn purples, softening in late sun, even when harsh in eye-dazzling noon whiteness, it is always sublime. And more so each visit.

So, even if your stay in Agra is short, it is well worth seeing the Taj under various lights. The white marble responds to each nuance, setting different moods. Visitors wandering the lush surrounding gardens contribute to the atmosphere — silent sunrise pilgrims, screeching coach parties, romantic honeymoon couples, incongruous hippies, and serious Western photographers laden with lenses. Oblivious of them, the daily life of the Taj continues. A *mali* (gardener) feeds a squirrel its breakfast; three or four help along the lawnmower drawn by two white bullocks; while others grow flowers in the nursery garden. Stonemasons repair marble and sandstone, and attendants watch over the museum and mosque. And as this is a living monument, the mausoleum of a Muslim queen (and her emperor), extra Muslim pilgrims come on Fridays, when entry is free of charge.

When Shah Jahan's beloved Mumtaz Mahal died in 1631, his despair was soon concentrated into creating her mausoleum. An estimated 20,000 labourers and craftsmen, some from Europe, began work the following year, completing this finest of Shah Jahan's buildings 21 years later. Probably

masterminded by himself (no architect has been agreed upon), it takes to
ultimate refinement the Mughal garden tomb first seen in Humayun's tomb in
Delhi (see page 85). But here the proportions are more satisfying from afar,
the detailed *pietra dura* work more precise seen close up. Furthermore, the
pure white marble, not sandstone, of the mausoleum stands silhouetted against
the Indian sky and receives additional reflected light off the Yamuna waters
behind. Painter William Hodges wrote in 1876 that it was 'like a most perfect
pearl on an azure ground.'

There are three gates into the complex, the west where the ticket office is,
the south found through tiny lanes which provide a striking contrast with the
tomb, and the east. From the last, a lane runs down to the river for more views
and, sometimes, ferries to the far bank. If the rains have failed, there are
splendid views of the Taj from the sands, but be careful not to trample the
entrepreneurial locals' cucumbers, watermelons and musk melons.

Inside, past the in-house school which meets on the lawns and the shops
where travellers once stayed, the inscription on the great gate prepares
visitors. It is chapter 89 of the Qur'an, called Al-Fajr (daybreak), and ends 'O
Soul that art at rest. Return to the Lord, at peace with Him and He at peace
with you. So enter as one of His servants. And enter into His garden.'

Through the gateway, the Taj stands across the lush garden divided by
water and surrounded by trees and a high wall. To the left of the platform is
the mosque; to the right the Mehman Khana (guest-house). Eleanor
Roosevelt, suffering cultural indigestion from Indian monuments, arrived here
somewhat jaded but 'held my breath, unable to speak in the face of so much
beauty. I wanted to drink in its beauty from a distance ... one's silence says
this is a beauty that enters the soul. With its minarets rising at each corner, its
dome and tapering spires, it creates a sense of airy, almost floating lightness
... I had never known what perfect proportions were before.'

Babur had introduced the Persian **char-bagh** (four-garden) concept to
India. It carries a threefold idea: a symbol of paradise to reward the faithful, as
described in the Qur'an; the secular tradition of the royal pleasure garden; and
an oasis from the dry desert heat. There is always water, as the main axis and
as crossings, to symbolize both the life source and, where the waters meet, the
meeting of man and God. The waters divide the garden into four, the char-
bagh. As for the original planting, this fell into such neglect that Lord Curzon
(Viceroy 1899–1905) cleared it up and replanted, hence the somewhat
municipal character.

Up on the platform, verses from the Qur'an, low-relief carving and
geometric and floral inlaid designs coat the outside, always perfectly balanced.
Inside, the memorial tombs of Mumtaz (central) and Shah Jahan (pen-box
shaped) lie within the trellis screen in the octagonal chamber. Below them,
down the dark and steep steps, lie the real tombs, the inscription over Shah
Jahan's firmly awarding him the posts of Razwan (guardian of paradise) and

Marble Inlayers
Descendants of Taj Mahal Craftsmen

Nai ki Mandi is an area north of the Jama Masjid in old Agra. The narrow whitewashed lanes are punctuated by high stone steps leading to blue-painted doors. Behind many of them, groups of Agra's 5,000 *pietra dura* craftsmen sit on the courtyard floors quietly creating delicate floral patterns like those worked by their distant forefathers for the fort and the Taj Mahal.

Mohammad Naseem, a Muslim like most marble workers, is a master craftsman who runs a typical workshop. His dozen craftsmen work in the shaded, blue-pillared courtyard of his family *haveli*. He hopes his sons will follow his trade. An apprentice begins young, at eight years old, becomes full-time when schooling ends at 14 and is trained by 20−22 years old. The trained craftsman specializes as a marble-cutter, gem-cutter, gem-setter or chiseller, making his own simple tools and helping his master with special pieces.

The expensive raw materials are supplied to the head of the workshop by the merchant. The hard, non-porous (and so non-staining) white marble comes from Macrana, near Jaipur. The precious and semi-precious stones come from all over the world and include turquoise, coral, pink rhodonite, golden tiger eye and the rare, gold-speckled blue lapis lazuli. Naseem's work is distinguished by the fine chrysanthemum designs with feather-light petals. He uses coral, turquoise and malachite for their purity of colour, and lapis lazuli for its colour and luminosity.

Such fine work, originally introduced from Persia, takes time and considerable patience. First, the paper design is agreed upon between craftsman and merchant. The marble is cut, coated with red water-based paint and the design drawn through. The stones are selected for colour and clarity — a green might be of jade, malachite, variscite or amazonite. Then the slow precision work of cutting each stone and chiselling a bed for it begins. A large design is tackled by area, a small piece in one go. Big flowers are cut first, such as the fine chrysanthemum petals; Naseem often works with the hard and difficult lapis and cornelian because of the glorious finish they give. Each stone is cut, fitted, fine-tuned with an emery paste wheel and then glued and heated to fuse the stone. Leaves are done next, and finally the stems. To finish, the surface is polished with increasingly fine emery.

To make a large tray coated in multi-coloured flowers takes three workers about six months, working 9 am−9 pm except on Friday, the Muslim holiday. A small box takes ten days, and the top of a box about three. The master craftsman oversees and checks each piece, for it all goes out under his name. Such painstakingly slow work means it takes about 25 Agra workshops to keep Subhash Emporium in Gwalior Road well stocked. And when you go to browse and, inevitably, to buy, the Hindu family of Bansal brothers who run Subhash will show you some of Naseem's award-winning pieces.

Firdaus Ashyanai (dweller in paradise). Incidentally, there is little substance in
the theory that Shah Jahan planned a black Taj for himself across the river. It
is best to come early or late to avoid noise and crowds and to indulge in the
inlay work of the serene upper chamber into which soft light filters through
marble. Also, the platform is a good place to be for sunrise, when sounds of
the temple below waft up and locals cross the sands to wash in the Yamuna;
equally, sunset views across to the fort are magical.

Across the Yamuna
Views, Tombs and a Garden

This expedition allows you to see the Taj from its back side, reflected in the
Yamuna; to see its immediate precursor, the tomb of Itimad-ud-Daulah; and,
past another courtier's tomb, to explore Babur's untended but atmospheric
garden. As there are only two bridges across the Yamuna, one of them very
narrow and running under the railway bridge, it is best to go early or on a
weekend day to avoid the worst traffic.

Down Yamuna Kinara Road past Akbar's fort ramparts and Shah Jahan's
extravagant palaces perched on top, the railway road bridge (negotiable in a
taxi, not in a coach) crosses onto Aligarh Road which almost immediately
bends sharp left. But to see the Taj, go straight ahead along a lane which turns
right, crosses two railway tracks and, after a few bumps, arrives at **Nagla
Kachhpura** village. Then wander down towards the river through the fields.
From here the rural view of the Taj gives it a new peacefulness and,
contrasting with the tiny village, returns its scale to the hugeness it would have
had when first built.

Back on the main road running north from the bridge, you come next to
the **tomb of Itimad-ud-Daulah** (1622−8). Built by his daughter, Nur Jahan, this
was the first all-marble building in Agra. Legend says she really wanted to
build in silver but was warned that it would be stolen bit by bit. This small,
casket-like mausoleum sits on its platform in the centre of the char-bagh,
whereas the Taj is at one end. But like the Taj, it gains from the reflected light
of its riverside setting — there are good views across wallowing bullocks to the
old city. The outside walls have geometric patterns of perfect precision, which
some say are even finer than the Taj's. Inside, the chambers still retain their
panels of flower paintings lit through delicate jalis (cut-screens). Amid these
and the finely-carved screens and pietra dura inlay of arabesques on the floors
and trees, fruits and flowers on the walls, lie the tombs of Itimad-ud-Daulah
and other members of his extraordinary family (see page 109).

Further up the road, off left down a lane and across a field, the waterside
Chini-ka-Rauza (1639) gives an idea of how splendid the Mughal buildings
must have looked when originally coated with glazed tiles. It is the tomb of
Alami Afzal Khan Shirazi, a poet-scholar who entered royal service under

Jahangir and became Shah Jahan's prime minister and one of his most distinguished nobles. Although he lived and died at Lahore, he was buried here in the tomb he had already built. Its sides glow with huge panels of delicate Lahore-style enamelled plasterwork, verses from the Qur'an alternating with delicate floral panels in turquoise, mauve, yellow, green and midnight blue.

On up Aligarh Road, **Ram Bagh** (1526) lies quietly beside the river, its entrance set back just after the Agra Bypass crossing. This, probably the first Mughal garden in India, was, its seems, Babur's contribution to Agra; and he was buried here before being moved to his favourite garden at Kabul. Babur was a passionate gardener. In his *Baburnama* diary he devotes pages to the careful observations of a born naturalist. Paintings of Babur often show him enthroned in a garden, laying out a garden and even dictating his diary in a garden. Here at the Ram Bagh he introduced the 'order and symmetry' of the Persian char-bagh (four-garden, see Taj Mahal, above) into landscape typical of 'that charmless and disorderly Hindustan'. Recently much restored, the garden's divisions and pavilions are there, and a good imagination can plant flowers and trees to recreate Babur's lush oasis in the dry Indian plain.

Northern Fringes
Akbar's Tomb at Sikandra

Akbar's tomb is good preparation for a trip out to see his City of Victory, Fatehpur Sikri. Abandoning that dream city in 1585 for Lahore, the emperor then returned to Agra in 1599, where he died six years later. But he had already designed and begun building his own tomb, choosing a site on the outskirts of the ruined Baradari Palace built by Sultan Sikandar Lodi when he moved from Delhi in 1502; hence the district's name, Sikandra, and the odd ruin in and around the tomb's park.

The tomb was incomplete at his death. Jahangir's diary notes constant redesigning and interference during construction, and William Finch, visiting it in 1608–11, found 'nothing neere finished as yet, after tenne years worke.' But Akbar's ideas and hopes for a unified culture in his empire are as clear here as at Fatehpur Sikri. Indeed, Mughal historian Gavin Hambly reckons 'the cultural synthesis achieved in the architecture of Fatehpur Sikri reached its culmination in Akbar's tomb at Sikandra.'

Into the Mughal garden tomb format (see Taj Mahal, above) Akbar wove the ideas of his **din-i-Ilani** (religion of God). This was a mixture of Hindu, Muslim, Sikh and Christian thought based on a sort of mystical liberalism, which Akbar announced in 1582 and dreamed would help unite his empire. It was a deliberate policy. In 1564 he had revoked the *jizya*, a poll-tax on non-

Muslims stipulated in the Qur'an. Now he had coins struck with the new religion's ambiguous motto, 'Allahu akbar', meaning both God is great and Akbar is God. Akbar saw himself as temporal and spiritual leader, an idea helpfully promoted by two close courtiers: Abu'l Fazl, adviser and friend, who wrote the *Akbarnama* chronicling his reign and describing an ideal king who was both worldly and a symbol of God; and his brother Fayzi, one of the emperor's great poets, who wrote explicit lines such as 'Thy old fashioned prostration is of no advantage to thee — see Akbar and you see God.'

From the beginning, the tomb was revered by both Muslims and Hindus. The stone, quarried near Fatehpur Sikri, was used in the Indian tradition, cut into planks as if it was wood. The great gateway has magnificently bold polychrome inlay in geometric and floral patterns. Italian quack doctor Niccolao Manucci, who died in India in 1717, hurried to see paintings of the crucifix, Virgin Mary and St Ignatius before Aurangzeb whitewashed them over (but he claimed they were originally added for their 'novelty . . . not on account of religion'). Beyond, alleys lead to the tomb through the park where monkeys frolic and deer graze on lawns shaded by magnificent trees. It is best to ignore the bright red so-called restoration of the outside walls, and — as is sometimes possible — climb this exotic, stone, stepped wedding cake to reach the roof and see both Akbar's cenotaph inscribed 'Allahu Akbar' and, through Jahangir's fine marble screens, splendid views.

Opposite Akbar's tomb stands the confusingly named **Miriam's Tomb**. Found through a quiet garden, the remains of Baradari Palace proper were later used for the tomb of, perhaps, Akbar's first Hindu wife, the Amber princess who was mother of Jahangir and became known as Maryam al-Zamani (Mary of the age). This and Sikandra gardens are popular with locals who flock here for weekend picnics.

South Agra
The British Cantonment and a Mughal Gem

With British power so extensive in India at the end of the 18th century, ordered camps — or cantonments — were laid out on the edge of the main cities. **Agra cantonment** was typical. It had its wide avenues, elegant bungalows shaded by verandas and bougainvillea, gardens with tidy rosebeds, post office, lending library, church, club, jam-making and whist parties. In the cantonment — stubborn evocations of Home — the British were totally cut off from local life. As the sun set on the Raj in 1930, Aldous Huxley was astonished by what he saw. Without exception, from clerk upwards, everyone dressed for dinner 'as though the integrity of the British Empire depended in some magical way upon the donning of black jackets and hard-boiled shirts.' And everyone ate too much: 'five meals a day — two breakfasts, luncheon, afternoon tea and dinner — are standard throughout India.'

Common pariah kite

Hoopoe

Indian robin

Roller

Sarus crane

Redwattled lapwing

Indian myna

Baya weaver bird

Roseringed parakeet

Cattle egret

Peacock

Whitebacked vulture

Agra cantonment retains its Raj flavour. Cruising along Mall Road and Taj Road, you pass the odd castle fantasy and the decayed splendour of grand bungalows. At the west end of Taj Road, near Sadar Bazar, proud Queen Mary's Library is just before the handsome cantonment church, **St George's** (1826), designed by Colonel J T Boileau and set in a large grassy enclosure. Turn south down Gwalior Road, and then left along Grand Parade Road: the two **British cemeteries**, Church of England and Roman Catholic side by side on the right, are found through a red ochre and white Gothic gatehouse. Here ancestors of Agra's Christian community have been buried since the 17th century; John Mildenhall (died 1614), self-appointed envoy of Elizabeth I, is the earliest known. Tragic family histories of traders and empire builders, for

Birds

The richness of bird life in India makes the most reluctant feather fan reach for the binoculars. Here are a handful to spot, their Hindi names in brackets. If the sight of an elegant sarus crane whets your appetite, visit splendid Keoladeo National Park (see page 178) and the bird houses of Delhi Zoo (see page 85). Illustrations are on pages 124−5.

Hoopoe (hudhud) Fawn with black and white zebra markings on back, wings and tail; sexes alike. With jaunty crest and curved bill, the hoopoe skittles across well-mown lawns around Delhi and Agra monuments, hunting out insects, occasionally chanting a soft, musical 'hoo-po-po'.

Roseringed parakeet (lybar tota) Green with black and rose-pink collar and short, hooked red bill; female lacks the collar. This Indian symbol of love perches in flocks on telephone wires and in trees, when not destroying crops and fruits, and loudly screeches 'keeak, keeak'.

Peacock (mor; mayura) Male midnight blue with extravagantly long, ocellated, green train-like tail; hen mottled brown, green touches on neck, lacks the showy tail; both crested. The national bird of India and also a symbol of passion, the proud peacock struts across lawns and in wild undergrowth, screeching occasionally. Karttikeya, god of war, rides a peacock.

Indian myna (desi myna) Rich brown with bright yellow bill, eye surround and legs, white patch on wing; sexes alike. Loudly chattering 'radio-radio-radio' and 'keek-keek-keek' and bobbing its head, the myna eats fruits and insects, catching grasshoppers off the backs of grazing cattle.

Sarus crane (saras) Pale grey with long red legs and red head and neck; sexes alike. The tall crane dwells in marshy areas and has a sonorous trumpet call. Pairs remain devoted for life, performing spectacular dancing displays before breeding. Brahma, premier god of the Hindu Trinity, rides a sarus crane.

whom early death by disease, accident or battle was common, are carved on tombstones built in the latest British architectural styles. One recounts that 'Frederick Nichterlien indigo planter, Mudrock Factory, Allygarh' died aged 23 in 1867.

On down Gwalior Road for a Mughal treat. After the roadside stalls of Madhunagar area, a small turning to the right has a signpost to **Firoz Khan's tomb**. Down the lane, a tiny village typical of thousands in India continues its daily life in modest houses surrounding a lake. And on the far side a most beautiful tomb stands on a high plinth, reflected in the water. If you hover in front, the *chaukidar* will soon arrive, as will most of the village children, and you can clamber up the very steep steps to go inside.

Cattle egret (surkhia bagla; gai-bagla) Pure white with yellow bill; orange-buff head and back when breeding (June−August); sexes alike. The elegant egret darts between the legs of cattle and rides on their backs catching grasshoppers, flies and lizards.

Roller or **blue jay** (nilkant; sabzak) Colourful chestnut back, blue head, mauve throat and pale and dark blue banded wings; sexes alike. Perched on a countryside telephone wire, it may chuckle loudly before spreading its brilliant blue wings to dive for a frog or lizard; spectacular courting acrobatics.

Indian robin (kalchuri) Male black with white wing patch and russet red undertail; hen ash-brown. Hops about the countryside and villages seeking spiders and other insects.

Whitebacked — or **Bengal** — **vulture** (gidh) Dark brown with white back, scrawny naked head and neck, and hooked beak; sexes alike. Parties of this large, ungainly but useful scavenger screech and hiss as they demolish a carcass — even a large camel knocked down by a lorry on the high road — with astonishing speed.

Common pariah kite (cheel) Chestnut hawk, with distinctive forked tail; sexes alike. Their dexterous acrobatics of elegant gliding, swooping and twisting create a glimmer of calm over congested town centres.

Baya weaver bird (baya) Dark-streaked brown with white tummy, short snub bill, square-cut tail; sexes alike. Flocks chirping 'chit-chit-chit' nest near grain fields. Their vessel-shaped nests have long entrance tubes and dangle from twigs, often overhanging water.

Redwattled lapwing (titeeri; tituri) Plover with bronze back, white belly and side-neck, black breast and head and crimson eye surround and beak; sexes alike. Its vigilance and speed in detecting intrusion have surely helped its penetrating call to be interpreted as 'did-he-do-it?'.

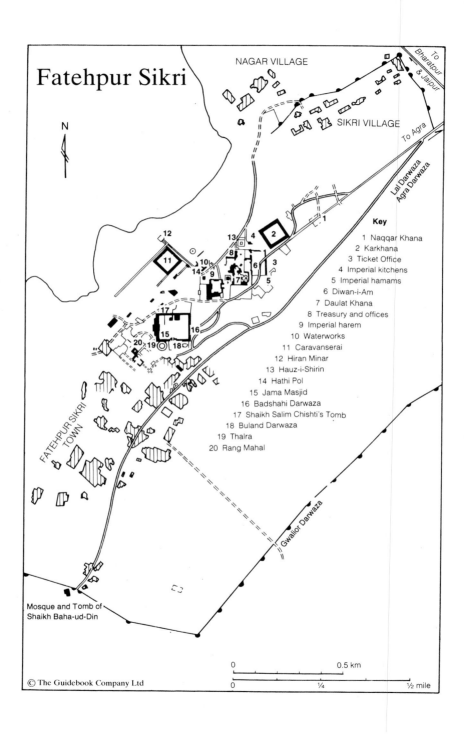

Fatehpur Sikri

N

NAGAR VILLAGE

SIKRI VILLAGE

To Agra

To
Bharatpur
& Jaipur

Lal Darwaza
Agra Darwaza

Key

1 Naqqar Khana
2 Karkhana
3 Ticket Office
4 Imperial kitchens
5 Imperial hamams
6 Diwan-i-Am
7 Daulat Khana
8 Treasury and offices
9 Imperial harem
10 Waterworks
11 Caravanserai
12 Hiran Minar
13 Hauz-i-Shirin
14 Hathi Pol
15 Jama Masjid
16 Badshahi Darwaza
17 Shaikh Salim Chishti's Tomb
18 Buland Darwaza
19 Thalra
20 Rang Mahal

FATEHPUR SIKRI TOWN

Gwalior Darwaza

Mosque and Tomb of
Shaikh Baha-ud-Din

0   0.5 km

0   ¼   ½ mile

© The Guidebook Company Ltd

Fatehpur Sikri
A Young King's Short-lived Ideal City

Fatehpur Sikri is one of the world's most perfect ghost cities. It was conceived and built by emperor Akbar, a man of exceptional intelligence and enlightenment, in thanks for the birth of his sons. For just 14 years this was his personal dream palace-city. His son, Jahangir, who spent his childhood there and imbibed its creative atmosphere, described how 'that hill, full of wild beasts, became a city containing all kinds of gardens and buildings.'

Here Akbar's patronage of the arts reached its apogee. It matched his military feats which stabilized and extended the empire to include most of the sub-continent, his social and administrative reforms which changed the very structure of Indian life, and his personal dynamism and political skilfulness which brought Muslim and Hindu factions into lasting union. Bursting into life in 1571, the city was an instant artistic and intellectual centre. Just as suddenly, it was abandoned in 1585, partly because of lack of water, partly because Akbar needed to consolidate the north-west borders of his empire.

Today, its pristine, red sandstone palace buildings are as crisp as when they were chiselled. It is easy to imagine the emperor, 'of good stature, sturdy body, broad shouldered', moving from building to building, sitting on finely-woven rugs to consult with ministers and advisers, learning about the world from visitors, or listening to the sublime music of his court musician, Tansen. One hour he might visit the court painting atelier to watch such masters as Basawan, Mansur, Miskin and Nanha at work. Another, he might check on Badauni's translation of the Hindu epic *Mahabharata* into Persian (when it was called the *Razmnama*) which was part of his plan to enlighten his Muslim courtiers about Indian culture (there is now a copy in Jaipur). Another time, he might meet a Jesuit missionary such as Father Monserrate who in 1580 described his eyes: 'small but extremely vivid and when he looks at you it seems as if they hurt you with their brightness, and thus nothing escapes his notice, be it a person or something trivial, and they also reveal sharpness of mind and keenness of intellect.'

This was the city of a young, powerful ruler. In 1568, the 26-year-old Akbar had been on the throne of his fast-expanding empire for 12 years. But he had no heir, despite copious diplomatic marriages which accumulated some 300 wives and a harem of, it was said, 5,000. So, after the defeat of the Rajput fort of Chittor, he made his annual pilgrimage to Ajmer to one Chishti saint and also visited another, **Shaikh Salim Chishti**, at Sikri. Shaikh Salim predicted he would soon have three sons.

The next year his first Rajput wife, Jodhai Bai of Amber whom he had married in 1562 on the way back from his first pilgrimage to Ajmer, gave birth to Salim, named after the saint. He was born here at Sikri. As the chronicler Abu'l Fazl grandly put it: 'In an auspicious moment the unique pearl of the

The Voice of Authority

ravelers are an enthusiastic lot. They do not mind any inconven-
ience as long as they have something to see. Why anyone should
want to forgo food and comfort and jolt a hundred-odd miles to see
some place, I could never understand, but it was not my business
to ask for reasons; just as I did not mind what people ate or smoked
in my shop, my business being only to provide the supply and
nothing more. It seemed to me silly to go a hundred miles to see the
source of Sarayu when it had taken the trouble to tumble down the
mountain and come to our door. I had not even heard of its source
till that moment; but the man who had gone was all praise for the
spot. He said, "I am only sorry I did not bring my wife and mother
to see the place." Later in life I found that everyone who saw an
interesting spot always regretted that he hadn't come with his wife
or daughter, and spoke as if he had cheated someone out of a nice
thing in life. Later, when I had become a full-blown tourist guide, I
often succeeded in inducing a sort of melancholia in my customer
by remarking, "This is something that should be enjoyed by the
whole family," and the man would swear that he would be back
with his entire brood in the coming season. . .

The age I ascribed to any particular place depended upon my
mood at that hour and the type of person I was escorting. If he was
the academic type I was careful to avoid all mention of facts and
figures and to confine myself to general descriptions, letting the
man himself do the talking. You may be sure he enjoyed the
opportunity. On the other hand, if an innocent man happened to be
at hand, I let myself go freely. I pointed out to him something as
the greatest, the highest, the only one in the world. I gave statistics
out of my head. I mentioned a relic as belonging to the thirteenth
century before Christ or the thirteenth century after Christ,
according to the mood of the hour. If I felt fatigued or bored with
the person I was conducting, I sometimes knocked the whole
glamour out by saying, "Must be something built within the last
twenty years and allowed to go to rack and ruin. There are scores
of such spots all over the place." But it was years before I could
arrive at that stage of confidence and nonchalance.

R K Narayan, The Guide

caliphate emerged from the shell of the womb, and arrived on the shore of existence in the city of Fatehpur.' Akbar again walked to Ajmer, this time to give thanks. In 1570 his second son, Murad, was born; in 1572 his third, Daniyal.

It was the impressive fulfilment of this prediction which decided the proud father in 1571, after just two sons were born, to build a new city where the saint lived, to be called Fatehpur Sikri, meaning City of Victory. This was to be the cultural, commercial and administrative centre of his empire. (Agra remained the military stronghold.) Of all the reasons given for leaving such an auspicious site, the most likely seem to be either a lack of water or Akbar's need to defend and then consolidate the northwest border of his empire by using Lahore as his base.

Arriving from Agra, 37 kilometres (23 miles) away, the visitor sees first the ruined walls of the town, then the ridge with the palace complex and behind it the tomb and mosque of the saint; the quiet town is behind. Best times for peacefulness and quality of light are early morning and late afternoon; noon-time is very hot, when hats and bottled drinks are vital accessories; the hawkers between palace and mosque are some of India's most insistent.

Agra Darwaza was just one of nine gates piercing the six kilometres (3.7 miles) of embattled walls; the western side was protected by the now-dry lake. Ahead, there is a distant view of the Buland Darwaza, a triumphal arch. To the right, is the much older Fatehpur Sikri village. Next, the Naqqar Khana (drum house) straddles the road, where music greeted important visitors and struck up at fixed hours of the day. Here too was a market square and just beyond, on the right, the large Karkhana (workshop) which operated under direct imperial control and pandered to the daily needs of the court.

And so into the palace complex. First, the **Diwan-i-Am** (public audience hall), a serene colonnaded space with the emperor's platform (fine star-design jali work) projecting on the far side. Akbar, seated on cushions and carpets, showed himself to his subjects every morning and dispensed justice, 'sternly and impartially' according to Monserrate, returning some afternoons to review the imperial animals and deal with court business.

A passage behind leads to the more private parts of the palace. Akbar revived the Timurid tradition of Persian court ceremonial and the splendour of Samarkand, blending it with the flourishing Indo-Muslim styles of his new country. Taking Persian principles, he built and decorated in a very Indian way, inspired by such buildings as Gwalior Fort and served by Indian craftsmen. There were three main parts to the palace: the Daulat Khana on the left of this inner court, the treasury and offices on the right, and the harem straight ahead.

The function of many buildings is still disputed; the location of others is a mystery, such as the extensive imperial library described in tantalizing detail by Monserrate; and the various firm names given by maps and guides confuse

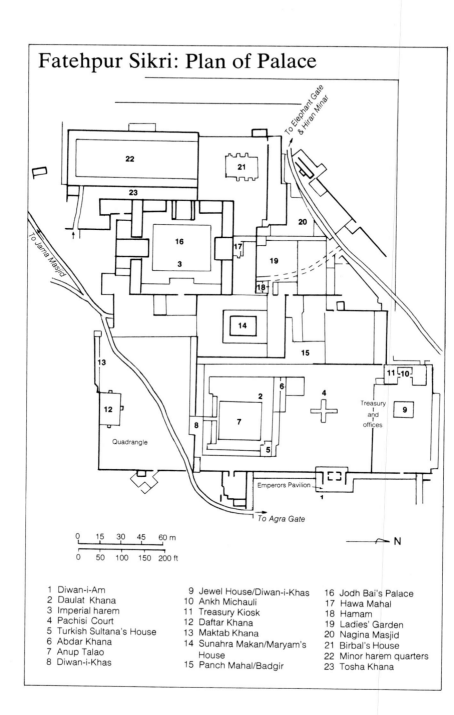

Fatehpur Sikri: Plan of Palace

To Elephant Gate & Hiran Minar

To Jama Masjid

To Agra Gate

Quadrangle

Treasury and offices

Emperors Pavilion

0 15 30 45 60 m
0 50 100 150 200 ft

N

1 Diwan-i-Am
2 Daulat Khana
3 Imperial harem
4 Pachisi Court
5 Turkish Sultana's House
6 Abdar Khana
7 Anup Talao
8 Diwan-i-Khas

9 Jewel House/Diwan-i-Khas
10 Ankh Michauli
11 Treasury Kiosk
12 Daftar Khana
13 Maktab Khana
14 Sunahra Makan/Maryam's
    House
15 Panch Mahal/Badgir

16 Jodh Bai's Palace
17 Hawa Mahal
18 Hamam
19 Ladies' Garden
20 Nagina Masjid
21 Birbal's House
22 Minor harem quarters
23 Tosha Khana

further. Here are one or two buildings worth seeking out for their architectural sake and for their presumed function.

From the Diwan-i-Am, the palace garden leads to the central **Pachisi Court** where, according to legend, Akbar sat on the platform playing the favourite *pachisi* game (similar to ludo), using his courtesans as pieces on the giant stone board.

To the left, surrounding the tank (pond), is the exquisite **Daulat Khana** (abode of fortune), the emperor's private palace rooms. The decoration is very Indian: elaborate brackets, broad overhanging eaves, richly carved bell-shaped column pedestals, elephant-head column capitals, lace-like chiselling on the walls to imitate painting, and intricate jali work. The pavilion on the north-eastern edge of the tank, known as the Turkish Sultana's house, is especially densely carved and casket-like. The rooms matching it, known as the Abdar Khana (water store), probably stored Akbar's drinking water and his much-loved melons, mangoes and grapes. The rooms at the back of the tank, known as the Anup Talao (peerless pool), were the most private of all: traces of painted tulips, poppies and roses survive in the smaller room; the larger is possibly the Diwan-i-Khas (private audience hall), where special visitors were received and where, perhaps, the emperor showed himself to his subjects daily (some would not eat until they saw his face and knew all was well with their ruler); and upstairs Akbar relaxed and slept surrounded by now-faded murals.

Back across Pachisi Court stand what were probably the **treasuries** and their offices. As the most important institutions of central government, their buildings were given appropriate status. Standing isolated is the Jewel House, or Diwan-i-Khas, Fatehpur Sikri's best-known and most controversial building. Architecturally it is extraordinary: a cube whose four doorways lead into a single, double-storey room where a huge central pillar carved to baroque richness supports a seat reached by four mid-air walkways. The steps to the walkways are in the room's walls and continue up to the roof (fine views). The building's purpose, despite all contemporary diaries, is not clear: perhaps it was the Ibadat Khana where Akbar initiated his religious discussions and devised his eclectic din-i-Ilani religion (see page 122), perhaps the Diwan-i-Khas for consulting with ministers, perhaps a place for dispensing justice, but most likely the storehouse for the vast hoards of imperial jewels. Akbar's chronicler, Abu'l Fazl, records three treasuries, for copper, for gold and silver, and for gems and jewels, and they are likely to have been close together.

The second treasury, known as the Ankh Michauli (blind man's buff house) for the stories that Akbar played hide-and-seek with his women here, stored the gold and silver. Traditional Indian monsters carved on the struts guard the treasury; the doors were of stone. Inside, the recesses were built-in coffers with stone slabs for doors. (Steps lead up to more good rooftop views.) The tiny kiosk at the south end, with its elaborate brackets inspired by Jain architecture, was most likely where Akbar's principal treasurer, the loyal

eunuch Phul Malik, sat keeping a watchful eye on the carrying and counting of the empire's coins.

The view northwards from the terrace behind the treasuries or from their roofs is a broad panorama of the city walls and, to the left, palace outbuildings such as waterworks, a caravanserai and the **Hiran Minar** (deer tower). The name of the tower relates to when Jahangir stayed here in 1619 (fleeing the plague at Agra) and had deer roaming beside the nearby lake; but the tower is of Akbar's time and was possibly both a place from which distances were measured and an *akash diya* (heavenly light), whose stone tusks were hung with lamps at night to guide travellers. The really keen can go through Hathi Pol (see page 138) and, if it is open, clamber the 53 steps to the top for magnificent views back to the palace and mosque. Just below the terrace, the rain-waters of the Hauz-i-Shirin (sweet tank) were mixed with Ganga water for the court food.

For more official buildings, explore the dusty courtyard behind the Daulat Khana to find the Daftar Khana (record chamber), whose double columns have elaborate brackets at the top and splendid double peacock's tail pattern at the bottom. The cloisters to the right of it were possibly the Maktab Khana (translation bureau), for Akbar's pet project of translating Sanskrit texts into Persian to promote cultural harmony.

Finally, to the **imperial harem**, where some 300 of Akbar's vast collection of wives and women took up two-thirds of the palace space. Contrary to Western assumption, women played an important role at the Mughal court and the harem was a major state institution. Their equivalent European position would have been ladies-in-waiting, even if they were not seen because their buildings were connected by covered passages and screened off from the rest of the palace. Individuals such as Nur Jahan and Mumtaz Mahal wielded enormous political power; courtesans ran lucrative trading businesses and were extensive landowners. The senior female in the emperor's family was both mistress of the royal household and guardian of two seals of the realm, without which the royal edicts were invalid. For Akbar, his mother Hamida Banu Begum (*c* 1527–1604) was the first lady, known as Maryam Makani (of equal rank to Mary) and one of his most important advisers.

In the harem above all, each palace's occupants are conjecture, despite the firm names the buildings have acquired. To see one or two of them, cross Pachisi Court and find the gap in the colonnaded wall to the west of the Daulat Khana. Sunahra Makan (golden house), known as Maryam's House, is in the first courtyard, remarkable for its surviving frescoes and its brackets richly carved with Hindu favourites — the hero Rama, the monkey god Hanuman, elephants and geese. One current theory is that Akbar's mother lived here. The dotty-looking Panch Mahal (five palace) or Badgir (wind tower) adjoins it, with its five decreasing storeys seemingly made of nothing but columns. Go up to the first floor for the column carving of blossoms, fleurs-de-lis, spirals, etc., and further on up to the top for views.

Southwest of Sunahra Makan, the Shabistan-i-Iqbal, known as Jodh Bai's Palace, is the largest, most important and central harem building. A current idea is that this was Akbar's private palace. There are baths to the south, a grand balcony to the north, minor harem quarters to the west, and the entrance to the east with watch-house for the 'guard of faithful Rajputs'. The rather solemn palace is saved by the glowing tiles of the azure-blue ribbed roof. Inside, the rooms around the little courtyard have carving by an assortment of Hindu craftsmen. To the north, the two-storey Hawa Mahal (palace of winds) is the traditional north Indian version of the Persian Badgir. Here Akbar would rest with his ladies and, according to Abu'l Fazl, sleep at night. The passage on the west side, leading towards the Nagina Masjid, has Fatehpur Sikri's only surviving arabesque stone screen, very lovely and worth a detour.

There are other harem buildings worth seeking out. Through the west exit from Sunahra Makan, there is the hamam, the ladies' garden and their simple Nagina Masjid. Further west, the so-called Birbal's House was another harem palace, probably the home of two of Akbar's senior queens, Ruqayya Begum and Salima Sultan Begum. Its two storeys are very delicately carved, its two upper rooms oddly arranged corner to corner. South of here, the large colonnaded enclosure housed the serving maids (not the stables as often thought, for they would have been far too messy to be near the ladies), with the Tosha Khana (storehouse) to the east.

North of here, the steep, rough road leads to the great **Hathi Pol** (elephant gate). Once the principal entrance for Akbar, the gate still has its two shattered stone elephants to give a royal welcome. 'What bliss his advent,' wrote Abu'l Fazl on Akbar's return to Fatehpur Sikri one time. 'On this day of joy the great officers, the loyal servants, and others were drawn up in two sides of the way for a distance of four *koss* from the city. The mountain-like elephants stood there in their majesty. The Khedive of the world proceeded on his way on a heaven-like elephant, attended by the Avaunt of the Divine Halo. The panoply was there in its splendour ... the noise of the drums and melodies of the magician-like musicians gave forth news of joy ... at the end of the day he sate in the lofty hall on the throne of sovereignty. He dispensed justice by rewarding the loyal and banishing the hostile and made the increase of dominion and success a vehicle for worship and supplication.'

The **Jama Masjid** (begun 1571) stands magnificently on the ridge peak. It is one of the biggest mosques in India. Architectural historian Percy Brown found it 'undoubtedly the most impressive part of Fatehpur Sikri'. Enter it up the steep steps of the Badshahi Darwaza (royal door), as Akbar did when he came to pray, and the huge and dignified courtyard opens beyond, with prayer chamber ahead and cloisters around the sides. The prayer chamber is worth exploring for its fine proportions and the carved, painted and inlaid decoration, 'unsurpassed in any other building in Akbar's reign.'

On the right, the shimmering, delicate white marble **tomb of Shaikh Salim Chishti** (died 1572) dominates the courtyard, given added focus on Fridays when musicians sit playing in front. Here pilgrims of all denominations come to pray, including childless women who tie a string to the jali work and pray for blessings equal to Akbar's. The original tomb was probably simple and of sandstone; Jahangir or Shah Jahan added the marble, whose carving is especially refined in the honeycomb capitals and serpentine brackets on the porch and in the exquisite jali work of the ambulatory (best enjoyed from inside). In the sanctuary, where the air is thick with incense, the catafalque built over the saint's actual tomb is coated with scales of mother-of-pearl.

A second, even more imposing gateway, the **Buland Darwaza** (gate of magnificence), soars up on the south side. This is Akbar's grandiose triumphal arch, probably added after his victorious conquest of Gujarat (1573), when he also decided to name his new city Fatehpur (city of victory) Sikri. Jahangir noted that on festivals it was hung with brightly coloured cloth and lamps. Through it, the Thalra (diving well) on the right is just that: hover about and some young lad or old boy will, for a fat tip, dive dramatically from the top of the gate. (It is sometimes possible for visitors to climb the gate; as the view is superb, it is worth asking.)

The ruined building on the left was probably the Langar Khana, the kitchen for feeding the poor. From the top of the very steep steps, the view is down over what remains of Fatehpur Sikri town, with old hamams in the foreground. On the far right, the Rang Mahal, built as Prince Salim's nursery and his mother's home, is now a weavers' factory but retains its fine carving. Round the back, past more hamams, the building hard by the mosque wall was probably another royal nursery (not Abu'l Fazl's home as once thought), placed here so the sons could gain maximum benefit from being close to the saint who had predicted their birth.

Perhaps the last word should be with Ralph Fitch, an English trader who carried letters from Elizabeth I and reached Fatehpur Sikri in 1584. 'Agra is a very great citie and populous, built with stone, having faire and large streetes, with a faire river running by it ... It hath a faire castle and a strong ... From thence we went for Fatepore ... The towne is greater than Agra, but the houses and streetes be not so faire. The king hath in Agra and Fatepore 1,000 elephants, thirtie thousand horses, 1,400 tame deere, 800 concubines: such a store of ounces, tigers, buffles, cocks, and haukes, that is very strange to see ... Agra and Fatepore are two very great cities, either of them much greater than London. Between [them], all the way is a market ... as full as though a man were still in a towne. Hither is great resort of marchants from Persia and out of India, and very much marchandise of silke and cloth, and of precious stones, both rubies, diamants, and pearles. The king is apparelled in a muslin tunic made like a shirt tied with strings on the one side, and a little cloth on his head coloured oftentimes with red or yellow.' Such was the capital of the Great Mughal.

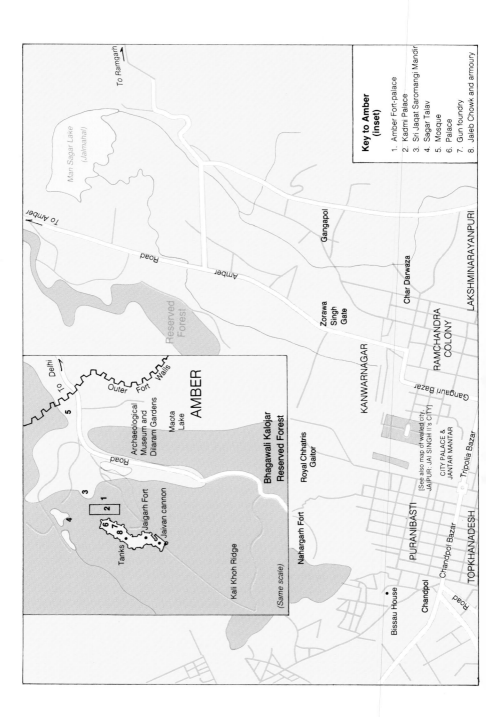

Key to Amber (inset)

1. Amber Fort-palace
2. Kadmi Palace
3. Sri Jaqat Saromangi Mandir
4. Sagar Talav
5. Mosque
6. Palace
7. Gun foundry
8. Jaleb Chowk and armoury

AMBER

Bhagawali Kalojar Reserved Forest

(Same scale)

To Delhi

Outer Fort Walls

Archaeological Museum and Dilaram Gardens

Maota Lake

Jaigarh Fort

Jaivan cannon

Tanks

Kali Khoh Ridge

Nahargarh Fort

Royal Chhatris Gaitor

Reserved Forest

Man Sagar Lake (Jalmahal)

To Ramgarh

To Amber

To Amber

Amber Road

Road

Zorawa Singh Gate

Gangapol

Char Darwaza

KANWARNAGAR

RAMCHANDRA COLONY

Gangaur Bazar

LAKSHMINARAYANPURI

PURANIBASTI

Bissau House

Chandpol

Chandpol Bazar

[See also map of walled city, JAIPUR: JAI SINGH II's CITY]

CITY PALACE & JANTAR MANTAR

Tripolia Bazar

TOPKHANADESH

Road

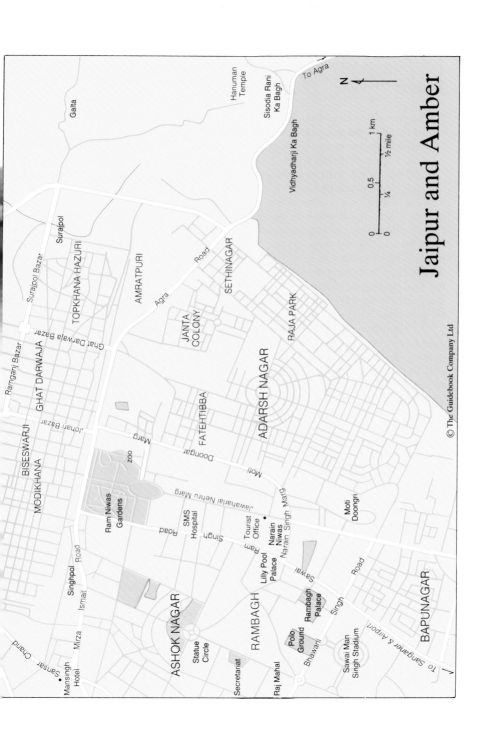

Jaipur and Amber

© The Guidebook Company Ltd

Jaipur

As the sun softens and the punishing Rajasthan heat eases off, the canny visitor to Jaipur hops in a taxi and spins out of town. On the road to Amber, a turning off left twists and turns up to the summit of a long, high ridge of the Aravalli Hills called Kali Khoh.

Clifftop Jaigarh Fort is at the end of the road to the right. Here the Rajput chieftain's built-in throne perches like an eagle's nest on the battlements. From it, there is a raja's-eye-view down to Amber fort-palace. The location is superb. The fort sprawls over its own hill in a valley protected on all sides by rugged mountains. As extra defence, castellated walls snake up the mountainsides, punctuated by watchtowers. From his seat, the clan chief of the Kachchwahas could survey the whole valley, espy any threats, receive warning signals from look-out posts and give orders to attack the enemy. For this was the nearest Rajput stronghold to Delhi, the capital of a succession of Muslim invaders: through the gap to the north lay the threat of first the sultans, then the powerful Mughal.

At the other end of the ridge, Nahargarh Fort mounts equally impressive guard over the later Kachchwaha capital, Jaipur. As the sun ripens to a glowing Rajasthani crimson, the honks, shouts and music waft up from the city. Standing on the walls to peer down onto the plain, you can easily pick out the original grid-plan, walled city in the foreground of Rajasthan's capital, whose tentacles now sprawl into infinity.

Jaipur contrasts sharply with tightly protected Amber Fort. Such comparative vulnerability reflected the confidence of its 18th-century builder, Maharaja Jai Singh II. With overflowing coffers and seven generations of Kachchwaha rulers behind him who had kept not merely a diplomatic peace with the Mughals but had married their princesses to Mughal emperors and led Mughal armies, he could leave off Rajput soldiering and indulge in more intellectual pastimes.

As the stars twinkle into life, the taxi zigzags down to the plain and through Zorawa Singh Gate into Jai Singh's city. This is the best hour to wander the streets. The locals are out in force. At Bari Chaupar crossroads, gaggles of girls in saffron saris barter for bangles, while housewives swathed in raspberry pink, turquoise and tomato red jingle their arm and ankle bangles as they glide about the jasmine-scented air of the flower stalls. Tall, dark-skinned, pink-turbaned men amble past sackfuls of fresh ginger and chillies lit by dangling naked lightbulbs. Behind the City Palace, men and women scurry through Jaleb Chowk to Govinda Deva Temple to do puja to the blue-skinned god Krishna. Down Johari Bazar, a magnificent parade of elephants, camels and floats carrying children dressed up as Krishna and his beloved Radha makes its stately progress, the way lit by women balancing gas lamps on their heads. At the gateways, piles of tempting sweetmeats glisten beneath rows of fairy lights.

And, up on the hill behind the palace, Nahargarh Fort is now floodlit like some extravagant prop for a Wagner opera.

Jaipur is no quiet provincial town. Built as the capital of the then most powerful Rajput state, it is now the capital of Rajasthan, the government seat for all the former states of Rajputana and their hilltop forts, fairytale palaces and exotic maharajas. The core may be pink and pretty, but it is also noisy and dusty and its bouncy black tempos (motorbike taxis) belch out polluting fumes into the dry heat. Best times to explore are early and late in the day, lolling in a palace or mansion-turned-hotel in between.

To see the warring Rajput at his most splendid, visit Amber first, going by car or bus. In town, Jai Singh's palace city is best seen on foot or by auto-rickshaw. More palaces and mansions, originally built in country suburbs, litter the rest of the city. Despite the encroachment of modern living, colourful processions for weddings and Hindu festivals are daily events, side lanes are crowded with traditional craftsmen and merchants, and the thoroughly royal game of polo thrives.

Amber
Fort-palace of the Kachchwaha Rajputs

Amber contains every ingredient to make it the classic romantic Rajasthan palace-fort. It was built by one raja and completed by another. Its forbidding, practical exterior belies a bejewelled interior whose richness reflects the nearby sumptuous court of the Mughal emperors.

The **Kachchwaha** story is a blend of myth, legend and history. For myth, there are the clan origins, which are traced to the sun. Then, the legends. One tells how, when the Kachchwahas took Amber from the Susawat Minas around 1150, the enemy infiltrated and persuaded them into drunkenness before butchering them wholesale. Then, historical reality. Once in power, the Kachchwahas kept Amber as their capital for six centuries and the loyal Minas became hereditary guards of their treasure. As for the city's name, it may derive from Ambikishwara, a name for the god Shiva, or Amba Mata, goddess of earth and fertility, or, mundanely, from Ambarisha, king of Aydohya.

The romance of the setting easily gives credit to myth and fact. The view on arrival from Jaipur, through the narrow pass between the cliffs, is stage-set perfect. The stern, anonymous exterior of honey-coloured stone ramparts and terraces seems to grow out of the rugged hill. Defensive walls snake up the hills on all sides. Jaigarh Fort hovers like a fiercely protective eagle on the hill above. All is reflected in Maota Lake in the foreground, where farmers wash and cool their beloved buffalo and white cranes stand decoratively by the shore. To complete the set, an elephant may plod along the road with young *mahout* on top, its huge ears flapping, and a packed lunch of grasses rolled up in its trunk.

At the fort base, through an arch on the right, the elephants find their mates in their special elephant café. Their jobs are well organized: more than 40 elephants work in strict rotation, each a paid-up member of one of the three elephant unions controlled by the Rajasthan government. Swaying their beautiful huge grey bodies from side to side, they relax and chew grass between shifts of plodding up the long hill to the fort, carrying visitors feverish with excitement at riding an elephant and playing the maharaja.

Before taking the trip, drop into the little **Archaeological Museum** (Greek coins, fragments of Ashoka pillars, etc.) set amid bougainvillea-coated trees and the well-restored, formal **Dilaram Gardens**; both are charming. And sometimes it is possible to hire a boat (Rs5 charge) to go out onto the lake, if the monsoon has been generous and the boatmen are about.

The natural advantages of the site become more obvious up near Jai Pol (victory gate), where increasingly spectacular views of the gorge and the hills are interrupted by malicious monkeys jumping about the battlements and a local serenading each arrival on his *ravanhatha*, a sort of lute. The east-facing gate is also known as Surya Pol (sun gate), a convenient reminder of the celestial origins of the Kachchwahas. It opens into Jaleb Chowk (sweet market), a large courtyard. There, a chaat-seller invariably squats amid ordered piles of saffron-yellow spicy snacks, flowerbeds fill the centre and, on the right, local craft shops have steps between them up to rooftop views.

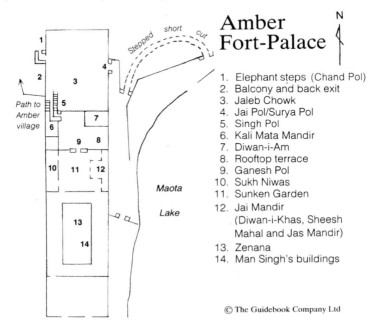

Amber Fort-Palace   N

1. Elephant steps (Chand Pol)
2. Balcony and back exit
3. Jaleb Chowk
4. Jai Pol/Surya Pol
5. Singh Pol
6. Kali Mata Mandir
7. Diwan-i-Am
8. Rooftop terrace
9. Ganesh Pol
10. Sukh Niwas
11. Sunken Garden
12. Jai Mandir
    (Diwan-i-Khas, Sheesh Mahal and Jas Mandir)
13. Zenana
14. Man Singh's buildings

© The Guidebook Company Ltd

Broken Song

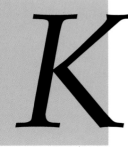

asinath the new young singer fills the hall with sound:
The seven notes dance in his throat like seven tame birds.
His voice is a sharp sword slicing and thrusting everywhere,
It darts like lightning—no knowing where it will go when.
He sets deadly traps for himself, then cuts them away:
The courtiers listen in amazement, give frequent gasps of praise.
Only the old king Pratap Ray sits like wood, unmoved.
Baraj Lal is the only singer he likes, all others leave him cold.
From childhood he has spent so long listening to him sing—
Rag Kafi during holi, cloud-songs during the rains, ·
Songs for Durga at dawn in autumn, songs to bid her farewell—
His heart swelled when he heard them and his eyes swam with tears.
And on days when friends gathered and filled the hall
There were cowherd's songs of Krsna, in rags Bhupali and Multan.

So many nights of wedding-festivity have passed in that royal house:
Servants dressed in red, hundreds of lamps alight:
The bridegroom sitting shyly in his finery and jewels,
Young friends teasing him and whispering in his ear:
Before him, singing rag Sahana, sits Baraj Lal.
The king's heart is full of all those days and songs.
When he hears some other singer, he feels no chord inside,
No sudden magical awakening of memories of the past.
When Pratap Ray watches Kasinath he just sees his wagging head:
Tune after tune after tune, but none with any echo in the heart.

Kasinath asks for a rest and the singing stops for a space.
Pratap Ray smilingly turns his eyes to Baraj Lal.
He puts his mouth to his ear and says, 'Dear ustad,
Give us a song as songs ought to be, this is no song at all.
It's all tricks and games, like a cat hunting a bird.
We used to hear songs in the old days, today they have no idea.'

Old Baraj Lal, white-haired, white turban on his head,
Bows to the assembled courtiers and slowly takes his seat.
He takes the tanpura in his wasted, heavily veined hand
And with lowered head and closed eyes begins rag Yaman-kalyan.
His quavering voice is swallowed by the enormous hall,

It is like a tiny bird in a storm, unable to fly for all it tries.
Pratap Ray, sitting to the left, encourages him again and again:
'Superb, bravo!' he says in his ear, 'sing out loud.'

The courtiers are inattentive: some whisper amongst themselves,
Some of them yawn, some doze, some go off to their rooms;
Some of them call to servants. 'Bring the hookah, bring some pan.'
Some fan themselves furiously and complain of the heat.
They cannot keep still for a minute, they shuffle or walk about—
The hall was quiet before, but every sort of noise has grown.
The old man's singing is swamped, like a frail boat in a typhoon:
Only his shaky fingering of the tanpura shows it is there.
Music that should rise on its own joy from the depths of the heart
Is crushed by heedless clamour, like a fountain under a stone.
The song and Baraj Lal's feelings go separate ways,
But he sings for all he is worth, to keep up the honour of his king.

One of the verses of the song has somehow slipped from his mind.
He quickly goes back, tries to get it right this time.
Again he forgets, it is lost, he shakes his head at the shame;
He starts the song at the beginning—again he has to stop.
His hand trembles doubly as he prays to his teacher's name.
His voice quakes with distress, like a lamp guttering in a breeze.
He abandons the words of the song and tries to salvage the tune,
But suddenly his wide-mouthed singing breaks into loud cries.
The intricate melody goes to the winds, the rhythm is swept away—
Tears snap the thread of the song, cascade like pearls.
In shame he rests his head on the old tanpura in his lap—
He has failed to remember a song: he weeps as he did as a child.
With brimming eyes king Pratap Ray tenderly touches his friend:
'Come, let us go from here,' he says with kindness and love.
They leave that festive hall with its hundreds of blinding lights.
The two old friends go outside, holding each other's hands.

Baraj says with hands clasped, 'Master, our days are gone.
New men have come now, new styles and customs in the world.
The court we kept is deserted—only the two of us are left.
Don't ask anyone to listen to me now, I beg you at your feet, my lord.
The singer alone does not make a song, there has to be someone who hears:
One man opens his throat to sing, the other sings in his mind.
Only when waves fall on the shore do they make a harmonious sound;
Only when breezes shake the woods do we hear a rustling in the leaves.
Only from a marriage of two forces does music arise in the world.
Where there is no love, where listeners are dumb, there never can be song.'

Rabindranath Tagore

Straight ahead are the elephant steps where more cautious visitors can take short rides around the courtyard. To the left of them, through the café, there is a wide balcony. From here you can look down on the abandoned-looking Kadmi Palace, where the chieftains lived before this fort was built. Old mansions and temples cluster around it; Jaigarh Fort towers above.

Amber fortunes took off when Akbar, cutting across Kachchwaha territory on his first pilgrimage to Ajmer in January 1562, summoned Raja Bihar Mal (ruled c 1548–74) and his whole family to attend the royal camp. The Rajput's daughter became the Mughal's wife and his adopted grandson, Man Singh, went into Mughal service. The next chief, Bhagwan Das (ruled 1574–89), continued to cement the relationship. And when **Man Singh I** (ruled 1589–1614) came to the throne, his Mughal military triumphs had reaped their reward. Coffers overflowed with booty and he ambitiously decided to build a new fort, inspired by the grand Mughal court.

Man Singh began his project around 1592; his descendant **Jai Singh I** (ruled 1621–67) added the most refined buildings and completed the embellishments. Although from the exterior the palace seems to ramble over the hill, the interior layout was given a new order, the formal gardens and rich decoration all influenced to an extent by Mughal styles. Among hilltop forts, it ranks second only to Gwalior in Madhya Pradesh. And according to historian Percy Brown, among Rajput forts it rivals 'even Akbar's deserted pavilions at Fatehpur Sikri in the richness of its architecture.'

Singh Pol (lion gate) is the principal entrance. But a detour up the steps to the right of it provides a little action to help bring the palace to life. Here sweet smells of incense and coconut announce the **Kali Mata Mandir** (Kali temple), the most sacred of all Kachchwaha family shrines and the only corner of state-owned Amber to remain in royal Jaipur hands today. Built by Man Singh I in 1604, it is dedicated to Sila Mata, one of the forms of Kali, the goddess of war who was revered by this soldiering people.

It is very much a living temple. Drummers and trumpets sound for the regular pujas. Inside, among the green marble pillars carved to imitate palm trees, the faithful come to ring the ceiling bell and offer sweets, coconut and flowers to the deity's image which Man Singh carried back from Jessore after he conquered East Bengal as Akbar's commander-in-chief. With the deity he brought a few Brahmin priests. One descendant was to be the architect of Jaipur (see page 157); more recent ones look after the temple today. Neither the move to Jaipur nor passing time has affected the temple's importance for the chieftains. The wife of Man Singh II, the last ruling maharaja of Jaipur, gave the solid silver entrance doors in 1939 in thanks for his recovery from a plane crash. And although the goat sacrifice was no longer a daily practice, he would sometimes arrive in his Bentley to sacrifice a live goat to the goddess with his own hands.

The arched, double gateway of Singh Pol leads up to another courtyard and the Diwan-i-Am (public audience hall). Of Jai Singh's additions, this is the best: a thoroughly Mughal borrowing of double pillars, clusters of brackets, wide eaves and high perforated parapet, surely built by masons trained in the Akbari stable. Set at the far corner of the dazzling white terrace, the building had such finesse that, the story goes, news of it aroused Jahangir to jealousy, and Jai Singh slapped over some stucco before the emperor's commissioners arrived to see if the successful Rajput was becoming a danger.

The magnificent **Ganesh Pol** (*c* 1640, elephant gate) is Jai Singh's ceremonial gate and also forms the facade and entrance to the private palace apartments. Its burst of colour seems even brighter under the fierce Rajasthan sun. Both structure and decoration are Mughal-inspired, but adapted to the more exuberant taste and exotic requirements of the Hindu ruler. To the Mughal foundation has been added extra arches and a bizarre decorative scheme (apparently inspired by Mughal tile-work) of glass mosaic, floral tempera paintings and pictures of gods. Over the doorway sits protective Ganesh, the elephant-headed Hindu god of learning and good fortune. Above, the palace ladies could peek through the jali screens to watch the splendour of court pageantry.

Inside, the geometric formality of the sunken garden is pure Mughal. Overlooking it, the **Sukh Niwas** (hall of pleasure) to the right is where the royals and courtesans came to find refuge from the heat, listening to the soothing sounds of water from a rooftop cistern tinkling down over the black and white marble cascades, and enjoying the fresh air cooled by water running through the hall and the cool colours of the ivory-encrusted doors. On the way back to Ganesh Pol, the room to the left of the gate has delightful wall-paintings.

The palace containing Jai Singh's private apartments overlooks the other end of the garden. Here Mughal and Hindu styles find their ultimate refinement, probably the best in any Rajasthan palace. Motifs are perfectly balanced: elegant green cypresses contrast with tiny flowers; larger areas are painted with favourite Rajput scenes of hunting and war. Colours are soft greens, pinks, blues and yellows. Walls were rendered perfectly smooth with a mixture of powdered marble, egg shells and pearls for the final coat. Precious stones and mirrors are set into the plaster but gaudiness, so often the criticism of Rajput decorations, is absent. To complete the scheme, the niches were filled with vases of flowers, Hindu deities and oil lamps which added sparkle to the mirror-work. While in these rooms you may spot a tiny thin old man, Gopal Lal, who has been restoring the traditional gold and silver mirror-work at Amber for ten years, with plenty of work yet to be done.

The **Diwan-i-Khas** (private audience hall) is on the ground floor. The scalloped, shade-giving arches of the gallery are decorated with flowers and butterflies. It surrounds a room whose walls and ceiling are coated with marble and mirror-work, except where they leave space for dancing Krishna and

Radha. It seems there could be nothing richer. But when the watchman shows you into the **Sheesh Mahal** (hall of mirrors), a tiny room off the Diwan-i-Khas, then closes the doors and lights a match and swirls it about, it is like being inside a vast twinkling diamond. Narrow steps in the courtyard wall lead up to the **Jas Mandir** (hall of glory), remarkable for its fine alabaster jali screens set at ground level so reclining royals could catch every little breeze and soothe their dusty-hot eyes with views of Maota Lake below.

Back towards Jaleb Court, an open corridor leads to a rooftop entertainment hall. In the cool of the evening the maharaja sat on his stone throne between picturesque pavilions to watch his ladies dancing on the central platform, with Jaigarh Fort as backdrop. Before leaving this area, it is worth going round to the top of Ganesh Pol to enjoy more fine jali screens and a ladies'-eye-view of the Diwan-i-Am.

Elephants
Symbols of Power, Knowledge and Good Fortune

Elephants are everywhere in India. They run around the gold borders of saris, cavort in the fine *ikat* weaves, parade in stone around temples and dance in wood above doorways. They stand in stone or painted plaster to protect palace entrances. They are cast in brass, fashioned into jewellery, moulded in plastic. Ganesh, the elephant-headed god of learning and good fortune, is a Hindu favourite and adorns doors, paintings, sweet-tins and auto-rickshaws. At festival time, the ex-Maharaja of Jaipur still rides an elephant richly caparisoned in gold. And visitors can journey up to the old Jaipur stronghold at Amber by elephant, after dropping in to the elephant café at the bottom of the hill, where the 40 or so magnificent beasts, each a paid-up member of one of the three local elephant unions, take their tea-break of grass and bamboo.

About 20,000 Asian elephants live in India; others live in Burma, Sri Lanka, Malaysia and Thailand. They differ from African elephants: smaller size, smaller ears, more domed forehead and only the male grows tusks. The largest land mammal, a female elephant undergoes an 18- to 22-month-long pregnancy before giving birth to a baby 75−90 centimetres (2.5−3 feet) tall and weighing about 100 kilos (220 pounds). For the first six months, the newborn lives solely on about 10 litres (18 pints) of mother's milk a day. Constant protection and love, with nudging trunk, are given by the mother and another female of the herd, her specially enlisted nanny. Soon calves are playing together, staging mock fights with flapping, almost muscle-free trunks. At two years, the tusks of a male begin to grow, two-thirds solid ivory visible on the outside, one third of hollow ivory in the skull. Elephants reach maturity

Man Singh's older buildings behind the garden court have a bold simplicity. This labyrinth of decaying, atmospheric minor palaces, *zenana* apartments, courtyards, terraces and gardens, is well worth exploring. Man Singh's wives each had separate rooms (the odd Krishna and Radha mural survives) opening onto a large courtyard, which is not too difficult to find.

If energy holds, a pleasant way to leave the fort is by the back door. (Alternatively, if you have real energy, leave by Jai Pol and stride 1½ kilometres, or about a mile, up to the Awani Gate of Jaigarh Fort, see page 154.) In Jaleb Chowk, near the balcony overlooking Kadmi Palace, a path leads down past temples including **Sri Jagat Saromangi**, built by Man Singh in memory of his eldest son, with sturdy stone elephants guarding its marble gateway and the sacred bird Garuda over the entrance indicating its dedication to Vishnu. Down past the Amber rulers' tombs, a right turn leads past ancient

aged 14 but continue to grow for life — if undisturbed, up to 80 years. A 35-year-old elephant may weigh 5,500 kilos (12,130 pounds) and be three metres (ten feet) tall, maintaining its huge bulk with 150 kilos (330 pounds) of green fodder each day, often chewing well into the night.

Water is crucial for washing and drinking. The daily bath is a delicious wallow and a good swim if the water is deep enough to float in. An elephant drinks about 140 litres (250 pints) of water a day, sucking it up with its hosepipe-like trunk and emptying it into the mouth. The highly sensitive multi-purpose trunk compensates for poor eyesight, for it is capable of emitting ultrasound noises to find family members and detect danger. And it is also used for mating. Contrary to myth, elephants mate on land and not in water, the male keeping his balance by sliding his trunk along the female's back.

To protect its back during the searing heat, the elephant scrapes the earth with its foot, then scoops up the dust with its trunk and sprays it over its back. This and a trunk-held flywhisk of tree branch help control the bloodsucking flies who cleverly find any chink in the armour skin. So do flapping ears, which double as cooling agents as elephants lack sweat glands. But during the hot hours the elephant needs shade. Here it sleeps, either lying down or standing up, as horses do, ears flapping throughout, trunk dipped into the mouth now and then to steal saliva and spray it over the hot body.

These magnificent, extremely gentle and loving creatures now live under threat from man. His cattle bring disease and disturbance to their grazing grounds; his concrete water-canals cut off centuries-old migration routes. And poachers have killed so many tuskers — a 1.8-metre (six-foot) -long pair fetches around US$8,000 — that they now kill five-year-old bulls for just a few inches of ivory, threatening the balance of the sexes.

painted mansions and temples of old Amber to the village centre. Turning left onto the road out to Delhi, then left again after the triple-domed mosque, you can clamber up the outer **fort walls**. A little further along the road, the tiny, open-fronted workshops on the right are busy with craftsmen cutting and polishing semi-precious stones, using the simple tools of wheel and water. Near them and near a lofty old gateway (found with a little local guidance from the children), the steep but more regular steps of further stretches of the fort wall have look-out posts for pauses and provide even better views.

Amber to Jaipur
Magnificent Forts and Royal Tombs

Of the 50 or so Kachchwaha forts, Jaigarh was most important. Opened to the public in 1983, it is well worth a long visit, afterwards nipping to the other end of the Kali Khoh Ridge to catch sunset over Jaipur from Nahargarh Fort. Gaitor, where the royals who lived down in Jaipur have their elaborately carved white marble tombs, lies between the City Palace and Nahargarh Fort. It is reached along a bumpy lane running right off the Amber–Jaipur road. But before the turn-off, the maharanis' less-grand tombs are on the left, on the roadside just after Man Sagar Lake. Beware: although Jaigarh Fort and Gaitor are both open daily, they currently close at 4.30 pm.

Jaigarh Fort is a fun fort — there is even a toy cannon which can be blasted off for Rs10. And it is in remarkably good condition. Its superb location has saved it from being attacked. In peacetime it was only accessible to the ruler (and it is one small section of Jaipur still belonging to the ex-royal family).

When the defeated Minas became the clan's loyal treasurers, they used their skills as archers and mountain fighters to guard this fort. Here Man Singh and his successors stored their fast-accumulating gold, silver and jewels which paid first for building Amber, then for Jaipur and for centuries of grand royal living. Legend tells how each new Kachchwaha chief was taken by the Minas into the treasury just once, where he chose a single item from the dazzling piles of war booty. Legends are tenacious. In 1976 the Indian taxmen dug here for six months, finding nothing. Some say Jai Singh II squandered it all on his new city; others claim it is still there. Certainly, the Rajmata of Jaipur, widow of the last maharaja, remembers the object her father-in-law Madho Singh II had chosen. It was a solid gold bird with ruby eyes and a huge emerald in its beak which sat on a Rambagh Palace mantlepiece. 'One day the emerald fell out of the beak and we put the bird away ... I wonder what became of it?'

Rajputs have always taken their hill forts very seriously. Belonging to the Hindu Kshatriya (warrior) caste, they found plenty of encouragement in the sacred Purana texts — 'a fort is the strength of a king', 'a force of one hundred, fighting from a fort, can encounter ten thousand', and so on. The Puranas even gave guidelines for the plan. Although this fort had existed for centuries, it was Jai Singh II who expanded, remodelled and renamed it in 1726, giving it its romantic character. Visitors can now ramble all over the area, pause at the café or watch a delightful puppet show. On arrival by road at Doongar Gate (where the ticket office is), it is best to head for the great cannon first, then visit the armoury, gun foundry and palace complex. If you are lucky, Thakur Pratap Singh, a handsome Rajput with a fine curly moustache, may be around to tell you more of Jaigarh's illustrious history.

Perched on a cliff, the fort is surrounded by huge battlements whose inside walkway provides stunning views on all sides. **Jaivan**, perhaps the world's largest cannon, stands at the southern end. The barrel is six metres (nearly 20 feet) long, and decorated with elephants, flowers and birds; the wheels have a diameter of two-and-a-half metres (eight feet). Jai Singh II had it built in 1720 and test-fired it once, landing the cannon ball about 38 kilometres (24 miles) away. But, as the notice proudly points out, 'because of strong defence system, management and the foresightedness of the rulers, enemy never dared to enter this fort.' So it was never used. However, Thakur Pratap Singh reckons it could be fired today, only 'in Jaipur many houses fall down; the hills have reverberation all round.'

On the way to the northern end, you can go down into the three damp, arched tanks in the courtyard, which stored water for emergency use; ever hopeful, the taxmen drained them in 1976. Through the great arch into Jaleb Chowk (sweet market), the fort's armoury kept in the closed verandas includes

the huge treasury lock with its five keys, great wine and oil jars, 17th-century time-bombs and a wonderful 1681 map of Amber. The far end of the square is where you get drinks and where you can have a mini cannon fired off with a surprisingly big bang.

To the right is the gun foundry, built by Bhagwan Das (ruled 1514−89) in 1584, with furnace, lathe, tools and a collection of cannons. Bhagwan Das's adopted son, who became Man Singh I, obtained the secret of gunpowder from Kabul in 1584 and cannons began to be made here three years later, much to the annoyance of the Mughals who had brought gunpowder to India in 1526 (when it helped them conquer the Lodis and the Rajputs) but carefully kept the secret to themselves. The royal look-out post up above the foundry includes a stone throne from which the chieftain surveyed the whole of Amber gorge and beyond.

The palace, which fills the north end, begins as usual with the Diwan-i-Am (public audience hall). But, appropriately, Khilbat Niwas (commanders' meeting hall), complete with secret back passages for royal escape, replaces the Diwan-i-Khas. Locals strike up charming puppet shows in one palace; lime plaster floors still shine smoothly; and the Aram Mandir (garden house) still traps every little breeze. At the end, the old 16th-century Vilas Mandir courtyard was where the royal ladies gossiped at their evening *janani-majlis*, best translated as hen-parties. The pavilions around it provide near-perfect views down over Amber on one side and the fort's reservoir, Sagar Talav, on the other.

Nahargarh (tiger) **Fort** is not in the same class as Jaigarh, but it is picturesque. Along the ridge-top road to it, there are magnificent views down to Man Sagar Lake, in the middle of which Jai Singh II built a thoroughly palatial duck blind for shooting parties. Alternatively, the keen can hike up the steep path found at the end of Nahargarh Fort Road at the northwest corner of Jaipur City Palace.

Jai Singh II built the fort in 1734. Known at first as Sudarshangarh, it was his new city's defence and the link back to Amber Fort via the Kali Khoh Ridge and Jaigarh. Ram Singh II gave it an extra floor in 1868−9; Madho Singh II made other additions in 1902−3. This fort was where official Jaipur time was boomed out across the city, where the ranis came to cool down and where the personal royal treasure was kept until Man Singh II moved it in the 1940s to Moti Doongri, the Scottish folly south of the pink city.

The royal tombs at **Gaitor** stand right below Nahargarh Fort. If the great doors at the top of the entrance steps are closed, just hover about and the watchman will come to open them. Inside, peacocks strut along the finely carved marble of Madho Singh II's enormous mausoleum at the front, while monkeys frolic among the trees around Jai Singh's beautiful mausoleum at the back. The 20 pillars richly carved with mythological scenes (except where vandals have snatched them) support a pure white marble dome. It is a suitably splendid memorial for the founder of Jaipur — who died of ill health in 1743 aged just 55 — had been one of the great soldiers and intellects of his time and one of the greatest Kachchwaha rulers.

Jaipur
A Humanist Maharaja's Model City

Jaipur is the perfect complement to Amber. Instead of being an empty museum, it bustles with life. And yet it still satisfies the most romantic imagination. Its exotic palace is matched by equally exotic stories of past inhabitants and a colourful streetlife today.

It was from the City Palace that loyal Madho Singh II left for Britain to attend the coronation of Edward VII in 1902, carrying huge silver water flasks to avoid drinking dangerous foreign water. Here, the birth in 1931 of Bhawani Singh provided the first male heir for two generations born to a ruling maharaja, Man Singh II. To celebrate, great marble elephants were carved for the palace entrance and so many champagne corks were popped that the baby prince's nanny nicknamed him Bubbles. Independence may have come to India but today the ex-prince still lives in the palace, is still regarded as the paternal maharaja by his citizens and still dresses in finery to parade on an elephant at the Hindu festivals, although visitors are more likely to glimpse him in informal clothes zipping through the palace courtyards in his Jeep.

When **Jai Singh II** (ruled 1699–1743) laid the foundation stone of his new city on 25 November 1727, the 38-year-old maharaja already had an enviable military and diplomatic career behind him in Mughal service. It had won him the hereditary title 'Sawai maharaja' from the emperor, meaning one-and-a-quarter great king, thoroughly upstaging his fellow Rajput rulers who were regularly reminded of it with the extra quarter-flag flown above Jaipur palaces. Now, turning from war to peace and using the Jaigarh treasury, he established his new city as the capital of expanding Jaipur state. Measuring more than 50,000 square kilometres (19,300 square miles), it was one of the largest in India and rivalled the two other powerful Rajput states, Mewar (capital at Udaipur) and Marwar (capital at Jodhpur). To keep control and to ensure his safety, Jai Singh ran a sort of secret service, an extensive network of men who were his eyes and ears throughout the state and at the Mughal court, and who sent in detailed reports on everything from monsoons, crops and crime to misconduct of local officials, traders' disputes and current rumours.

The city reflects Jai Singh's two passions: science and the arts. A young Bengali, **Vidyadhar Bhattacharaya**, was its chief architect. He was a key figure in the second part of Jai Singh's life. Descended from one of the Bengali priests brought back by Man Singh I to serve in Amber's temple (see above), Vidyadhar left the priesthood to enter the royal accounts department and rose to be engineer, scholar and senior state official, attaining the post of Desh

Jaipur: Jai Singh II's City

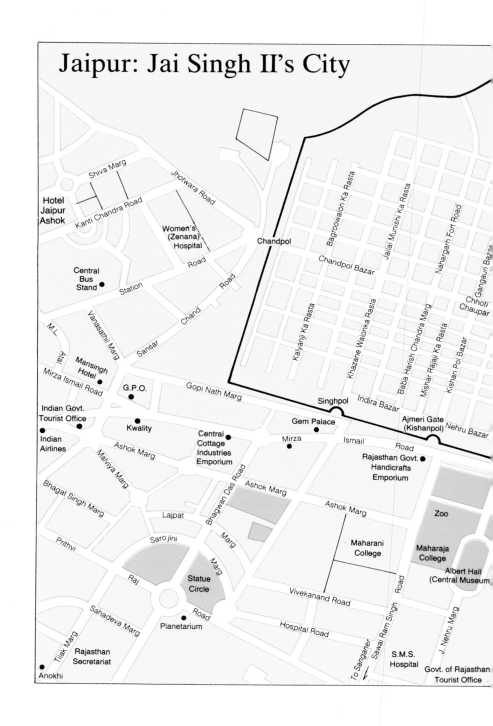

Hotel Jaipur Ashok

Shiva Marg

Jhotwara Road

Kanti Chandra Road

Women's (Zenana) Hospital

Chandpol

Bagroowalon Ka Rasta

Jallal Munishi Ka Rasta

Nahargarh Fort Road

Gangauri Bazar

Central Bus Stand

Station

Road

Chandpol Bazar

Chhoti Chaupar

Road

Chand

Sansar

Kalyanji Ka Rasta

Khazane Walonka Rasta

Baba Harish Chandra Marg

Mishar Rajaji Ka Rasta

Kishan Pol Bazar

M.L.

Vanasathli Marg

Mansingh Hotel

Alal

Mirza Ismail Road

G.P.O.

Gopi Nath Marg

Singhpol

Indira Bazar

Indian Govt. Tourist Office

Kwality

Central Cottage Industries Emporium

Gem Palace

Mirza

Ismail

Ajmeri Gate (Kishanpol)

Nehru Bazar

Indian Airlines

Ashok Marg

Malviya Marg

Bhagwan Das Road

Ashok Marg

Road

Rajasthan Govt. Handicrafts Emporium

Bhagat Singh Marg

Lajpat

Marg

Ashok Marg

Ashok Marg

Zoo

Prithvi

Saro jini

Marg

Maharani College

Maharaja College

Albert Hall (Central Museum)

Raj

Statue Circle

Vivekanand Road

Road

J. Nehru Marg

Sahadeva Marg

Road

Planetarium

Hospital Road

Sawai Ram Singh Road

Tilak Marg

Rajasthan Secretariat

To Sanganer

S.M.S. Hospital

Govt. of Rajasthan Tourist Office

Anokhi

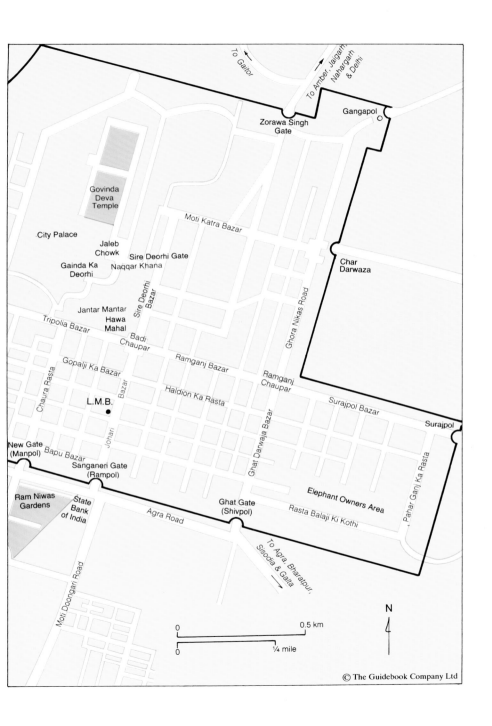

Diwan, roughly equivalent to prime minister. According to the historian James Todd, he also aided his master 'in all his scientific pursuits, both astronomical and historical.'

As recorded by a contemporary historian in 1739: 'Jai Singh said to Vidyadhar that a city should be founded here ... There should be many crossroads with shops on them. The backyards of the houses should meet together.' Furthermore, he envisaged his city as the capital of a united Rajputana, a centre of government, trade and worship. Two hundred years later, his dream came true: as capital of Rajasthan, Jaipur is one of the few former princely states to enjoy increased, rather than decreased, status since Independence.

Vidyadhar devised a simple grid plan following the principles of the ancient Hindu architectural treatise, the *Shilpa Shastra*. Seven blocks of buildings are divided by wide, tree-lined avenues. The palace is on the north side, covering another two blocks, and the whole is surrounded by high walls pierced by ten gates. Orientation is to the northeast, towards two hilltop temples. To this design Jai Singh added his humanist ideas of hygiene, beauty and commerce. But the pink colour symbolizing welcome followed much later, when Ram Singh II spruced up the whole city for the Prince of Wales's visit in 1876, having experimented with several colours before settling on pink. Unusually in India, his example of city maintenance was kept up. Today, every house-owner is obliged by law to maintain his facade, paying a high penalty charge for the city to do it for him if he fails.

Jaipur was the first sizable north Indian city — as opposed to collections of palace buildings such as at Fatehpur Sikri — to be built from scratch to a single plan of such order and detail and to be thriving almost unchanged today. Vidyadhar's was the controlling hand. Merchants were invited to come and build houses, but only to Vidyadhar's directions. All building materials were delivered to him and he personally oversaw all public and palace buildings.

Work moved fast. By 1729 many temples, markets, mansions and small houses had been built. By 1733, the main landmarks were completed, and on the Holi festival Jai Singh 'mounted on an elephant, and with Thakurs [landowning courtiers] too mounted on elephants, came via Chandni Chowk, playing Holi all the way ... then amidst revelries to Ramganj, then returned to the palace.' The following year, Jai Singh rewarded Vidyadhar for the speedy construction of his seven-storey palace and again in 1735 for completing the water canal from the Darbhawati River. Vidyadhar, one of the great architects of his time, became a living legend. One panegyric went: 'The wealth acquired by the possession of all lands, the province, the cities, and the forts and the whole population are on one side, and Vidyadhar like an ocean of all virtues is on the other.'

To see a little of the layout and drink in the lively Jaipur atmosphere before visiting the palace, start at **Badi Chaupar** crossroads. This is the city centre.

The road is a continuous confusion of honking cars, daring bicyclists, bouncy black tempos (motorbike taxis), scooters with sari-clad ladies sat side-saddle on the back, tooting auto-rickshaws, bullocks pulling small carts and camels heaving large ones loaded with wood or stones. Jaipur's main artery stretches east and west, 36 metres wide (118 feet) and running some three kilometres (1.9 miles) from Surajpol Gate to Chandpol Gate. When Father José Tieffenthaler came in 1739, he was mightily impressed by the 'wide and long streets' compared to the 'unequal and narrow streets' of other towns, and reckoned this especially fine one could take 'six or seven carriages driven abreast.'

To the south is busy Johari Bazar, the jewellery and cotton fabric centre; to the north is Hawa Mahal Bazar, where more camels plod in from Amber direction. Similar north−south arteries with market crossroads lie to the east (Ramganj Chaupar) and west (Chhoti Chaupar) of here, with smaller roads in between and beyond. The blocks they form were each designed for a particular trade or craft and planned with a precise number of shops and given a distinctive style. And many still retain their original function; today's craftsmen still live in courtyard houses with beautifully painted rooms, and practise skills passed down through the generations. They work happily side by side with the newer Jaipur industries of distilling, engineering, shoemaking, glass-making and sports equipment production.

On the far corner of Badi Chaupar, the bangle-sellers set up walls of glittering coloured glass and plastic to tempt local girls. Behind them rises the huge **City Palace complex**. The crazy **Hawa Mahal** (palace of the winds) borders this side of it, like a baroque folly stuck onto the outside wall. Its five-storey facade of pink sandstone encrusted with fine jali work and balconies has 953 niches and windows and is just one room deep. It was built in 1799 by the architect Lalchand Usta for the aesthete Pratap Singh (ruled 1778−1803). One of his poetry couplets suggests that this building was dedicated to Krishna and Radha. Its function was a royal grandstand so that the palace women, trapped in purdah, could watch the streetlife, including processions. (Visitors today can climb up to enjoy the same views.)

Before exploring the City Palace, take a quick look at the north side of **Ramganj Bazar**. Here are the shoe shops selling traditional black embroidered Jaipur slippers. Diving down Neel Garo ka Mohla, you can find women nimbly working at tie-and-dye. Along on the left, Sri Mohammed Siddique's tie-and-dye factory is in a cool, dark haveli. Opposite Hawa Mahal, more shoe shops are interspersed with puppet-makers in **Sire Deorhi Bazar**. The 'magic', double-headed puppet is especially good; he is the court magician character essential for recounting royal tales. Across on the Hawa Mahal side, fireworks shops advertise their tinsel-coated Catharine wheels. Just beyond, a turn left leads through Sire Deorhi gate into the palace complex. The second part of the gateway is the Naqqar Khana (drum house), where beating drums and wailing

shehnai reed instruments would announce important visitors and tell locals the time. Beyond is Jaleb Chowk (sweet market), now a large public square with cafés and the odd mini-temple to Ganesh or Krishna.

Before the left turn to the palace proper, there is a good detour to the right. **Govinda Deva Temple** is found through the archway and round to the left, past holy men and stalls selling sweetmeats and temple mementos. This is an excellent place to appreciate the Hindu atmosphere of Jaipur and the local devotion to Krishna, the blue-skinned god who is the human, eighth incarnation of the god Vishnu. Govinda is Krishna's name when he is a cowherd, flirting with the *gopis* (female cowherds), teasing them, stealing their clothes while they swim, and enjoying a fiery romance with the beautiful Radha, all of which is believed to have taken place just north of Agra, in Vrindaban village. It was from there that Jai Singh brought back an image of Govinda and installed it here in 1735, to be the guardian deity of Jaipur rulers. From this time, their public addresses began meekly with 'subjects of Govinda Devi', implying that they were humble, temporal instruments of the all-powerful god.

Looking back from the temple across the City Palace garden, you can see how the central room was lined up so the devout maharajas had a direct view of their god and could worship in palace comfort. Locals come daily to offer their puja (worship) of songs, music, sweetmeats and devout words, timing their visits with one of the priests' seven pujas, when the curtain is drawn back to reveal the deity. Each puja celebrates part of the god's daily life — he wakes at 5 am, and dresses at around 10.30 am. But as most people come after work, it is best to pop down for the 6 pm and 8 pm ones. Past the temple, down a ramp to the right, holy men sit around the garden and an old tank where crocodiles were once bred; and there are more little Krishna temples along the left side.

Back through Jaleb Chowk, a right turn after the narrow archway leads directly to Gainda ka Deorhi (rhinoceros gate) and the core of **City Palace** buildings (ticket office by the gate). These are Vidyadhar's showpiece. Although he followed the Rajput fort plan seen at Amber, with public buildings leading to increasingly private ones, he wove in the Mughal idea of having buildings for different functions standing entirely separate from one another. Thus, through a series of courtyards, the simple stables and offices lead ultimately to the colourful and richly decorated royal rooms in Chandra Mahal. The private rooms are still lived in by the ex-maharaja. But many of the others are open to visitors and constitute the **City Palace Museum** (founded 1959), housing a tiny part of the fabulous royal collection. The Kachchwaha rulers had a good eye. They took advantage of the Mughal alliance to acquire fine Mughal pieces and, led by Jai Singh II, became art patrons themselves.

Mubarak Mahal (palace of welcome) stands in the middle of this courtyard like a great carved ivory box. It was added by Madho Singh II (ruled 1880–1922) in 1900 as a guest-house, later served as the Mahakma Khas (Royal

Secretariat) and is now the Tosha Khana (royal wardrobe) of the museum. The first floor houses fine muslins, Benares silks, local hand-printed cottons and embroidered coats from north India. But the star is surely the *atamsukh* (long quilted robe) of Madho Singh I (ruled 1750–68), a huge man whose legendary height of two metres (6.6 feet) and weight of 225 kilos (496 pounds) is almost believable from seeing the quantity of gold-encrusted raspberry-pink silk needed to envelop him. Beautiful musical instruments, many inlaid with ivory, are also here, as are Jaipur blue pottery, Mughal glass, hookah bases and delightful toys for young royals. And do not miss a close look at the balcony which runs round the whole suite of rooms.

Before going further into the palace, there are two other buildings worth seeing. First, the **Sileh Khana** (armoury) in the corner. Upstairs, past huge paintings of great Jaipur battles, one of the finest collections of Indian weaponry — both Hindu and Mughal — is displayed in prettily painted and decorated rooms. It reflects the real love of every Rajput warrior. There is a dagger with an inlaid ivory handle in the shape of a parrot, a finely chiselled

Jaipur City Palace

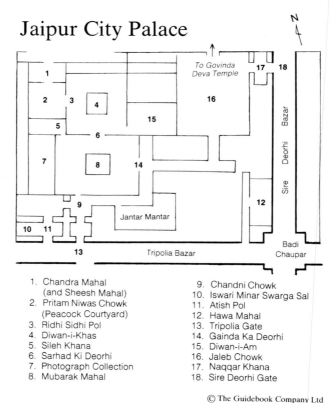

1. Chandra Mahal
   (and Sheesh Mahal)
2. Pritam Niwas Chowk
   (Peacock Courtyard)
3. Ridhi Sidhi Pol
4. Diwan-i-Khas
5. Sileh Khana
6. Sarhad Ki Deorhi
7. Photograph Collection
8. Mubarak Mahal
9. Chandni Chowk
10. Iswari Minar Swarga Sal
11. Atish Pol
12. Hawa Mahal
13. Tripolia Gate
14. Gainda Ka Deorhi
15. Diwan-i-Am
16. Jaleb Chowk
17. Naqqar Khana
18. Sire Deorhi Gate

helmet and shield, swords belonging to Man Singh I and emperor Shah Jahan, Jai Singh I's ingenious turban-helmet and devilish warring devices such as the lotus-bud steel mace which, when jammed into the enemy's guts, would spring open into a fan of sharp spikes.

Turning from such horrors, you find the royal photograph collection next door. It was made by Ram Singh II (ruled 1835–80), who gave Jaipur its pink welcome and whose enlightened rule under the watchful British eye brought revolutionary improvements to the city: a state postal system (1861) carried by camels and runners, a Public Works Department (1860), a formal municipality (1868) and, installed to great excitement, piped water (1874) and street lighting. He also laid out Ram Niwas Public Gardens and founded the cultural centres inside it (see below). He was also intrigued by the new art of photography. Helped by an Englishman, T Murray, he clicked his cameras around Jaipur, developed the films in the palace dark-rooms and left a fascinating record of everything from progress reports on his pet projects to Parsi theatre companies playing Shakespeare.

The great **Sarhad ki Deorhi**, also known as Singh Pol (lion gate), is a typically Hindu square gatehouse flamboyantly decorated with carved marble and flanked by the elephants which celebrated the present ex-maharaja's birth in 1931. The bronze double doors lead to a more intimate courtyard whose frilly white arches on the salmon-pink walls are also pure Rajput taste. But the little **Diwan-i-Khas** (private audience hall) in the centre returns to the sedate Mughal traditions of Fatehpur Sikri. Here are the two great silver urns the craftsman Govind Narain made so that Madho Singh II could take Ganga drinking water to Britain in 1901. Probably still the largest pieces of silver in the world, each used 242.7 kilos (535 pounds) of silver and holds 8,182 litres (1,800 gallons). Before starting his trip, the ruler took other precautions: he chartered a liner, built a temple on board and threw bags of gold, silver and silk into Bombay harbour to invoke a safe passage.

To the right, the great enclosed Diwan-i-Am (public audience hall) has none of the Diwan-i-Khas's sophistication or airiness. Originally entered from Jaleb Chowk, this was the setting for the elaborate panoply of court pageantry and durbars, watched by the ranis from behind high screens. Today, a few of the greatest Jaipur treasures are shown here. The walls are hung with magnificent carpets made at Lahore, Herat and Agra, their burgundy red fields littered with bold flowers. The showcases contain a few of the collection's exquisite miniature paintings (the best are in the vertical cases), both those of the Jaipur school encouraged and refined by Jai Singh II (there should be at least one portrait of the great man on show) and many Mughal ones including an amusing Holy Family evidently inspired by European models brought by Jesuits, and a family tree of the Mughal dynasty.

A narrow doorway in the diagonally opposite corner of the Diwan-i-Khas courtyard leads under the ladies' corridor and through Ridhi Sidhi Pol to the more intimate part of the palace. **Pritam Niwas Chowk** comes first, a magical enclosed courtyard, recently restored and painted, whose four doorways thickly encrusted with elaborate polychrome inlay have given it its nickname, the Peacock Courtyard. It is as fanciful as the Hawa Mahal and was built by the same ruler, Pratap Singh. Each doorway represents a season, and the doors are decorated with scenes from Krishna's life. The interior of Pritam Niwas is in sharp contrast: it is painted in Wedgwood blue and hung with portraits of recent royals. This marks the beginning of Chandra Mahal (moon palace), the inner sanctum and usually not open to the public. Its seven tiers of private rooms begin with the Chandra Mandir, from where the elderly, pious Jai Singh II would gaze down the garden to Sri Govinda Temple, and is topped by the Sheesh Mahal, a jewel-like room whose walls and ceilings are entirely coated with coloured glass inlay, floral designs and quantities of gold.

Back outside the Gainda ki Deorhi, a turn right leads to the most interesting and influential of Jai Singh II's scientific experiments. It looks like a children's park filled with the giant geometric shapes of a modern sculptor. But it is his very serious **Jantar Mantar** (jyantra: instrument; mantra: magic formula), an open-air observatory of outsize astronomical instruments. As a keen mathematician and astronomer, Jai Singh had already built the first observatory in India at Delhi in 1724—7 (see page 69). Then, while governor of Agra, he built more at Ujjain, Varanasi and Mathura, all ancient centres of learning and Hinduism. All the while he was not only aware of European progress in the field by Flamsteed, Cassini, Newton and others, but he sent to Europe for the latest books and instruments.

Between 1728 and 1734, he built this one at home, the biggest of all his observatories and the only one built of stone. This he used daily, often accompanied by his astronomy gurus, Pandit Jagannath and Kewal Ram. The function of each instrument is rather complex (and local guides give contradictory, long-winded versions), although time is the dominant theme. For the amateur, it is enough to understand just the basic ideas (several have similar functions) and enjoy their splendid shapes.

The Samrat Yantra (supreme instrument) is a good first stop. It is really a giant sundial. Until the 1940s, this was the time-piece for Jaipur's own solar time, the hours read off the quadrants either side of the vast gnomon (right angle) and then announced to the citizens on drums at the top of its steps and at the Naqqar Khana and with gunfire from Nahargarh Fort. Turning back from it, you come to the Jai Prakash Yantra, Jai Singh's invention: two sunken hemispheres which told both the time and the sun's path in the heavens. The Kapala Yantra next to them performed a similar job. The little Dhruva Yantra also helped determine the hour. So did the Nari Valaya Yantra, the two huge circles placed back-to-back at an angle: the north-facing one was read in winter, the other in summer.

The Raj Yantra had a different function. This ancient instrument was used to calculate the height and position of celestial bodies; the circular Unnatansha Yantra behind it did much the same; and the great Disha Charkra seems primarily to have indicated the northern direction. Beyond, the Dakshina Yantra was for calculating the position of celestial bodies when they passed the meridian. The biggest instrument of all is merely another sundial, its 27-metre (89-foot) height aiding greater accuracy. The dozen triangles of the Rashi Valaya Yantra represent the signs of the zodiac and were used to work out relationships between the celestial bodies. Finally, the large, circular Ram Yantras and Digamsha Yantra are for reading altitudes and azimuths (distances in the sky).

After such concentration, a relaxed wander through the streets. Turn left out of the Observatory, and Atish Pol (stable gate) is found past the palace stables of Chandni Chowk (moonlight square). Immediately to the left is the **Tripolia** (triple-arched) **Gate**, the grand entrance through which the maharajas, decked in silk, gold and huge diamonds and pearls, would emerge seated on their equally grandly dressed elephants. In festival processions, the thakurs (landowners) would follow, competing with one another to give an opulent show — on one occasion this century, the Thakur of Isarda piled Rs25,000 worth of jewellery on. They came in from their estates to dance attendance on their ruler for a few days and stay in their town houses, at first in the pink city, then in more spacious homes outside the walls. To the right, **Iswari Minar Swarga Sal** (minaret piercing heaven) was built by Iswari Singh (ruled 1743– 51), the weak and ineffectual successor to Jaipur's builder. When the Maratha army advanced, he committed double suicide by taking poison and making a

Jaipur Blue Pottery and Tile-work

Spacious bungalows lie west of the Pink City. Among them, you know when you have found Kripal Singh Shekhawat's. The front garden is his pottery studio. Right behind the gate, trays of buff, undecorated pots dry in the sun. By the front door, the splash of hazy blue against the cream wall is a pile of vases and storage jars painted with pale and inky-dark blue geometric and flower patterns. Where front garden roses might be, the shoulders of his massive kiln rise above the earth.

The studio proper is the deep, open-fronted garage to the left of the house. A young potter sits cross-legged in the shaded porch patiently painting the outline of a flower onto a square vase; completed jars stand in a neat row at his side. Beyond him, another worker inspects large jars for faults. Further back, another dips cups into a large bowl of white slip, carefully placing them on wooden trays to dry. Around him, shelves up to the ceiling are stacked with finished pots while more clutter up all available floor space, giving the whole room a mesmerizing blue glow.

Kripal Singh presides over his 15-man studio. It was Man Singh I of Amber who in the 16th century, as Commander-in-Chief of Akbar's army, caught some of the Mughals' artistic tastes. One was for Persian and Chinese blue-and-white tiles and pottery. Later, potters came to live in Jai Singh II's new city, Jaipur. Then, when in 1866 Ram Singh founded the Jaipur School of Art to stimulate the city's stagnating crafts, top potters were brought from Delhi and Bharatpur to revive the skills. Royal patronage continued: Ram Singh's grandson, Man Singh II, commissioned master potter Jamuna Prasan to make the glorious fountain in what is now the Rambagh Palace's Polo Bar.

Today, award-winning Kripal Singh is one of a dozen potters in Jaipur; others work in nearby Sanganer. All follow the Jaipur tradition of using local quart clay to make the pots, then painting and glazing them before a single firing. Originally from the Shekhavati region of painted houses, north of Jaipur, Kripal Singh is a painter-turned-potter who takes inspiration from the old Jaipur pieces with their simple shapes and geometric patterns in dark sapphire and pale aquamarine blues. His most effective pieces are the big, bulbous *surahi* pots and the huge storage jars which Ali Baba's 40 men could have hidden in. (He promises they survive being shipped home.)

Some pots he enriches with his experiences in Persia and Japan and with elements from Rajasthan folk crafts. Using a fine squirrel-hair brush, he may paint a Simurgh, the mythical Persian bird, amid sinuous flowers of blue, green, yellow and a special warm pink he gets from Amritsar, not shirking from adding chemicals to enrich the tones. On a tile he may use cobalt oxide for the deep lapis blue outline of another Persian design, large flowers within delicate arabesques, filling it in with copper oxide for turquoise blue and dashes of antimony oxide for yellow, manganese oxide for brown and chromium oxide for green.

cobra bite him. But his wives behaved with more Rajput style: three took poison and 21 committed sati on their ruler's funeral pyre. (Further along, Nahargarh Road on the right leads up to the fort, see above.)

Now for a taste of inner Jaipur life, almost unchanged since the city was built. Indeed, British journalist Bernard Levin was delighted to find that Jaipur 'really is a rose-red city, and looks — though it is not — half as old as time', and went on to describe a street 'with rows of tiny shops and tinier booths, and still tinier pushcarts, where one trader has spread out his wares on the pavement ... The dishes are full of colourful miniature seas of the various grains: white, yellow, red, brown, purple ... like the palette of a giant artist.' In Tripolia Bazar, cooking utensils compete with costume jewellery. Down Maniharon ke Rasta, craftsmen make multicoloured lacquer bangles. Down Chaura Rasta, a left turn into narrow Gopalji ka Rasta leads past lanes lined with havelis and the occasional temple, with sweetmeat and jewellery sellers lining the far end. It opens into **Johari Bazar**. Straight across is Haldion ka Rasta, where portly dealers in precious and semi-precious stones sit cross-legged in their kiosks and, through the painted archway on the right, the great Jaipur jeweller Surana keeps his exclusive, twinkling shop.

Back and down Johari Bazar — a favourite shopping area for bright, unpatterned cottons (sold by weight) and elaborate tie-dye creations — the LMB Restaurant is found on the right. It is always crowded with foreign visitors tucking in to irresistible fresh mango and pistachio ice-creams. Across the road are grand merchants' houses and, behind them, a market for vegetables and herbs. At the bottom of the street, Bapu Bazar and Nehru Bazar are on the right. Here are dozens of little shops selling locally block-printed cotton (see page 172), cheap meenakari jewellery and bangles, and heady perfumes to shock any man into retreat.

New Gate between the two bazaars leads out of the city, piercing its high, thick protective wall. Like all ten gates, it is topped by two kiosks and was until this century locked at night against all strangers (unknowing European travellers arriving on night trains were left stranded until sunrise).

Outside the Pink City
Gardens and Palaces in Modern Jaipur

Ignoring the dust and braving the quite long distances, spend some time exploring the Jaipur overspill. Ram Singh II's splendid cultural park is hard by the city walls, and its museum is a real treat. The splendid Rambagh Palace is south of it, and the beautiful Sisodia Palace lies out to the east.

Ram Singh II laid out his **Ram Niwas Gardens** right outside New Gate, employing a certain Dr de Fabeck to landscape what is now reduced to 14.5 hectares (36 acres). The view down the central road, Jawaharlal Nehru Marg, is closed by the palatial Central Museum. On the way there it passes first The

Gallery of Modern Art, the zoo, a crocodile breeding farm and the Maharaja College (founded 1845) which taught Urdu, Persian and English. Ram Singh also founded the School of Art (1868) which revived and promoted so many of Jaipur's crafts, including the blue pottery (see page 168).

The Albert Hall, housing the **Central Museum**, is the park centrepiece. It is a triumph of Raj influence, having been modelled on the Victoria and Albert Museum in London. The Prince of Wales laid the foundation stone on his 1876 visit and the architect was Colonel Sir Samuel Swinton Jacob (1841–1917), a British engineer whose knowledge of Indian buildings later earned him a job as consultant for the British capital of New Delhi. Inside the thoroughly Indian palace, locals wander about enjoying models of their festivals, collections of puppets and costumes, and exhibitions of top-quality Jaipur brasswork. The separate room at the front is the Durbar Hall, usually locked but just ask and it will be opened. It houses several exquisite carpets including the magnificent Persian Garden Carpet, one of India's finest art treasures. Made in 1632 in Kerman, Persia, its design is a paradise garden on char-bagh lines (see page 117). Fish swim in canals and mother birds feed their young in blossoming trees. It is one of the best of its kind, its fine silk colours still fresh and bright.

Further down the road, Narain Singh Marg leads past Narain Niwas, a thakur townhouse. Built in 1881 by Narain Singh, Madho Singh II's emissary, it was furnished in the heavy Raj taste so fashionable at the Jaipur court. At the end of the road, Lilly Pool Palace opposite is where the Rajmata of Jaipur lives. She is the widow of the last maharaja, Man Singh II. Her autobiography, *A Princess Remembers*, describes a queen's fairytale life before Independence and, to a great extent, after it.

The Rajmata lived much of her married life at **Rambagh Palace**, found by turning left down Sawai Ram Singh Road, then right at the large crossroads. It was Ram Singh II who made what were originally a few pleasure pavilions outside the city into a hunting lodge, Ram Bagh (garden of Ram). Then, with Sir Swinton Jacob's help, Madho Singh II transformed it into a royal play-ground, with English herbaceous borders, squash court, tennis court, indoor swimming pool complete with trapeze, and polo field next door. Not surprisingly, his adopted son, who succeeded him as Man Singh II in 1922 aged just 11 years, later chose it as his principal home. And when in 1940 he made a love match marriage with his third wife, Gayatri Devi, Lalique fountains and the latest sleek black marble bathrooms and bold geometric furniture were added.

Here the handsome, glamorous couple known to friends as Jai and Ayesha lived, ruled and played out a fairytale life, mixing medieval with thoroughly modern. The maharaja's water was brought in daily from a special well by four men and a soldier guard, yet the couple jetted about the world to New York, London and elsewhere. Jai died after a fall during a polo game at Cirencester in England in 1970.

Today the palace is a hotel, so the courtyards, public rooms and glorious gardens are easy to see (good shops; tea on the lawn a treat). And Madho Singh's polo grounds next door are also fun to visit if there is a game on or even a practice — the annual season is March. From here, you can look south to Moti Doongri, the fort, built like a Scottish castle, where the royal treasure was once stored (see Nahargarh Fort, page 156). You can then move west and see Jai and Ayesha's later home, the relatively modest **Raj Mahal Palace**, built at the British Residency and now, like the Rambagh, a hotel. Here they entertained Prince Philip, the Duke of Edinburgh, on his 1965 visit which coincided with the Hindu festival of Holi. His letter of thanks shows that the couple, although by then reduced to commoner status, could still entertain royally: 'Every moment was sheer joy and it's only the bruises from polo and the pink stain on my fingers which remain to convince me that the whole thing wasn't some marvellous dream.'

Block-printing and Paper-making in Sanganer

Sanganer lies 16 kilometres (ten miles) south of Jaipur. Approaching it over the Aman-i-Shah River, you can often see lengths of cloth drying in the sun on high wooden frames propped up on the left bank. Beside them, Radhamohan Udaiwal's dimly-lit block-printing workshops evoke the days when this was the metropolis of calico-printing.

In his first room, eye-smarting smoke billows up from the wood-fed fires heating huge copper vats of dye. Men stir and prod the soaking fabric, then heave it out to drain. Next door, mountains of cloth are rinsed, while in the bright courtyard lengths are stretched out for three days of natural sun-bleaching, helped by a soak in cowdung beforehand. The largest room is silent but for the thud of printing as several craftsmen speedily work down the long tables on which a whole length of cloth is pinned. Each puts his wooden block onto a dye-soaked pad and then with steady hand and keen eye prints square after square with remarkably accurate matching. Before the end is reached, the first yards are dry enough for another man to start printing the next colour on top — there may be six or seven colours in all. The blocks are stored in the basement, a hundred thousand of them neatly stacked on shelves by subject: flowers, gods, elephants, birds and floral borders.

It was the river's fixing powers that brought Sanganer its wealth, making fast the colours of the delicate flower and animal designs on the gathered Rajasthani skirts. Today, several thousand craftsmen work in the village. Many follow the traditional methods: the designer separates the colours onto tracing paper, the woodblock-cutter pricks each colour onto a block before precision-cutting it with hammer and chisel; and the printer prints the cloth. Others have capitulated to screen-printing which

One last trip makes a delightful end to a city day. Just outside town, on the road eastwards out of the Ghat Gate towards Agra, Jaipur's great architect is honoured with a little garden, **Vidhyadharji ka Bagh**, which is now sadly in need of some restoration. Almost opposite, **Sisodia Rana ka Bagh** is pristine perfect. This country palace was built by Jai Singh II for his Udaipur queen whom he married to cement a Rajput alliance. Large, chirpy, bright murals surround the exterior, lush terraced gardens overlook the open plains, and the watchman will unlock the palace to show you a hideaway home still full of royal atmosphere. Drive on behind the palace to the hillside **Hanuman Temple** dedicated to the monkey-god. It surges into life each day at 4 pm. Crowds of langur monkeys come to meet the priest who arrives in an auto-rickshaw with sacks of bananas which the animals grab greedily and then sit gobbling in mid-road. The keen can do a small hike from here, up to Galta's hilltop **Temple of the Sun God** — worth it for the views.

---

gives less character to the cloth but demands less skill and is 20 times as fast and therefore more profitable.

Chemicals have replaced both the soft natural dyes and the local waters in most workshops. But sometimes you can see a dye cauldron being brewed up. Faith Singh has helped sustain old ways. A talented British woman, she started her Jaipur shop Anokhi in 1971 and now exports worldwide and has 150 quality workers in Sanganer, Jaipur and Bagru (southwest of Jaipur). Of the 40,000 metres (44,000 yards) of fabric she has printed every month, a quarter is coloured with vegetable and mineral dyes. For black, she mixes molasses with iron from the disused horseshoes of *tonga* ponies. For red, there is alum (aluminium silicate); and blues are modified to subtle shades with turmeric and pomegranate skins. The dye is mixed with mud, lime, gum and wheat chaff and ground to a paste before being used to print.

Not far from Mr Udaiwal, up the main road and past J K Arts and Saadh (two shops stocking his prints), a right turn leads to another busy Sanganer workshop. This one makes paper, Sanganer's spin-off industry which uses cotton and silk off-cuts. Squares of rough pink and blue paper cover the green lawns. In the large, cool, surrounding rooms the fabric is churned and bleached to pulp in huge stone vats, then strained and sieved. Next, diluted to a slurry in a square tub, the pulp is stirred furiously before a wooden ladder and screen are deftly floated on top, whisked off and turned onto a muslin sheet. Like the weekly wash, these fragile wet sheets of paper are pegged up on lines to dry. To finish, they may be dyed, starched, trimmed and even gold-sprinkled like the exquisite album leaves that perfectly set off fine Mughal portraits and court scenes. For fabric and paper stockists, see page 49.

The Triangle on Wheels
Detours to Palaces, Parks and Villages

A day spent on the road, pausing to see a village or some wildlife, can be one of the most precious and memorable of a visit to India. For the country's magic is not restricted to its cities and monuments. Despite urbanization, the pulse is in the villages and the land, where the vast majority of Indians still live.

There is plenty to see: painted lorries and overloaded cars jostle for road space with camels hauling loads of wood, cartfuls of locals off to a wedding or festival, and door-to-door bicyclist salesmen with colourful plastic buckets and other household temptations. On the roadside, lapis-blue peacocks and apple-green parrots decorate the trees, children attend school beneath a shady tree, and boys play cricket on any available space. In the villages, men and women go about their traditional life: women sing as they draw water from the wells; roadside markets have piles of bananas, blood-red chillies and purple onions; little houses have dung pats drying on or around them, to be burnt as fuel; and men loll about on *charpoys* (string beds). In the fields, men work their bullocks and pump up irrigation water over carpets of yellow-flowering mustard seed.

There are good places to stop and explore. At Vrindaban, the tiny lanes are suffused in the atmosphere of the god Krishna. In Bharatpur bird sanctuary, birds from all over Asia and Europe gather on the lakes. And at Sariska or Ranthambore National Parks, you may be lucky and spot a tiger.

Each road connecting the cities has a distinct character. The Delhi–Agra road (197 kilometres/122 miles) is dotted with Mughal ruins. This is a stretch of the Grand Trunk Road which ran from east Bengal right across to the Indus. Sher Shah (see page 83) laid it out in the 16th century to improve communications and defence, lined it with shade-giving trees and equipped it with separate *serais* (rest-houses) for Hindus and Muslims. The Mughals, who made it part of the great Lahore–Agra road connecting their headquarters, improved it, as did the British. In 1663, François Bernier described it as having 'a double row of trees planted by order of Jehan-Guyre [Jahangir] ... with small pyramids, or turrets, every two miles or so. Wells are frequently met with, affording drink to travellers.'

The quieter Agra–Jaipur road (228 kilometres/142 miles) is best taken via Fatehpur Sikri for magical morning light, reaching Jaipur at the end of the day when it is drenched in a ruddy sunset glow. The Jaipur–Delhi road (259 kilometres/161 miles) thunders with lorries and is reputedly India's busiest stretch of highway. So, if you have time, it is best to leave it to enjoy the countryside, possibly stopping overnight to visit Sariska Park or Alwar.

It is an easy area to visit by road: the distances are not great by Indian standards and, for perfect overnight peace, several ex-maharajas' beautiful countryside palaces are now hotels (see pages 209 ff.). Here a few suggestions that merit a detour, and one or two that merit a trip out from Agra or Jaipur. For tips on trains, buses and car hire, see pages 32–4. It is wise to take a picnic and plenty to drink, ordered the night before from your hotel. It is also advisable to have a map; the Discover India map of Rajasthan includes Delhi and Agra.

Delhi—Agra

The monuments of south Delhi, such as the Qutb Minar complex and Tughluqabad, open at sunrise and may make convenient first stops.

State Boundaries Always some action here, where lorry and bus drivers patiently battle with bureaucracy to pass into first Haryana, then Uttar Pradesh.

Mughal Ruins Just after the milestone announcing Agra is 144 kilometres (90 miles) away, there is a beehive-shaped *kos* (milestone) in the field on the right, one of several along this road.

Kotwan On the right after the Uttar Pradesh border, Raja Batsu Singh's ruined palace sits on a hillock surrounded by a tiny, peaceful and typical Indian village — this is one of the nicest along this route. A little further on, the great battlements of Chhata Fort stand on the left.

Vrindaban One of a clutch of villages sacred to the mischievous blue-skinned god, Krishna. Others include Mahaban, where the young god was looked after by his foster-father, Nanda; Gokul, where he lived; Barsana, where his beloved Radha was born; and Goverdhan Hill, which Krishna balanced on one finger for a week as an umbrella for the cowherds while the god Indra's rainstorms poured down. Vrindaban, nearest to the main road, is full of life and interest. Walk through the tiny lanes to seek out Gobind Deo, Banki Behari and Krishna Behari temples; Vrindaban Garden where Krishna came daily from Gokul to dance with the gopis (milkmaids) and play his flute and where Radha still comes to sleep; and the Yamuna riverside tree Krishna climbed with the gopis' clothes while they were swimming. Vrindaban is a good place to be at Holi, Diwali or Janmashtami (see Festivals, page 187). A freelance guide may, for once, be useful.

Mathura Krishna's birthplace, and as such a pilgrimage centre since early times; later a thriving Buddhist centre (fifth century BC—AD sixth century); now a large, chaotic town. Two stops, not close together, are recommended. Mathura Museum's gallery around a central garden houses top-quality sculptures including ravishing ones of the Kushana period (fifth century BC). Down at the old town, a turn right at Tilak Dwar (Holy Gate) and a left down to Bhangali Ghat leads to the Yamuna; from here you can walk down the lanes to the river to find Sati Burj Tower, Vishram Ghat and Vishram Temple.

Wine, Women and Song

"Your majesty, there is nothing so beneficial as gambling. It develops an unexampled magnanimity, since you drop a pile of money like a straw. With its alternations of winning and losing, it liberates you from servile joy or despondency. It nourishes impetuosity, the basis of all manliness. It compels a continuous exercise of quick intelligence in detecting tricks (very difficult to perceive) with dice, sleight of hand, the board, and other equipment. Demanding exclusive attention, it gives superb training in mental concentration. It makes for delight in audacity, the companion of brisk resolution; for ability to hold one's own while rubbing up with the toughest customers; for the cultivation of self-reliance; for getting a living without stinginess.

"Or again, take the society of good-looking girls. That makes money and virtue worth having. That means genuine manly pride; skill in thought-reading; conduct untainted by sordid greed; training in all the social arts; quickness of wit and speech because you must be forever devising means to get what you lack, to keep what you get, to dream of what you enjoy, to pacify the peevish , and so on; public deference for your well-groomed person and stunning clothes; social acceptability; great respect from servants; smiling address; dignity; gallantry; the winning, through children, of salvation on earth and salvation in heaven.

"Then again, take alcohol. This fortifies the charm of youth through steady use of spirituous antidotes to numerous diseases. It neutralises all misfortunes by increasing self-esteem. It kindles sexual desire and improves the capacity for pleasure. It drowns the consciousness of sin, so counteracting morbidity. By removing the fetters of reticence, it conduces to mutual confidence. By repressing envy, it makes for pure joy. It encourages continual enjoyment of music and other sense-impressions; the acquisition of countless and varied friendships; unrivalled beauty of person; unparalleled graces; martial spirit, resulting from the loss of fear and depression."

Dandin, The Ten Princes, (circa 700 A.D.)
translated by A W Ryder

Trips out from Agra

In addition to the Krishna villages, trips to Fatehpur Sikri, Bharatpur and Deeg — all towards Jaipur — make good outings. But here is one very special trip down into Madhya Pradesh state, to Gwalior, Datia and Orchha. It is best taken with two overnight stops, at Gwalior and Orchha.

Gwalior fulfills the romantic maharaja image even today. Its hilltop fort, built by the Tomar chief Man Singh (ruled 1486–1517), is perhaps the best of its kind, surpassing Amber, with precision-cut animal carving and glittering tiles. Its grossly extravagant Jai Vilas town palace (1872–4), built by Maharaja Jayaji Rao, and now partly open to the public, is where in 1987 the family daughter married the eldest son of the ex-Maharaja of Kashmir, watched by more than a hundred ex-maharajas, in a sensational (and controversial) revival of royal panoply. In the unspoilt, provincial town lurk the tombs of Tansen (Akbar's musician) and Muhammed Ghaus (Akbar's spiritual guru), the richly-carved royal mausolea, and the town's local steam train built by Jayaji Rao (well worth a ride).

Then, to **Datia** and Orchha, where remarkable palaces were built by Raja Bir Singh Deo, the Rajput ruler who was a partner in crime with the rebellious Prince Salim before he became Emperor Jahangir (see page 107). Datia's seven-storey palace with stone elephants poking out at the top is surrounded by quiet village lanes. It gets better and better as you climb up, with fine jali work, perfect pavilions and surviving ceiling paintings (the curator lives next to the great entrance). **Orchha** has three palaces built on an island in the Betwa River: one built for Jahangir (worth scrambling up and around the roofs); one whose rooms are coated in brightly coloured murals including one of the raja out hunting; and one to stay in. In the rest of this perfect, forgotten medieval city, find more paintings in Lakshmi Narayan Temple, explore the chhatris and other deserted buildings, and enjoy the sunset from the far side of the Betwa.

Agra–Jaipur

Worth leaving early to enjoy the soft morning light and peace at Fatehpur Sikri. Continuing to Bharatpur, do not miss the fine views back to Fatehpur's walls. Soon after, the pink posts announce the Rajasthan state border.

Keoladeo National Park, Bharatpur One of world's most important bird sanctuaries. Originally a freshwater swamp, this was where the Maharaja of Bharatpur dug out the lake and, from 1902, entertained the British to splendid duck shoots. Today, a sunrise trip on the lake is magical, silent but for the flutter of waking Chinese coots, large painted storks and some of the other 350 species of visiting birds — sharp eyes may espy the rare Siberian crane between November and March. Antelopes, fishing cats and porcupines live in the surrounding park, where pythons sunbathe in the noonday sun. The information centre has a big wall-plan, lists of wildlife to spot and excellent ornithologists to hire as guides (their acute observation transforms a visit). To see the park, either take the dawn boat onto the lake, hire a bicycle rickshaw (with bicyclist) to go up the paths between the water, hire a bicycle, or take a picnic and follow the trails. Best months November–January (October and February are also good); bring binoculars (none for hire), hat, walking shoes and bird books (see page 186); well worth staying overnight for evening animal and morning bird sightings and to see Stanley and Belinda Breedan's film shown 6.30 most evenings at Shanti Kutir Rest House (which is also the nicest place to stay inside the sanctuary).

Bharatpur The walled Jat stronghold retains a certain decayed splendour at its 18th-century Lohargarh Fort where one of the three palaces is now a museum. Good for spotting sculptures and rulers' nicknacks as you ramble up and down steps to the various rooftops and peer down into courtyards where locals inhabit apartments once occupied by princesses. If you are staying at Golbargh Palace, once a royal guest-house, Mr Cheema may take you to another one at Baretha (25 kilometres/16 miles south).

Deeg The Bharatpur maharajas came to this glorious palace (1750) for the summer, enjoying the cool air of the tanks either side. Their magnificent apartments, still partly furnished and partly frescoed, overlook sunken water-gardens where 500 fountains would splash coloured water during royal fireworks displays. Visitors feel they are nosing around a still-used home. An excellent guidebook, available on site, describes every room.

Trips out from Jaipur

As well as the detours off the Delhi road, here are three trips in other directions. For Sanganer, see page 172.

Samode The keen can abandon cars for camels for part of this short trip (42 kilometres/26 miles from Jaipur) to a tiny rural village where Jai Singh's finance minister built a palace which nestles in the hills beneath the older cliff-top fort. The giveaway on the simple exterior is the grand staircase. It leads up to rooms decorated with large murals, fine mirror work and quantities of gilding; and as it is a hotel, you can also stay here.

Ajmer This city is 138 kilometres (84 miles) southwest of Jaipur. The shrine of Sufi saint Khwaja Muin-ud-din Chishti is as sacred to Muslims now as when Akbar first visited it (see page 131). Tiny streets lined with kiosks selling lace caps, flowers and sacred texts lead to the holy complex where emperors from Humayun to Aurangzeb added the buildings. Rich pilgrims pay for sweet rice to be cooked up in vast iron cauldrons for the poor, qawwalis are sung in the hall and pilgrims flock daily to worship under the colourful awnings around the tomb. See also the Adhai-Din-Jhopra (Hut of Two-and-a-Half Days), a mosque which incorporates fabulous carvings from Hindu temples and a Sanskrit college; Akbar's palace; and the hilltop Taragarh (star) Fort for views. Outside the city, the man-made Ana Sagar Lake has pretty pavilions, ghats and temples along the west side. Nearby Pushkar is where the annual camel fair is held. For a countryside overnight stop on the way back to Jaipur, stay at Kishangarh Palace-hotel (Ajmer and Pushkar accommodation breeds complaints).

Bundi and Kota A long trip south but worth it for two truly magnificent palaces. In 1579 Rao Ratan Singh of Bundi gave his son, Madho Singh, the tiny principality of Kota. Both flourished. Bundi's Taragarh (1372 onwards) Fort-palace coated with murals (1744–71) sprawls over the hillside above the narrow lanes and blue houses of its town, a delightful time-warp even today. Kota's palace, found through the extravagant elephant gate, has equally wonderful murals (ask to see the locked room which is covered in them). The road down to these treats passes hilltop forts near Chatsu and Nawai and brushes past Tonk, worth stopping at to see Sunehri Kothi (golden mansion). Best to stay overnight (or longer) at the riverside Brijraj Bhawan Palace, so there is also time to visit Sir Swinton Jacob's Umed Bhawan (soon to be another hotel), the royal tombs and nearby Mandalgarh Fort.

Ranthambore Tiger Reserve If seeing a tiger is going to complete a trip to India, here is your best chance. The 400 square kilometres (154 square miles) of deciduous forest rambling over the Aravalli and Vindhyan hills is a perfect habitat for tigers, which have multiplied since Project Tiger was launched in 1973 by the Government of India and the World Wildlife Fund. Ranthambore Fort and the Jaipur maharajas' pavilions add romance to the setting (the Maharaja's Lodge has re-opened, see page 214). Essential to stay overnight, preferably longer, and equally essential to arrive with a firm booking (made in Jaipur) for the small government lodge; unprepared visitors have to sleep in their cars.

Jaipur—Delhi

If you pound up the main highway, there is not much to see. But by turning right just after Shahpura there is a pretty, quiet road which goes through the undulating countryside of Sariska Park, past Siliserh Lake, through Alwar town and then up via Tijara to rejoin the main Delhi road.

Sariska National Park Like Ranthambore, this is a Project Tiger reserve; but it is less compact, set in 800 square kilometres (309 square miles) of the Aravalli Hills which takes in local villages, roads, temples and Kankwari Fort. Where the Alwar maharajas would have gone on hunts mounted on trained elephants, today's visitors go by Jeep with a guide to try their luck at glimpsing one of about 50 tigers at dawn, dusk or during the night from a *machan* (hide). Other animals range from leopard and sloth bear to caracal and wild dog; and there is usually a good variety of birds. Essential to book in writing (mentioning the machan and guide if wanted); best to stay at least two nights (choice of one palace, a tourist lodge and a forest rest-house) and to bring binoculars and a sleeping bag if staying out in a machan.

Alwar Past Siliserh Lake and its overlooking palace-hotel, Alwar is the next stop. Alwar state separated from Jaipur only in 1776, but its capital soon had a cluster of palace buildings at the foot of a huge hilltop fort. Vinai Vilas (1840), the great City Palace, is now filled with bureaucrats and all sorts, conjuring up the sense of a bustling prince's household when the rulers were living at their most extravagant (the stables held 3,000 horses). The top floor is a wonderful museum housing royal treasures and nicknacks, including some good miniatures, musical instruments, and items displaying Raj loyalty. Also worth seeking out are the Musi Maharanai ki Chhatri (mausolea), the mini Simla in Company Bargh, the 16th-century Mughal tomb of Fateh Jung and beautiful Vijay Mandir where the late maharaja lived (permission to visit obtained can be from his son's on-site secretary). To visit the hilltop fort, seek permission (usually given instantly) from the Superintendent of Police at the City Palace, then hire a Jeep and driver and set off by noon (taking a picnic), to return by 5 pm.

Dynastic Chart

The Delhi Sultanate 1206−1526

Slave Sultans	1206−90
Khalji Sultans	1290−1320
Tughluq Sultans	1320−1413
Sayyid Sultans	1414−51
Lodi Sultans	1451−1526

Emperors of the Mughal Empire 1526−1858 (the six Great Mughals are Babur to Aurangzeb)

Rulers of Amber, then Jaipur

Babur, lived 1483−1530, reigned 1526−30	Bihar Mal, ruled c 1548−74
Humayun, lived 1508−56, reigned 1530−40 (deposed), then 1555−6	Bhagwan Das, ruled 1574−89
	Man Singh, ruled 1589−1614
Akbar, lived 1542−1605, reigned 1556−1605	Bhau Singh, ruled 1614−21
Jahangir, lived 1569−1627, reigned 1605−27	Jai Singh I, ruled 1621−67
Shah Jahan, lived 1592−1666, reigned 1627−58 (deposed)	Ram Singh I, ruled 1667−88
Aurangzeb, lived 1618−1707, reigned 1658−1707	Bishan Singh, ruled 1688−99
Bahadur Shah I, reigned 1707−12	Jai Singh II, ruled 1699−1743
Jahandar Shah, reigned 1712−13 (killed)	Ishvari Singh, ruled 1743−50
Farrukh-siyar, reigned 1713−19 (murdered)	Madho Singh I, ruled 1750−68
Muhammad Shah, reigned 1719−48	Prithvi Singh, ruled 1768−78
Ahmad Shah, reigned 1748−54 (deposed)	Pratap Singh, ruled 1778−1803
Alamgir II, reigned 1754−9 (killed)	Jagat Singh, ruled 1803−19
Shah Alam II, reigned 1759−1806 (blinded 1788)	Jai Singh III, ruled 1820−35
Akbar Shah II, reigned 1806−37	Ram Singh II, ruled 1835−80

Bahadur Shah II, reigned 1837−58
(deposed, died in Burma 1862)

Madho Singh II, ruled 1880−1922
Man Singh II, ruled 1922−49
(position abolished, died 1970)

Prime ministers of India

Jawaharlal Nehru	August 1947−May 1964
Lal Bahadur Shastri	June 1964−January 1966
Indira Gandhi	January 1964−March 1977 (Emergency 1975−7)
Morarji Desai	March 1977−July 1979
Charan Singh	July 1979−January 1980
Indira Gandhi	January 1980−31 October 1984 (assassinated)
Rajiv Gandhi	October 1984–December 1989
Vishwanath Pratap Singh	December 1989—November 1990
Chandra Shekhar	November 1990—present

Recommended Reading

Here is a springboard of good reads focusing on the Golden Triangle. Books From India, 45 Museum Street, London WC1, probably has the largest stock of books about India kept outside of India; for bookshops in India see page 218.

General History and Culture
Good overviews are F Watson's *A Concise History of India* (London 1974) and P Spear and R Thapar's two-volume *A History of India* (London 1978), all in paperback. *The Cambridge History of India, vols I-VI*; Volume IV is on the Mughals—Cambridge's new 30-volume *History of India* is currently emerging, each volume thematic rather than chronological, eg C A Bayly's *Indian Society and the Making of the British Empire* (1987). For a well-illustrated Mughal introduction, read B Gascoigne's *The Great Moghuls* (London 1979); for Delhi, R E Frykenberg's *Delhi through the Ages* (New Delhi 1986); and for Jaipur, Q Crewe's *The Last Maharaja: A Biography of Sawai Man Singh II* (London 1985). M Brand and G D Lowry's *Akbar's India: Art from the Mughal City of Victory* (New York 1985) probes into Mughal culture, while N Patnaik's *A Second Paradise: Indian courtly life 1590-1947* (New York 1985), and C Allen and S Dwivedi's *Lives of the Indian Princes* (London 1985) celebrate exotic court life in general. P Mason's *The Men who Ruled India* chronicles Britain's role; M K Gandhi's *An Autobiography* (Ahmedabad 1927, reprinted 1982), J Nehru's *An Autobiography* (New Delhi 1936, paperback 1980) and M J Akbar's *Nehru The Making of India* (London 1989) provide background for India's struggle for independence; and M Tully's *From Raj to Rajiv* (London 1987) charts India's story since independence. The monthly *India Magazine*, published in Delhi, covers all aspects of Indian culture.

Religion
The Hindu epics touch every part of daily life. But their tales of heroic gods with several forms and names apiece are confusing. R K Narayan's *The Mahabharata* (London 1978) and S R Rao's delightfully illustrated *The Mahabharata* (Hyderabad 1985) and *The Ramayana* (Hyderabad 1988) provide plot and personality outlines. C Rajagopalachari wrote the clear paperback editions of *Ramayana* and *Mahabharata* (Bombay 1978 and 1979). And the strip-cartoon comics telling separate episodes are sold on news-stands in India.

Art
S C Welch's *India: Art and Culture 1300-1900* (New York 1985, available in paperback) is a mammoth tome crammed with illustrations and information on

all visual arts. While G Michell and Linda Leach's *In the Image of Man* (London 1982), is good on painting and sculpture. P Chandra's *The Scultpure of India 3000 BC–AD 1300* (Washington 1985) and A G Mitchell's *Little Hindu Gods and Goddesses* (London 1982), based on Victoria and Albert Museum pieces, both cover sculpture. For every-day art, *Aditi* (New Delhi 1982, available at the Crafts Museum, Delhi), and A Nath and F Wacziarg's *Arts and Crafts of Rajasthan* (Ahmedabad and New York 1987) are useful.

Architecture
The magnificence of Indian building has at long last received thorough attention in the new *Penguin Guide to the Monuments of India*, volume 1 on Hindu and Buddhist buildings by G Michell, *Volume II on Islamic, Rajput and British building* by P Davies (London 1989). Others to seek out: C Tadgell's lavish *The History of Architecture in India* (London 1990); P Brown's *Indian architecture,* vols I & II (Bombay 1942, later reprints);

Y D Sharma's *Delhi and its Neighbourhood* (New Delhi 1982), a paperback published by the Archaeological Survey of India; and Louise Nicholson's *The Red Fort, Delhi* (London 1989). On British Building P Davies's *Splendours of the Raj : British Architecture in India 1660-1947* (London, 1985), and R G Irving's *Indian Summer, Lutyens, Baker and Imperial Delhi* (New Haven and London 1981).

Photographic Books
R Rai's *Taj* (Singapore 1986, available worldwide) has stunning photographs; *Henri Cartier-Bresson in India* (London 1987) contains the observations of six trips, 1947–86; Jean-Louis Nou's photos with Indira Gandhi's text make up *Eternal India* (New Delhi 1980); and B Lloyd's *The Colour of India* (London 1988) is just that. R Rai and K Singh's *Delhi, A Portrait* (New Delhi 1983).

Wildlife
For birds, two useful books are S Ali's *The Book of Indian Birds* (Bombay 1979) and M Woodcock's *Collins Handguide to the Birds of the Indian Sub-Continent* (London 1980). For wildlife, T Sinclair's *Indian Wildlife* (Singapore 1987) is excellent. K Singh's delightful *Nature Watch* opens visitors' eyes to Delhi's birds and trees.

Personal Views, Travel Writing and Novels
A copy of Babur's illustrated *Baburnama* is in the National Museum, Delhi, some of it published as M S Randhawa's *Paintings of the Baburnama* (New Delhi 1983), available at the museum; and some of Akbar's diary kept in the Victoria and Albert Museum, London, is published in G Sen's *Paintings from the Akbarnama* (Varanasi 1984). Two good anthologies of writing through the centuries, including the emperor's diaries, are M Alexander's *Delhi & Agra, a traveller'' companion* (London 1987) and H K Kaul's Historic Delhi, *An Anthology* (New Delhi 1985). M M Kaye has edited an illustrated Victorian diary of Delhi life by Emily Metcalfe, *The Golden Calm* (London 1980) and written her own autobiography, *The Sun in the Morning* (London 1990). More contemporary accounts are provided by J Nehru's *Discovery of India* (Bombay 1946, London 1947) and G Devi and S R Rau's *A Princess Remembers, The Memoirs of the Maharani of Jaipur* (London 1976), both Indian views; and T Fishlock's *India File: Inside the Subcontinent* (London 1983) and J Keay's *Into India* (London 1973), two British views. Also recommended are S Rushdies's *Midnight's Children* (London 1981), V T Vittachi's *The Brown Sahib Revisted* (New Delhi 1987), V S Naipaul's *India: A Million Mutinies Now* (London 1990). Novelists who portray Indian life with acute observation include R K Narayan and Anita Desai.

Practical Information

Major Festivals and Holidays

Indians celebrate with gaiety and gusto. Happiness is to cry out 'What a tamasha!' — what a to-do! A festival, like a train ride, is part of a visit to India and quite easy to find. The major Hindu festivals have local variations in each town. Their dates, although keeping to roughly regular times, are fixed each year according to the lunar calendar. The dates of Muslim festivals move right around the year. Government of India Tourist Offices have the latest list of festivals; local tourist offices will advise on how best to enjoy them and will know the extent and duration of any related public holiday. In addition, a string of cultural festivals keeps Delhi sparkling throughout the winter; for these and other events in the capital, check through *City Scan* magazine, *Delhi Diary* (free from hotel bell captains) and the newspapers.

National Festivals

Republic Day: 26 January Commemorates the inauguration of the Republic of India in 1950. Best in Delhi, the capital. Lutyens's Raj Path is the stage and Rastrapati Bhavan the backdrop for splendid parades of elaborately decorated floats, dancers, camels, elephants and the armed forces. Rastrapati Bhavan is outlined in fairy lights . ll week (best views from the Taj Mahal Hotel rooftop restaurant). Every moment is televised.

   Beating Retreat: 29 January, Delhi Utterly magical and worth standing for. Camels stand on the walls of North and South Blocks silhouetted against Rastrapati Bhavan and the sinking sun while the massed bands of the armed forces parade up and down the lower slopes of Raisina Hill from Vijay Chowk. Twilight approaches to the music of Gandhi's favourite hymn 'Abide With Me', the drummers' call, haunting bugle sounds from a high pavilion and a burst of fireworks. The bands retreat to 'Sare Janan Se Achha', a poem by Iqbal set to military music.

   Independence Day: 15 August Best in Delhi, where at midnight on 14−15 August 1947 Lord Louis Mountbatten made the official transfer of power to India's first Prime Minister, Jawaharlal Nehru, at Rastrapati Bhavan. On this day the building is outlined in fairy lights, while the Prime Minister delivers an address from the Red Fort ramparts.

   Gandhi Jayanti: 2 October Mahatma Gandhi's birthday is celebrated throughout India but especially in Delhi at the Gandhi Memorial Museum and at Birla House where he was assassinated.

   Children's Day: 14 November The birthday of India's first Prime Minister, Jawaharlal Nehru, is celebrated throughout India and especially in the capital at the Nehru Museum and at India Gate.

Art, Cultural and Social Festivals

International Film Festival: January Held in Delhi on odd years (1989, etc.), another Indian city on evens.

Kite Festival: 14 January On this day brightly coloured paper kites made in city backstreets flutter beautifully like giant confetti; by sunset, many are trapped in tree branches.

Crafts Mela: February, Delhi Beside the waters of South Delhi's Surajkund — a vast, circular, stepped pool built in the tenth century — craftsmen from all over India demonstrate their skills for a fortnight and have plenty of finished goods to sell. Worth stopping to see Tughluqabad Fort on the way.

Tansen Music Festival: February, Delhi Named after the musician Tansen, Akbar's court composer from 1562. Tansen elaborated the stately *dhrupad* form of Hindustani classical vocal and instrumental music and also developed the simpler Gwalior *gharana*, a form of singing easier on Western ears.

Dhrupad Music Festival: February, Delhi A chance to hear strictly classical, orthodox music.

Maharaj Kalka Bindadi Kathak Mahotsave: February, Delhi Performances of the refined, classical *kathak* dance of north India that was developed in the Mughal court and tells stories with a feat of mime and fast footwork dancing.

The Delhi Flower Show: February–March, Delhi Held at Pragati Maidan with the Purana Qila as backdrop.

All India Rose Show: March, Delhi Organized by the Rose Society of India at Pragati Maidan. Rose-growing in India is as serious as in Britain. Some roses are indigenous to north India. It was the Mughals who made rose cultivation popular, a pursuit continued by the British.

Pushkar Cattle Fair: November–December, near Ajmer Ten days of hard desert trading by tribes and dealers who barter cattle, camels, goats, sheep, cloth, jewellery and more, running camel races to show off their wares. Beware: all prices are high and accommodation needs careful planning.

Hindu Festivals

Shivarati: February–March A day of fasting dedicated to Shiva includes processions, mantra chanting and *lingam* anointing at Shiva temples throughout India.

Holi: February–March The arrival of spring is celebrated across northern India but particularly in Rajasthan and the Krishna villages north of Agra. On the eve of Holi, bonfires of unwanted possessions symbolize the destruction of the demon Holika by the infant Krishna and also the death of winter ready for spring rebirth. On a perfect Holi, social conventions are suspended until noon while men and women flirt, shower each other with pink powder and water, and sing and dance in the streets to the beat of the big *chang* drum. But the drinking and merriment can be overpowering for visitors, if not downright aggressive; so beware how and where you play Holi. In Jaipur, the ex-maharaja plays Holi in the City Palace and is likely to put in a public appearance around the city. In Vrindaban and the other villages sacred to Krishna, Holi is very special: a fortnight of Krishna plays precedes Holi, the pink water is coloured with roses and not chemicals, cows are dressed up, the faithful plunge in the Yamuna and women take a turn at chasing their men.

Gangaur: March−April, Jaipur Incantations for marital bliss continue for 16 days after Holi; women, dressed in best saris, chant special songs to painted wooden images of Gauri (another name for Parvati, Shiva's wife), goddess of fertility. On the 17th day, the image of Gauri is processed from the City Palace accompanied by drummers, dancers and gaily caparisoned elephants and camels.

Elephant Festival: March−April, Jaipur To honour Ganesh, the elephant-headed son of Shiva and Parvati, a magnificent procession of elephants moves through Jaipur to Chaughan Stadium where the animals play polo and Holi.

Ramanavami: March−April The birth of the god Rama, hero of the epic *Ramayana*, is celebrated in temples by all devotees.

Teej: July−August, Jaipur Women dressed in striped green veils sing, dance and play on swings suspended from trees to welcome the monsoon and to venerate the goddess Parvati in hopes of her gift of marital bliss. The festival marks the occasion when Parvati and Shiva were reunited after separation. In Jaipur, caparisoned elephants escort Parvati's image from her parents' home to her husband's.

Sawan: July−August, Agra Celebrations honouring Shiva in various areas of the town focus on the four Shiva temples on successive Mondays. Kailash Fair follows, held 12 kilometres (seven miles) outside Agra at a temple built where Shiva is believed to have appeared in the form of a stone lingam.

Raksha Bandhan: July−August Across northern India, girls tie tinsel and silk amulets known as *rakhi* around men's wrists to commemorate the god Indra's battle triumph after his wife gave him a rakhi.

Janmashtami: August−September This is Krishna's birthday, celebrated with *ras lila* dances in many Krishna temples, especially in the Krishna villages (see Holi, above).

Dussehra: September−October A major all-India festival celebrating the god Rama's victory over the demon Ravana who had captured his wife Sita. Especially colourful in Delhi where it is known as Ram Lila (Rama play). Ten days of dance, theatre and music programmes in cultural halls, and processions in Old Delhi are inspired by the *Ramayana* epic. The festival ends with a fair, a massive fireworks display and the burning of huge coloured effigies of wicked Ravana, all on Ram Lila Maidan between Old and New Delhi. In Agra, Dussehra includes the Rambarat sunset-to-sunrise procession through the city, when thousands join the caparisoned elephants, camels and cartloads of dressed-up Ramas and Sitas, ending at the special grounds in front of the Fort. In Jaipur, there are plays, processions and fireworks with effigies.

Karwa Chauth: October, Delhi To honour their mothers-in-law, women fast for a day, dress up in their best saris and make offerings to their husbands' mothers.

Diwali: October—November A major north India festival, known as the festival of lights and celebrating two events: Rama's return north with Sita; and the welcome of Lakshmi, goddess of good fortune and wealth, into every home at the start of the Hindu financial new year (official New Year is 13 April, a public holiday). Friends and relatives visit newly spring-cleaned homes bearing gifts of sweetmeats. There is much gambling; those who win will have Lakshmi's luck for the coming year. In the evening everyone lights tiny oil lamps or candles in rows along the walls of gardens, roofs and balconies to show Rama and Sita the way home, while fireworks fill the skies. The family atmosphere is like Christmas. In Jaipur, women also wear black veils edged with gold tinsel and celebrate for five days, ending by putting the red tikka mark on their brothers' foreheads.

Muslim Festivals

These are best seen in the Old Delhi and Nizamuddin areas of Delhi, in the old streets around Agra's Jama Masjid and at Ajmer, three hours' drive west of Jaipur.

Ramadan For the 30 days of the ninth month of the Muslim calendar, all the faithful over 12 years old fast between dawn and sunset, pray five times daily and attend *tarawih* (congregational prayers). The 27th night is called Lailat-ul-Kadr (night of power), when the Qur'an came down from heaven.

Id-ul-Fitr Celebrates the end of Ramadan, when the new moon is seen; a climax of gourmandising and merriment.

Id-ul-Zuhar Abraham's attempted sacrifice of Ishmael is remembered with prayers and presents for children.

Muharram A ten-day-long mourning period for the murder in AD 680 of Imam Hussain, the Prophet Mohammad's grandson. Drummers and mourning men parade giant *tazias* (tinsel, brass or silver replicas of Hussain's tomb); *ulema* (religious scholars) give readings in mosques; there are passion plays and men lash themselves in sorrow.

Urs The Ajmer Urs celebrates the death anniversary of the Sufi saint Khwaja Muin-ud-din Chishti with six days of music, fairs and night-long qawwali singing. The two Nizamuddin Urs celebrate the death anniversary of another Sufi saint and the poet Amir Khusrau (see page 203) with poetry readings and all-night qawwali singing.

Other Religions

Mahavir Jayanti: March—April Jains celebrate the birth of Mahavira, the 24th and last Tirthankara (teacher) who lived in the sixth century BC.

Buddha Purnima: May—June Buddhists celebrate the Buddha's birth, enlightenment and achievement of nirvana on one day, even though the events happened in different years.

Pateti: August Parsis celebrate their migration from Persia, although one sect does so a month earlier.

Nanak Jayanti: November Sikhs celebrate the birthday of Guru Nanak, founder of their religion, with prayers and processions, best seen along Chandni Chowk in Old Delhi.

Christmas: 25 December Christians celebrate Christ's birth.

Hindi Survival Vocabulary

English is widely used by Indians working in the tourist, hotel and commercial worlds. It is also the language of communication between two Indians of different mother tongues. However, a few Hindi words may be useful in markets or while travelling. Here is a minimum survival kit.

Basics

hello, goodbye, good-day (spoken hands together, fingers up)	*namaste*
yes/no	*han/nahin*
please	*meharbani se, kripaya*
thank you	*shukriya, dhanyawad*
OK, good	*atcha*
correct, genuine	*pucka*
bad	*kharab*
hot/cold	*garam/thanda*

Numbers

1 *ek*; 2 *do*; 3 *tin*; 4 *char*; 5 *panch*; 6 *chhe*; 7 *sat*; 8 *ath*; 9 *nau*; 10 *das*; 100 *sau*; 1,000 *hazar*; 100,000 *lakh* (written 1,00,000); 10,000,000 *crore* (written 1,00,00,000).

Getting Around

where is (the tourist office)?	*(turist afis) kahan hia?*
how far is?	*kitne dur hai?*
how much?/too much	*kitne paise?/bahut zyada hai*
what is this?/what is that?	*yeh kya hai?/who kya hai?*
what is your name?	*apka shubh nam?*
what is the time?	*kya baja hai?*
today	*aaj*
let's go, hurry up/stop	*chalo/ruko*
left/right	*baya/dhaina*
straight ahead	*seedha*
big/small	*bara/chota*
festival, fair	*utsav, mela*
road/alley	*marg/gulli*
market place	*chowk*
large lake/artificial lake	*sagar/tank*
gate	*pol, darwaza*
garden/gardener	*bagh/mali*
palace	*mahal*

The Right Man for the Job

'*I am sure you will never guess what my duties are.*'

He was middle-aged, thin, sharp-featured, with spectacles. His eyes were running and there was a drop of moisture on the tip of his nose. It was a winter's morning and our second-class railway compartment was unheated.

'*I will give you a little assistance. I work for the Railways. This is my pass. Have you ever seen one?*'

'*You are a ticket inspector!*'

A smile revealed his missing teeth. 'No, no, my dear sir. They wear a uniform.'

'*You are from the Police.*'

His smile cracked into a wet laugh. 'I see that you will never guess. Well, I will tell you. I am an Inspector of Forms and Stationery, Northern Railway.'

'*Forms and stationery!*'

'*Indeed. I travel about, night and day, winter and summer, from railway station to railway station, inspecting forms and stationery.*'

'*But how did this begin, Mr Inspector?*'

'*Why do you ask, sir? My life has been a failure.*'

'*Please don't say that, Mr Inspector.*'

'*I might have done so much better, sir. You have no doubt observed my English. My teacher was Mr Harding. I was a Bachelor of Arts, you know. When I joined the Service I expected to go far. I was put in Stores. In those days I would take down bundles of forms and stationery from the shelves and hand them to the porter. This was, of course, after the indents had been approved.*'

'*Of course.*'

'*From Stores to the office: it was a slow business. Steady. But slow. Somehow I managed. I have remained in Forms and Stationery all my life. I have kept my family. I have given the boys an education. I have married my daughter. One son is in the army and the other is in the air force, an officer.*'

'But, Mr Inspector, this is a success story.'

'O sir, do not mock me. It has been a wasted life.'

'Tell me more about your job, Mr Inspector.'

'Secrets, you are after my secrets. Well, I will explain. Let me show you, first of all, an indent.'

'It's like a little book, Mr Inspector. Sixteen pages.'

'It goes to the head of a stationmaster sometimes. Once a year these indents are sent out to our stationmasters. They prepare their indents and submit three copies. What you see now, by the way, is an elementary type of indent. There are others.'

'And when the indents are submitted—'

'Then they come to me, you see. And I pay my little visits. I get off at the station like any other passenger. It sometimes happens that I am insulted by the very stationmaster whose indents I have come to prune. Then I declare myself.'

'You are a wicked man, Mr Inspector.'

'Do you think so, sir? An Inspector of Forms and Stationery gets to know his stationmasters. They show themselves in their indents. You get to recognize them. This might interest you. It was yesterday's work.'

The indent, filled in in black, was heavily annotated in red.

'Turn to page twelve. Do you see? A hundred note-pads were what he required'.

'Goodness! You've only given him two.'

'He has six children, all of school age. Ninety-eight of those pads were for those six children. An Inspector of Forms and Stationery gets to know these things. Well, here we are. I shall get off here. I believe I am going to enjoy myself today. I wish I had the time to show you what he has indented for.'

'I met one of your Inspectors of Forms and Stationery the other day.

'You met what?'

'One of your Inspectors of Forms and Stationery.'

'There are no such people.'

'I didn't dream this man up. He had his indents and everything.'

It was a good word to use.

'It just goes to show. You can work for the Railways for years and not know a thing about it.'

V S Naipaul, An Area of Darkness

big building, big house	*bhavan*
mosque (Friday Mosque)	*masjid*
(Jama Masjid) temple	*mandir*
sandals	*chappals*
ruler	*raja*
master, term of respect	*sahib*
mistress, term of respect	*memsahib*
tip, gift to beggar, bribe	*baksheesh*

Drink and Food

food	*khana*
water	*pani*
ice	*baraf*
tea	*chai*
coffee	*kafi*
sugar	*chini*
milk	*dudh*
yoghurt drink	*lassi*
yoghurt	*dahi*
egg	*anda*
fruit (banana, lime)	*phal (kela, nimbu)*
vegetable	*sabzi*
rice	*chawal*
pulse (lentil, split pea, etc.)	*dhal*

Glossary

Here is a handful of gods, terms and words you are likely to encounter in this area of India. Among the vast plethora of Hindu gods, only the most common are included, together with the principal Hindu texts. The English words are included because they have unfamiliar meanings in India.

ahimsa non-violence, reverence for life

apsaras beautiful nymphs who are consorts to the gods and seduce men

ashram spiritual retreat, centre for yoga and meditation

bagh garden; a char-bagh (four-garden) is the formal geometric Persian garden layout introduced into India by Babur

Bhagavata Purana epic Hindu chronicle of Vishnu and his incarnations which include Krishna, the eighth incarnation

Bhagavad Gita Song of the Lord, the section of the epic *Mahabharata* where Krishna reveals himself as god incarnate and expounds on the human struggle for light and love

Brahma Creator of the universe; head of the Trimurti (the Hindu Trinity) of Brahma, Vishnu and Shiva. Saraswati is his daughter or consort; Hamsa the goose is his vehicle. The lotus that sprang from Vishnu's navel to give birth to Brahma is a popular symbol in Hindu art and architecture.

Brahmin highest of the four Hindu castes; see caste

Buddha The Enlightened One, from buddhi (intellect); see also page 23

cantonment military and administrative area of a town, built and used by the British during the Raj

caste one of four stations of life into which a Hindu is born — Brahmins (priests and religious teachers); Kshatriyas (kings, warriors, aristocrats); Vaisyas (traders, merchants, professionals), and Shudras (cultivators, servants, etc.), called Untouchables until Gandhi coined the name 'Harijan'

chaukidar doorman, watchman

chhatri mausoleum, tomb, cenotaph

dargah shrine or burial place of a Muslim saint

Diwan-i-Am public audience hall

Diwan-i-Khas private audience hall

durbar court audience or government meeting

emporium shop, often large and selling local crafts

fakir Muslim holy man who has taken the vow of poverty; also applied to Hindu ascetics such as *sadhus*

Ganesh elephant-headed god of learning and good fortune, son of Shiva and Parvati; also called Ganapati; his vehicle is a rat

Ganga sacred river of the Hindus, rising near Gangotri, up in the Himalayas, and flowing 2,500 kilometres (1,554 miles) across the northeast plains of India to empty into the Bay of Bengal. Named after the goddess whose waters trickled down through the god Shiva's tousled hair over the great souls of the world, freeing them to go to heaven.

ghat steps down to a river or lake
ghazel light Urdu song, often with a sad love theme
godown warehouse
gurdwara Sikh temple
guru spiritual teacher, holy man; his pupil is a *chela*; the audience he gives is a *darshan*; 'export' guru is the nickname for a guru whose following is mainly Westerners
hamam bath-house
Hanuman the monkey god; Rama's ally in defeating Ravana in the epic *Ramayana*
Harijan Children of God, the word coined by Mahatma Gandhi to replace the term 'Untouchables' for the lowest Hindu caste
haveli courtyard town house
hookah hubble-bubble pipe which cools the tobacco smoke by passing it through water
howdah elaborate seat on top of an elephant
imam Muslim leader; an *imambara* is the tomb of a Shi'ite Muslim holy man
Indra god of rain and thunder
jali carved and pierced stone or marble screens
kama desire, physical love, worldly pleasure; one of the four goals of life in Hindu philosophy; Kama is the god of love
karma the Hindu idea that good and bad deeds in previous existences dictate the pleasant or unpleasant form of man's current and future incarnations
kathak classical dance of northern India using dance and mime to tell stories (*kathas*)
Krishna the blue-skinned god in human form, worshipped in his own right or as the eighth incarnation of Vishnu; protagonist of the Bhagavad Gita; consort and love of the gopi (milkmaid) Radha
Lakshmi or Laxmi goddess of wealth and good fortune, consort of Vishnu; especially worshipped during Diwali festival
lingam phallic symbol of energy; see Shiva
liquor spirits, alcohol; thus liquor store. IMFL is Indian Made Foreign Liquor, that is, beer or gin etc. made in India
Lok Sabha House of the People; this and the Rajya Sabha (Council of States) are the Lower and Upper Houses of the Indian Parliament
Mahabharata Hindu epic poem of about 90,000 couplets, recounted orally until first written down in the fourth to second centuries BC; it recounts the war for succession between the Pandava and Kaurava princes around 1500 BC, with the Pandava Arjuna as hero
maharaja king; see raja
Mahatma Great Soul, as in Mahatma Gandhi
mahout elephant keeper/rider
mandir Hindu temple, composed of a *mandapam* (entrance), a *vimana*

(sanctuary) with the *garbhagriha* (unlit shrine), and a *sikhara* (spire) topped by a *kalasa* (finial)

Marathas the Hindu, warring, stocky people of central India who rose in the mid-17th century under their hero-king Shivaji; they won vast territories and menaced both Mughals and British; their ruler, the Maharaja of Gwalior, is called The Scindia

masjid mosque, thus Jama Masjid (Friday Mosque) for the principal mosque of a town. The *mihrab* (prayer niche) contains the *qibla* (indicator) for the direction of Mecca; outside, the muezzin calls the faithful to prayer from the minaret (often an amplified recording now); the *mullah* is the priest

moksha enlightenment, release from worldly existence; like kama, one of the Hindu goals for life

Mughals Muslim dynasty who were the dominant rulers in northern and central India from the 16th to the 18th century and nominally ruled until 1857; hence Mughal art, architecture and design, Mughlai cuisine, etc.

namaste respectful greeting when people meet or depart, accompanied by putting the hands together, fingers upwards

nirvana the achievement of total peace on release from the cycle of rebirth; a term adopted by Hindus from Buddhist philosophy

paan a digestive of betel nut and other condiments wrapped in a leaf, chewed and spat out

Parvati Daughter of the Mountains, goddess of peace and beauty. The female energy of the gods, she is the consort of Shiva. When known as Devi her destructive powers are manifest in various forms including Kali (goddess of death and destruction) and Durga

puja Hindu worship, usually a mixture of prayer, incantation and offerings of flowers and food (prashad) to a deity, performed with or without a priest

pundit teacher/professor of the Hindu scriptures, classical music, etc.

Puranas the traditional Hindu myths and legends arranged in 18 collections

purdah Urdu for veil, curtain. The practice of Muslim women living in purdah, screened from men and strangers, spread to Hindus with Muslim conquests of India

pyjama baggy trousers, usually worn with a *kurta* (long shirt)

qawwali mystical poems set to music, sung in chorus by Muslims

Raj Hindi for reign, rule; usually refers to British rule in India

raja Hindu ruler, prince; a maharaja is a king. They sit on *gaddis* (thrones) and have ranis and maharanis as their princesses and queens. The Rajputs (sons of princes) were the Hindu warrior caste who ruled Rajasthan (abode of the princes) and the Punjab

Rama Vishnu's seventh incarnation, the human god-hero of the epic *Ramayana*; his brothers are Bharata and Lakshmana; his wife is Sita

Ramayana Hindu epic poem of about 24,000 couplets, possibly written by Valmiki in the sixth–fifth century BC, then told orally until written down in the fourth−second centuries BC; it recounts how the god-king Rama, helped by monkey and bear allies, rescues his wife Sita from abduction by Ravana, the multi-headed demon king of Lanka (Sri Lanka)

raga the musical mode providing the framework for improvization by a musician. The ragas for each time of day and each mood inspired poets and the development of a complex iconography in Indian miniature painting

Rajya Sabha see Lok Sabha

sadhu Hindu ascetic

sati a widow's honourable self-immolation, often on her husband's funeral pyre. It was outlawed by the British in 1829 but continued, and is now undergoing a revival

Shiva or Siva The Auspicious; third member of the Hindu Trinity (see Brahma) and the symbol of both destructive and creative energy manifested in such forms as Nataraja (Lord of the Dance) and the lingam (see above). Parvati is his consort; Ganesh and Kartikeya (god of war) are his sons; Nandi the bull is his vehicle; the lingam is his emblem. A Shaivite is a worshipper of Shiva

Sita wife of the god Rama

Surya god of the sun; Aruna, god of dawn, is his charioteer

tikka dot of paste, often red, worn by Hindus; the dot worn by married Hindu women is called a *suhag*

Tirthankaras the 24 Jain teachers

urs death-anniversary of a Muslim saint, when he was united with God

Vedas the ancient, spiritual and orthodox Hindu texts. The earliest Hindus practised Vedism, the worship of Nature, through songs and prayers called vedas in which the three chief gods were Indra (rain), Agni (fire) and Surya (sun)

Vishnu The Preserver; second member of the Hindu Trinity (see Brahma). He symbolizes the creation and preservation that maintain the balance of the forces which sustain the universe. His ten principal avatars (incarnations) include Matsya (first, fish), Kurma (second, turtle), Varaha (third, boar), Narasimha (fourth, man-lion), Rama (seventh, hero-king), and blue-skinned Krishna or his brother Balarama (eighth, both human; opinions differ as to which is the avatar). Lakshmi is his consort; Garuda the eagle or mythical sunbird is his vehicle; the disc-like *chakra* is his weapon; Shesha is the snake on which he reclines on the Cosmic Ocean. A Vaishnavite is a worshipper of Vishnu

wallah fellow, as in rickshaw-wallah, dhobi-wallah (washerman)

yoga psycho-physical discipline involving the practice of meditation, exercise positions and breathing control to increase spiritual and physical well-being

zenana women's quarters of a Hindi household; harem is the Muslim equivalent

Useful Addresses

UK

Missions: **High Commission for India**, India House, Aldwych, London WC2 (tel. 071 836 8484). There is also an Assistant High Commission at 86 New Street, Birmingham (tel. 021 643 0366).

Airlines: **Air India**, 17-18 New Bond Street, London W1 (tel. 071 491 7979; flight information 081 897 6311); **British Airways**, 156 Regent Street, London W1 (tel. 081 897 4000; flight information 081 759 2525). British Airways Regent Street has an immunization centre.

Government of India Tourist Office, 7 Cork Street, London W1 (tel. 071 437 3677/8).

Trailfinder, 194 Kensington High Street, London W8 (tel. 071 938 3939, economy; 071 938 3444, business and first class) and 46-48 Earls Court Road, London W8 (tel 071 938 3366 economy). The Kensington High Street office also has a full immunization centre (tel. 071 938 3999) and provides travel insurance, hotel discounts, currency and traveller's cheques, visas (tel. 071 938 3848), permits, books (tel. 071 938 3999) and information for clients (tel. 071 938 3303).

London booking for the main Indian hotel chains: Oberoi, LRI, 113-19 High Street, Hampton Hill, Middlesex TW12 1PS (tel. 081 941 7400, free-phone 0800 282811, fax 081 941 5169): Taj Group, Utell International House, 2 Kew Bridge Road, Brentfort, Middlesex TW8 OJF (tel. 081995 8211, fax 081 995 2474); Welcomgroup hotels in the Sheraton group, Sheraton Reservations System (tel. freephone 0800 353 535, fax 071 731 0532).

US

Missions: **Embassy of India**, 2107 Massachusetts Avenue, NW, Washington, DC 2008 (tel.202 939 7000/7069). There are also three **Consulates General**, 3 East 64th Street, New York, NY 10021 (tel.212 879 7888); Suite 1100, 150 N Michigan Avenue, Chicago, 60601 (tel.312 781 6280); and 540 Arguello Boulevard, San Francisco, Ca 94118 (tel.415 668 0998).

Airlines: **Air India**, 400 Park Avenue, New York, NY 10154 (tel.212 407 1460); **British Airways**, 1 World Trade Center, New York, NY 10048 and 530 Fifth Avenue, New York, NY 10036 (tel. freephone 1-800-Airways); **Pan Am.** 600 Fifth Avenue and 48th Street, New York, NY 10020 (tel.212 687 2600/625 5555; freephone 800 221 1111); 721 Market (between 3rd and 4th Streets), San Francisco, Ca 94103.

Fifth Avenue and 48th Street, New York, NY 10020 (tel.212 687 2600/625 5555; freephone 800 221 1111); 721 Market (between 3rd and 4th Streets), San Francisco, Ca 94103.

Government of India Tourist Offices 30 Rockefeller Plaza, 15 North Mezzanine, New York, NY 10020 (tel.212 586 4901); 201 North Michigan Avenue, Chicago, Ill 60601 (tel.312 236 6899); Suite 204, 3550 Wilshire Boulevard, Los Angeles, Ca 90010 (tel.213 380 8855).

To make bookings for hotels, cars, etc, either use a reputable travel agent or tour operator who is a member of **ABTA**, or book direct with the Delhi office of **SITA** or **TCI**, who both have offices in all three cities.

US booking for the main Indian hotel chains: **Oberoi Hotels** (tel. freephone 800 223 0888 PIA or 800 8005 OBEROI): **Taj Group**, Utell International, 10605 Burt Circle, Omaha, Nebraska 68114 (tel. freephone 800 44 UTELL); **Welcomgroup Hotels** in the Sheraton Group (tel. freephone 800 325 3535).

Delhi

Missions: **British High Commission**, Shantipath, Chanakyapuri (tel.601371); **US Embassy**, Shantipath, Chanakyapuri (tel.600651).

International airlines: **Air India**, 124 Connaught Place (tel.3311225); **British Airways**, 1a Connaught Place (tel.3327630); **Pan Am**, Chandralok Building, 36 Janpath (tel.3313161).

Indian Airlines: Kanchenjunga Building, 18 Barakhamba Road (tel. 3310052).

Railway bookings: Tourist Guide, Northern Railway, New Delhi Station (tel.3313535) has a special foreign tourist booking office selling tickets, seat reservations and Indrail passes.

Bus bookings: Interstate Bus Terminal, Kashmiri Gate, Old Delhi.

Government of India Tourist Office, 88 Janpath (tel.3320005, 3320342), with a counter at the domestic airport.

State tourist offices: **Delhi Tourism Development Corporation** (DTDC), N-36 Connaught Place (tel.3313637, 3315322), with counters at New and Old Delhi railways stations, the Interstate Bus Terminal and the international airport; offices for **Rajasthan** (tel.322332) and **Uttar Pradesh** (tel.322251) are both upstairs in Chandralok Building, 36 Janpath.

City tours: Indian Tourism Development Corporation (ITDC)'s am, pm and day-long tours leave from L-Block, Connaught Circus (tel.3320331, 3322336); Delhi Tourism Development Corporations (DTDC)'s from their office. ITDC also do day and overnight tours to Agra and day tours to Jaipur, leaving from Hotel Janpath and the Ashok.

Archaeological Survey of India, Janpath (tel.3012058), next to the National Museum; has good publications, advises on antiques.

Government Gem Laboratory, Gem & Jewellery Export Promotion Council, Barakhamba Road (tel. 3313204).

Travel agents: **SITA World Travel**, F12 Connaught Place (tel.3311133, 3311122; telex 3165141, 316663) have offices in Agra and Jaipur; **Mercury Travels**, 4A Ground Floor, Jeevan Tara Building, Parliament Street (tel.312167; telex 7207) and **TCI**, Hotel Metro, N49 Connaught Circus (tel. 3315181, 3312570; telex 65656; fax 3316705) both have offices in Agra. **American Express** is at A Bock, Connaught Place (tel.344119, 3324119; telex 62781, 66420). **Mountain Travel**, 1 Rani Jhansi Road (tel. 523057), **Abercrombie and Kent**, Chiranjiv Tower, Nehru Place (tel. 6434417, 6436207).

Agra, Uttar Pradesh

Airlines: **Air India**, Janta Travels, Hotel Clarks Shiraz, Taj Road (tel.76983); **Indian Airlines**, Hotel Clarks Shiraz, Taj Road (tel.73434, 73862).

Government of India Tourist Office, 191 The Mall (tel.72377), with a counter at the airport.

State tourist offices: **Uttar Pradesh Tourist Bureau**, 64 Taj Road (tel.75852), with a counter at Agra Cantonment Railway Station; the **Rajasthan** office is in the Taj Mahal Precinct (tel.64582).

City tours: ITDC day-long tours of Fatehpur Sikri and Agra pick up at their office and then at the railway station (passengers on the Taj Express train will have an on-board ticket-seller). There are also separate am tours to Fatehpur Sikri and pm Agra tours.

Archaeological Survey of India, Mall Road

Travel agents: **Mercury Travels**, Fatehabad Road (tel.65365); **SITA World Travels**, A2 Shopping Centre, Taj Road, Sadar Bazar (tel. 66181, 749222; telex 0565-213); **TCI**, Hotel Clarks Shiraz (tel.64111).

Jaipur, Rajasthan

Airlines: **Air India**, Rattan Mansion, opp. All India Radio, M.I. Road (tel.65559); **British Airways**, Nijhawan Travel Service, Park Street (tel.74929); **Pan Am**, Amber Tours Railway Station Road (tel.69664); **Indian Airlines**, Mundhra Bhawan, Ajmer Road (tel.74500, 72940; airport 822222).

Government of India Tourist Office, State Hotel, Khasa Kothi, M.I. Road (tel.72000), with a counter at the airport (tel.822222).

State tourist offices: **Rajasthan Tourism Development Corporation** (RTDC), Usha Niwas, Kalyan Path (tel.79252, 69714); **Rajasthan** information counters at the railway station (tel.69714) and at Amber (tel.40764).

City tours: RTDC's am, pm and day-long tours leave from the railway station.

Railway station enquiries (tel.72121) and reservations (tel.72122) are open 9 am – 6.30 pm.

Archaeological Survey of India, Sub Circle Pundrikji-ki-Haveli, Shastri Chowk, Brahampuri.

Gem Testing Laboratory, Ministry of Commerce, Government of India, Rajasthan Chamber Bhavan, M.I. Road (tel.67940), for advice on jewellery buys.

Travel agents: **SITA World Travel**, Railway Station Road (tel.66809, 68226; telex 0365-438); TCI A/3 Jamnalal Bajaj Mong (tel.68371); **Rajasthan Tours**, Rambagh Palace Hotel (tel.76041, 66784); **Rajasthan Mounted Sports Association,** Dundlod House, Civil Lines (tel.6627).

Hotels

There is usually a bed shortage in all three cities, so it is crazy to arrive without a booking. The Taj Group and Welcomgroup have hotels in all three cities. Rates for a standard double room in Delhi hotels range from about Rs700 (Nirula's) to Rs2,000 (Taj Mahal). In Agra, Jaipur and other destinations, hotel tariffs are 20-40 percent cheaper.

Top of the market — all modern, with good restaurants, shops, pool and health club:

Taj Mahal Hotel, 1 Mansingh Road, New Delhi 110011 (tel.3016162; fax 3017299). 300 rooms, modern, well-positioned; sustains the rare combination of efficiency and warm friendliness; a favourite with Delhi society.

Oberoi, Dr Zakir Hussain Road, New Delhi 110003 (tel.363030; fax 360484). 288 rooms. Delhi's pioneer highrise luxury hotel has been totally revamped and is now the top business hotel with excellent restaurants.

Welcomgroup Maurya Sheraton, Sarda Patel Marg, Diplomatic Enclave, New Delhi 110021 (tel.3010101; fax 3010908). 500 rooms in an imaginative new building furnished with contemporary art; Tower Block has the best service; good food; sited on the centre's fringes.

Hyatt Regency, Bhikaji Cama Place, Ring Road, New Delhi 110066 (tel.609911; fax 678833). 535 rooms in a gleaming highrise with special executive floor, but located in south Delhi; the favourite local for Delhi's smartest residents. Location and atmosphere is for businessmen.

Taj Palace Inter-continental, 2 Sardar Patel Marg, New Delhi 110021 (tel.3010404; fax 3011252) 431 rooms; next door to the Maurya Sheraton and as big but lacking its style; excellent service, good food.

Le Meridien, Windsor Place, Janpath, New Delhi 110011 (tel.383960; fax 384220). 375 rooms in this monstrous landmark designed by Mr Raja Aderie.

Holiday Inn Connaught Plaza, Barakhamba Avenue, Connaught Place, New Delhi 110001 (tel.3320101; fax 3325335). 500 rooms around an atrium with a thundering waterfall.

Park Hotel, 15 Parliament Street, New Delhi 110001 (tel.352477; fax 352025). 234 rooms whose best views overlook Lutyen's Rajpath.

Good hotels with old character and modern facilities (but sometimes less polished service); all have a pool:

Ashok, 50-B Chanakyapuri, New Delhi 110021 (tel.600121). 571 Raj style spacious rooms (110 suites) and public areas; some rooms with balconies; good food, charming service, excellent shops; best of the old hotels.

Imperial, Janpath, New Delhi 110001 (tel.3328511; fax 3314542). 175 rooms in a stylish 1930s building; Raj style maintained in rooms; a perfect base for keen explorers. Lovingly restored.

Oberoi Maidens, 7 Sham Nath Marg, Delhi 110054 (tel.2525464; telex 66303 OMDL). 46 rooms in Mr Maiden's hotel built in 1900 just north of Old Delhi; colonial spaciousness in renovated rooms.

Ambassador, Sujan Singh Park, New Delhi 110003 (tel.690391; telex 3277). 73 spacious rooms in well located hotel built in 1951 by Sir Shoba Singh, an engineer of New Delhi.

Practical and good value, with simple, clean rooms.

Manor House, 77 Friends Colony West, New Delhi 110065 (tel.6832171). 24 rooms. A small hotel built in 1951 with colonial spaciousness and a large garden; located in a smart residential area in south Delhi.

Hotel Marina, G59 Connaught Circus, New Delhi 110001 (tel.3324658). 93 rooms; Well located for Old and New Delhi exploration. Good service.

Nirula's Hotel, L Block, Connaught Place, New Delhi 110001 (tel.3322419). 29 rooms on top of their much-patronized restaurants.

Park Hotel, 15 Parliament Street (Sansad Marg), New Delhi 110001 (tel.352477; telex 031-65231; fax:(011)352025). 234 rooms, some overlooking the Jantar Mantar, only 100 metres from Connaught Place.

York Hotel, K Block, Connaught Circus, New Delhi 110001 (tel.3323769). 28 rooms; room service from their York and Ginza restaurants.

Hotel Fifty-Five, H-55 Connaught Circus, New Delhi 110001 (tel.3321244). 15 rooms with manager Mr Joshi's homely atmosphere.

Central Court Hotel, N-Block, Connaught Circus, New Delhi 110001 (tel.3315013). 36 rooms, the deluxe ones opening onto a wide terrace.

Hotel Hans Plaza, 15 Barakambha Road, New Delhi 110001 (tel.3316868; telex 031-63126 HANS IN). 67 rooms at the top of one of Delhi's highest buildings and without a pool. Only a few minutes walk from Connaught Place.

Note: the airport **Centaur Hotel** should be avoided.

Agra

Despite being a tourist centre since the Mughals arrived, there are only three deluxe hotels and a handful of modest places. None has greater character or old charm.

Top of the market — all newish, with pool, health club, shops and garden
Mughal Sheraton, Tajganj (tel.64701; telex 0565-201). 282 rooms in a magnificent, Mughal-inspired new building set around fountain-filled courtyards and extensive landscaped gardens; new wing of rooms.

Taj View, Tajganj (tel.64171; telex 0565-202 TAJV IN). 100 rooms. Rooms with sofas from which to gaze endlessly on the monument through a picture window; high floors best.

Hotel Agra Ashok, 6B Mall Road, Agra (tel.76223; telex 0656-313). Recently upgraded and set in a pleasant garden.

Clarks Shiraz, 54 Taj Road (tel.72421; telex 0565-211). 147 rooms; an older hotel that compensates for dull decor and food with a good garden, shopping arcade and the only rooftop bar and restaurant in town for Taj views.

Middle market and practical— small, well-serviced and friendly hotels
Mumtaz, 181/2 Fatehabad Road (tel.64771; telex 0565-222). 50 rooms, upper front ones with Taj view; the smartest of the set.

Amar, Fatehabad Road (tel.65696; telex 0565-341 AMAR IN). 68 rooms. Clean and simple.

Mayur Tourist Complex, Fatehabad Road (tel.67302). 30 rooms; clean, unpretentious and with a pretty, spacious garden.

Ratan Deep, Fatehabad Road (tel.63098). Small hotel on the cheap 'n' cheerful model with very thougtful staff, plenty of hot water etc.

Grand, 137 Station Road (tel.74014, 76311). 46 rooms; with the demise of old Lauries, this is the only possibility for colonial style; simple, friendly and cheap but located west of The Mall, a 15-minute ride to the Taj.

Jaipur

A chance to stay in a grand palace or experience the friendly intimacy of a
courtier's town mansion. Here is the best choice in India of hotels brimful of
the atmosphere of past grandeur.

*Top of the market — three royal palaces, all run by the Taj Group. All
are well outside the Pink City; to avoid over-priced taxis wander to the
end of the drive to take an auto-rickshaw into the centre:*
Rambagh Palace, Bhawani Singh Road (tel.75141; telex 0365-254;
fax:(041)73798). 110 rooms; a rambling palace amid magnificent gardens which
Maharaja Man Singh II vacated to launch the palace-hotel concept in 1957; if
the purse permits, go for the elaborate suites with original furnishings and live
in a dream for a few days; avoid back and basement rooms; food has
improved, but beware of sleepy service and astronomical hotel taxi rates.
Jai Mahal Palace, Jacob Road, Civil Lines (tel.73314; telex 0365-250
JMPH IN). 102 rooms in the refurbished, yellow-painted palace set in
extensive well-kept grounds; efficient staff and very good food.
Raj Mahal Palace, off Hawa Sarak Road (tel.61257; telex 0365-313 JAI IM;
fax:c/o(0141)73798). 14 rooms; a cosy, characterful palace in a large garden;
once the British Residency, later the maharaja's modest home after he left the
Rambagh and still furnished with royal nicknacks. More often used for
elaborate weddings on the extensive lawns.

*Nobleman's homes — several former thakurs of Jaipur state have
opened their delightful town houses as small, friendly and peaceful
family-run hotels, all well-priced and well-located. Service may not be
extensive and meals may be prepared only to order:*
Narain Niwas, Kanota Bagh, Narain Singh Road (tel.65448). 22 rooms; Narain
Singh Ji's haveli built in 1881 retains the splendid fin de siécle furnishings, and
is run by Mr Mohan Singh; garden; good food to order.
Haveli Hotel, Statue Circle (tel.75024). 10 rooms; Mr Vinay Podar lives
upstairs in the 1940s family haveli where rooms with family furnishings
surround a small central courtyard; beautifully kept gardens with lawns, lake
and swimming pool.
Samode Haveli, Gangapole (tel.42407). 11 rooms; by the north wall of the Pink
City, found through a decorated gateway; splendidly painted and furnished
public rooms open onto a large garden-courtyard with tables and wicker chairs
(open to non-residents).
Achrol Lodge, Civil Lines Road (tel.72254). 8 rooms; a large, simple house
with large garden run by Mr Mahandra Singh; very peaceful; Indian food to
order.

Bissau Palace, Chandpole Gate (tel.74191). 28 rooms; Bissau descendants Mr and Mrs Sanjay Singh keep their heirlooms in the public rooms; garden; Rajasthani food if wished; Pink City walls just a stroll away.

Mandava House, Sansar Chandra Road, Jaipur 302001, (tel.75358). 17 new rooms in an old family house near the centre of town, 1km from the railway station.

Others
Welcomgroup Mansingh, Sansar Chandra Road (tel.78771; telex 0365-344). 100 rooms; modern hotel located just west of the Pink City, three minutes' walk away, and well equipped with shops and an excellent rooftop restaurant; negligible garden.

LMB Hotel, Johari Bazar (tel.48844) has 33 simple rooms above its famous restaurant. Located in the Pink City

Note: **Jaipur Ashok** (tel.75171) and **Clarks Amber** (tel.822616, both modern, are emergencies for up-market hotels; the **State Hotel**, Khasa Kothi, in an old building with extensive gardens at the west end of M I Road, is a cheap-with-character hotel if the noblemen's homes are full.

Hotels for Off-beat Travellers

Here are some more unusual places to stay. Many are ex-palaces, as ideal for a lunch stop as for an overnight stay. Some are such beautiful buildings in idyllic settings that two nights of rural relaxation is irresitible.

Gwalior
Usha Kiran Palace, Jayendragunj (tel.23453, 22049; telex 566-225). 22 rooms in a mini-palace, the guest-house of the massive Jai Vilas palace next door; good garden and food, stylish 1930s furniture, splendid top room with balcony. Part of the Welcomgroup chain.

Orchha
Hotel Sheesh Mahal, bookable in writing to Madhya Pradesh Tourist Office, 19 Ashok Road, New Delhi (tel.351187). Just a handful of rooms in the palace jammed between two grander palaces. Very relaxed, top room with veranda best.

Bharatpur
Golbagh Palace Hotel, Bharatpur (tel.3349). 18 rooms in the guest-house set in the grounds of the ex-maharaja's palace. Rooms and halls hung with royal pictures and hunting trophies; good food; large garden; all run by the charming Mr Cheema who indulges guests with thoughful care.

Shanti Kutir Forest Rest House, Keoladeo National Park (book in writing). 5 clean and neat rooms in the maharaja's old hunting lodge; much nicer than the Bharatpur Forest Lodge (ITDC).

Saras Tourist Bungalow, Fatehpur Sikri Road, Bharatpur (tel.3700). A dozen or so rooms, all practical and clean, a few yards from the park entrance.

Samode

Samode Palace Hotel, Samode, 303806 Jaipur (tel.34; Jaipur office tel.42407). 20 rooms of all sizes in this painted palace run by the young ex-royals; beware of group travellers who may destroy the tranquillity.

Kishangarh

Mahjhela Palace, Kishangarh (tel.1). A few rooms in one of the royal palaces, bookable through Mr Veer Singh.

Kota

Hotel Brijraj Bhawan, Kota (tel.23071). Riverside palace with lush, immaculate, terraced gardens down to the wide river; large rooms, the best one upstairs and with large balcony; Mr Ishwar Singh pampers guests with good food and great care.

Ramgarh (30 km northeast of Jaipur)

The Ramgarh Lodge, above the dam holding back Jaipur's water supply. The Lodge, with 9 rooms, has recently been renovated by the Taj Group of Hotels and can be booked through the Rambagh Palace. Excellent birds and a few crocodiles on, in and around the lake. Good walks and the Lodge has tennis and squash courts and a billiard room.

Ranthambore

The Sawai Madhopur, recently renovated by the Taj Group of Hotels, may be booked through their central reservations office at Chandralok, 36 Janpath, New Delhi 110001 (tel.3016162).

Government Lodge has a handful of rooms which must be pre-booked in Jaipur at the tourist office (see above).

Sariska

Hotel Sariska Palace, Sariska District, Alwar (tel.22). 27 rooms in the maharaja's palace which he modestly called his hunting lodge. Deep verandas overlook the gardens; bonfires and barbecues on some nights; plenty of original furniture and fittings; right opposite the park entrance.

Tiger's Den, Sariska, Alwar; clean and well-organized lodge at the park gates run by the Rajasthan State Tourism Corporation.

Siliserh
Lake Palace, Siliserh, Alwar (tel.22991). 11 rooms in a hideaway palace overlooking Siliserh Lake, midway between Sariska and Alwar. Top rooms with own verandas are the best. Boating and bird-watching available for the more energetic.

Alwar
Phool Bag Tourist Palace, opposite New Stadium, Alwar (tel.2274). Small hotel, not palatial but clean, charming and set in a lush, well-kept garden in the town centre.

Restaurants

Hotel restaurants are listed first; their full address is found above, in the hotels section. Although they are often the best and grandest, it is more fun to eat out in a city restaurant sometimes. A good way to taste Mughlai and north Indian food is to try several dishes at a lunchtime buffet; and there is often Indian dance or music to sample, too. Note: coffee shops in the bigger hotels tend to stay open 24 hours, making them handy for travellers hungry at odd times; they usually have a broad multi-cuisine menu and quicker service than restaurants; breakfast and lunch are often buffets.

Delhi

A large choice of restaurants but locals are keen on the good Indian and Chinese hotel restaurants so evening tables need to be booked. Here are just a handful of suggestions; fashions and chefs change so see *City Scan* and weekend newspapers for the latest opinions.

Mughlai
Dum Pukht, Maurya Sheraton; **Darbar**, Ashok (good buffet); **Haveli**, Taj Mahal; **Moghal Room**, Oberoi; **Gulnar**, Janpath Hotel (tel.3320070), with good singing. Around Connaught Place: **Degchi**, 13 Regal Building (tel.311444); **Minar**, L11 Connaught Place, (tel.3323259); **Mughlai**, M17 Connaught Circus (tel. 3321101). With Old Delhi atmosphere for the adventurous: **Karim**, Jama Masjid, Old Delhi (tel.269880, see page 73) (its Nizamuddin outpost entirely lacks atmosphere); **Moti Mahal**, Daryaganj (tel.273011), best when locals come to cheer on the evening ghazel singers; **Jawahar**, Jama Masjid, Old Delhi (tel.270839); **Flora**, Urdu Bazar, Jama Masjid, Old Delhi (tel.264593); **Maseets**, Jama Masjid.

North Indian and Northwest Frontier
Bukhara, Maurya Sheraton; **Frontier**, Ashok; **Kandahar**, Oberoi; **Handi**, Taj

Palace; **Tandoor**, President (tel.277836); **Aangan**, Hyatt Regency; **Corbett's**, Claridges. Just by Old Delhi: **Khyber**, Kashmiri Gate. Around Connaught Place (and all serving Chinese and Continental as well): **Gaylord**, B16 Regal Building (tel.352677); **Standard**, 44 Regal Building (tel.389251); **Kwality**, 7 Regal Building (tel.350110); **Embassy**, 11D Connaught Place. For snacks, **Nathu's** in Bengali Market (tel.389784, 385660, see page 68). **Amber**, N-Block, Connaught Circus; **Darbar** L-Block Connaught Circus.

South Indian
Dasaprakash Ambassador; **Woodlands**, Lodhi Hotel (tel.362422); **South Indian Boarding House**, opposite Shanker Market; **Sona Rupa**, Janpath; **The Coconut Grove**, Ashok Yatri Niwas; **Nathu's** (see North Indian); **Sagar**, Defence Colony Market.

Chinese
Tai Pan, Oberoi (rooftop views); **Pearls**, Hyatt Regency; **Tea House of the August Moon**, Taj Palace; **House of Ming**, Taj Mahal; **China Town**, Ashok; **Bali Hit**, Maurya (rooftop views). Around Connaught Place: **Nirula's Chinese Room**, L-Block (tel.3322419); **Ginza**, K-Block (tel.3320427); **Dynasty**, M-17 Connaught Place (tel.3321102); **Noble House**, Holiday Inn. In Chanakyapuri: **Fujiya**, 12/48 Malcha Marg (tel.3016059). **Nathu's** also serves Chinese (see North Indian).

Continental
Usually unsatisfactory, and often accompanied by equally unsatisfactory European live music: **Casa Medici**, Taj Mahal (Italian, rooftop views); **Takshila**, Maurya Sheraton (rooftop views); **Burgundy**, Ashok (French); **Orient Express**, Taj Palace (in a train carriage); **The Taj**, Oberoi.

Tea
Gaylord, B16 Regal Building, Connaught Place (tel.352677) for a splendid blow-out; imperial hotel lawns for colonial style. To buy Western cakes, **Nathu's** cake and bread shop in Bengali Market is best; the up-market hotels with in-house bakeries include the **Maurya, Ashok, Oberoi, Taj Mahal** and **Nirula's**.

Cocktails
Oberoi Skylark Bar (rooftop); **Imperial** (on the lawns); **Hyatt** (with piano);

Agra

Few restaurants and often disappointing food inside them; so feast your eyes on the buildings. For the best hotel eating: **Mughal Sheraton** for good Mughlai food (booking essential for dinner, musicians); a multi-cuisine buffet restaurant; also Italian, Northwest Frontier, Chinese and Continental restaurants; good poolside sandwiches, good bar; **Taj View** for good Coffee Shop and bar (main restaurant opening soon); **Clarks Shiraz** for fair Indian, Chinese and Continental in the rooftop restaurant (with band, avoid dreary ground-floor restaurant); cocktails with Taj sunset in next-door bar. In the city, even less to recommend: no good Mughlai restaurants despite the high percentage of Muslim population; **Kwality**, Sadar Bazar, serves all cuisines; **Lakshmi Vilas** in Sadar Bazar, **Achman** on the bypass opposite Siri Talkies, and **Awadh** and **Panchratan** in Sanjay Place are all vegetarian.

Jaipur

Several good places in the city and the hotels; if the purse does not stretch to a palace-hotel bed, have a glimpse at royal living over a drink or meal, although none serves good Rajasthani food.

Mughlai and North Indian
Jai Mahal (extra tables on the veranda and, at lunchtime, on the lawns); **Man Singh** (rooftop, good qawwali singing), vies with Jai Mahal to serve the best Indian food; **Samod Haveli** (beautiful setting). In town on M.I. Road there are Nero's (tel.74493) (the best), Handi (in Maya Mansions), **Rainbow** and **Kwality**.

Chinese
Golden Dragon; **Niro's**, M.I. Road.

Vegetarian
LMB (tel.48844), Johari Bazar (a favourite; takeaway treats from upstairs include delicious ice-creams; sit-down basement); **Eats** (tel.69098) (downstairs) and **Rituraj** (tel.75162) in Hotel Mangal, both on Sanar Chandra Marg; **Natraj**, Chandralok (next to Canara Bank) and **Chankya** on M.I. Road; the open-air restaurant in pretty **Ram Niwas Gardens**.

Snacks, tea and cocktails
Rambagh, on the veranda, lawns and in the beautiful Polo Bar (avoid dreary dining room); **Jai Mahal** lawns and another beautiful bar.

Practical Shopping

To save time, the up-market hotels have good in-house shops which conveniently keep long hours. But their prices (especially for film) may be higher than in town, and they may fall down on the odd practical need.

Delhi

Excellent in-house shops in all the top-of-the-market hotels, especially the **Taj Mahal**, the **Taj Palace, Ashok, Maurya** and **Oberoi**. Books and maps, **Bahri Sons** in Khan Market, **Book Worm** at 29-B Connaught Place, **Famous Book Store**, 25 Janpath and **Oxford Book and Stationary Co** at Connaught Circus are just some of the many good stores; chemist **Kemp & Co,** E-Block, Connaught Circus; photography/film, **Mahatta & Co** 59-M Connaught Place; shoes, **Metro** 16-F Connaught Place, is one of a clutch selling sandals and high fashion shoes at good prices, and **Bata** at D-4 Connaught Place has branches throughout India.

Agra

All three up-market hotels have good shops. Books and maps, **Modern Book Depot**, Sadar Bazar; chemist, **Chacha Medical Store**, Pratabpura Crossing; photography/film from **Priyalal and Sons**, Pratabpura; shoes, shops in **Sardar Bazar**.

Jaipur

The Rambagh has many good shops including Mr **Jain's** excellent **bookshop**; he stocks all sorts of other useful things including film and may be able to mend a broken camera. Books and maps, **Books Corner**, M.I. Road; chemist, **Medicos** on M I Road, near Niro's restaurant; photography/film, **Pictorial Photographers**, M.I. Road at Panchpati Crossing; shoes, **Fancy Nagra Shoe Store** is one of several on Ramganj Bazar, and there is also **Bharat Boot House** on Johari Bazar.

Index